Duty
Faithfully
Performed

Also by John M. Taylor

While Cannons Roared: The Civil War Behind the Lines

Confederate Raider: Raphael Semmes of the Alabama

William Henry Seward: Lincoln's Right Hand

General Maxwell Taylor: The Sword and the Pen

Garfield of Ohio

From the White House Inkwell

Korea's Syngman Rhee
      (writing as Richard C. Allen)

Raiders and Blockaders: The American Civil War Afloat
      (with William N. Still Jr. and Norman C. Delaney)

DUTY
FAITHFULLY
PERFORMED

ROBERT E. LEE AND HIS CRITICS

John M. Taylor

with a foreword by Rod Paschall

BRASSEY'S

Library of Congress Cataloging-in-Publication Data

Taylor, John M., 1930–
    Duty faithfully performed : Robert E. Lee and his critics / John M. Taylor. — 1st ed.
      p.   cm.
    Includes bibliographical references and index.
    1. Lee, Robert E. (Robert Edward), 1807–1870. 2. Generals—Confederate States of America Biography. 3. Confederate States of America. Army Biography. 4. Generals—United States Biography. I. Title.
E467.1.L4T39   1999
973.7'3'092
[B]—DC21   99-29910
                                                    CIP

ISBN 1-57488-297-X (alk. paper)

Printed in the United States of America on acid-free paper that meets the American National Standards Institute Z39-48 Standard.

Map on p. vi by Albert D. McJoynt

Brassey's
22883 Quicksilver Drive
Dulles, Va. 20166

10 9 8 7 6 5 4 3 2 1

For Katharine Shaibani,

who shares many virtues with Robert E. Lee

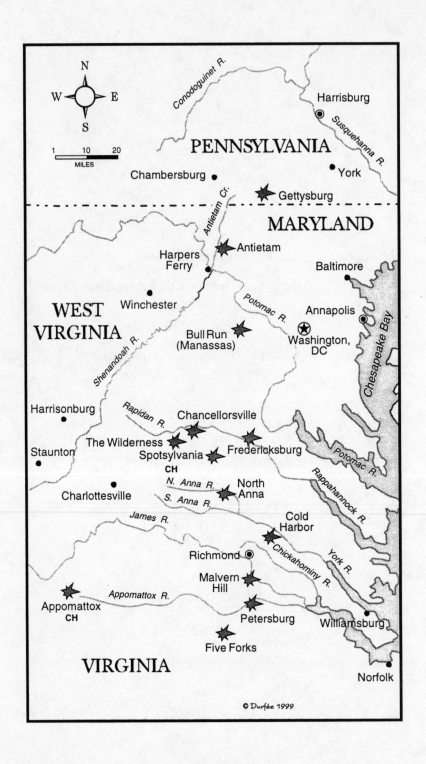

© Durfee 1999

CONTENTS

Map		*vi*
Foreword	*Rod Paschall*	*ix*
Preface		*xiii*

1	The General and the Historians	1
2	Son of the Old Dominion	10
3	The Young Soldier	24
4	Duty, God, and Slavery	32
5	"I Shall Share the Miseries of My People"	44
6	War	54
7	Saving Richmond	67
8	Suppressing Pope	79
9	Determined Valor	89
10	High Tide at Fredericksburg	101

11   "May God Have Mercy on General Lee"   112

12   The Road to Gettysburg   128

13   "This Is All My Fault"   142

14   A Military Sacrament   156

15   "We Have Got to Whip Them"   167

16   Never Call Retreat   179

17   Siege   189

18   A Surrender of Quality   202

19   A Dry and Thirsty Land   215

20   Meet General Lee   228

Appendix: Lee's Reflections   *240*

Notes   *245*

Index   *261*

FOREWORD

This thoughtful book is aimed, first, at answering the question, who? Just who *was* Robert E. Lee? What were the general's attitudes, relationships, beliefs, abilities, and what were his weaknesses? But, the ultimate and overshadowing target of John Taylor's quest is far greater game, finding an answer to the question, why? If one can know Lee's character, then it may be possible to understand why the Army of Northern Virginia's commander was so successful in one battle and so disappointing in another.

Why did the man who was offered command of the Union armies turn down that lofty perch for a more humble position in the fledgling and highly doubtful Confederate service? Why was Lee fighting for a cause that would defend and extend an institution he believed to be deeply flawed, slavery? Why was this man, among all other American field commanders, the most revered by the troops he commanded? What was it in Lee that attracted such loyalty and respect from those who knew him well?

Aimed at defining a man's character, this book has much more to say about America's most tragic event. It is an important and worthy book because the course, the cost, and the length of that terrible war were, in the main, determined by Robert E. Lee.

Among the three pre–twentieth century Americans leaders who have attracted great and continuing attention from historians, Lee has been the most mysterious. Like Washington and Lincoln, Lee has had his share of wholly uncritical, worshipful biographers. The damage these writers have wrought is to have turned away readers who came in search of answers. They have seen glowing, moral, flawless, and unbelievable descriptions. They disbelieve, then neglect the story of a life that begs study.

Sadly, Robert E. Lee's life has drawn a peculiar breed of writer. They seek acclaim by attacking Lee's most pronounced and storied reputation, that of the superb tactician. These critics set out to belittle the general armed with little more than convenient and selective hindsight and novice military opinion. Unfortunately, the result has been to drive the debate over Lee to his brief spate of battlefield aggressiveness. This is indeed thin gruel in comparison with the much more important and rewarding field of exploring Lee's views on slavery and secession, his appraisal of subordinates, his relationships with superiors, and his closely held ideas about the strategy of a long, vast, and devastating war.

John Taylor plunges into the debate over Robert E. Lee's knack for attack but goes much further. The author not only treats the influence of Lee's experience in the Mexican War, but provides a sound discussion on the alternatives to seizing opportunities to assault Union forces. And Taylor describes a pronounced character trait in his subject: an abundance—maybe an overabundance—of physical courage. This book also explores the effect of Lee's emotional and religious makeup. Lee has long been described as a religious man, but here the reader will discover how Lee's piety might have affected his judgment on several crucial aspects of the Civil War. The author describes Lee's occasional flashes of temper. Taylor uses these incidents to provide the reader insights into this otherwise controlled and reserved man's innermost convictions.

Before reading this book, it is important to keep several facts in mind. Beginning in 1862, President Lincoln's attempt to reunify America depended on the defeat of General Lee's Army of Northern Virginia. In the 1860s, the liberation of slaves in the United States would not be achieved without the defeat of General Lee's Army of Northern Virginia. In early 1863, the Confederate Army of Northern

Virginia had become an extension of its commander, General Robert E. Lee. In the summer of 1863, with antiwar riots breaking out in the North, the ability to hold the Federal coalition together depended on the defeat of General Lee's Army of Northern Virginia. And in 1864, the reelection of Abraham Lincoln and the triumph of the Union cause depended on the prospect of defeating General Lee's Army of Northern Virginia.

To date, Robert E. Lee has been the most dangerous and worthy opponent the United States has ever faced. For that distinction alone his character should be studied.

ROD PASCHALL

PREFACE

Back in 1946, Harry Truman was president of the United States, the Cold War was beginning, and hernias were not taken lightly. I was 16 at that time, and my operation for a hernia entailed a hospital stay that I recall as more than a week, followed by extensive bed rest.

What I remember best about my convalescence is that much of it was spent reading Douglas Southall Freeman's three-volume *Lee's Lieutenants* rather than doing homework assignments. Freeman's volumes, an extension of the author's Pulitzer Prize–winning *R. E. Lee*, generated an interest in the Civil War on my part that has never completely abated. Winston Churchill called the American Civil War the noblest and least avoidable of the great wars up to that time. My own conviction is that the cast of characters in our Civil War was uniquely interesting, and this belief prompted me to undertake biographies of a prominent Northerner, William Henry Seward, and a less prominent Southerner, Adm. Raphael Semmes.

But why Robert E. Lee? A recent compendium of writings on Lee, Gary W. Gallagher's *Lee the Soldier*, includes a bibliography of 200 books related to Lee. Although Lincoln is unchallenged as the subject of more books than any other American, there is no shortage of books on Lee, some of them of high quality.

By any criterion, Lee was one of the most gifted soldiers to come out of America. He was a thoughtful strategist, with as good a plan for a Confederate victory as any Southerner put forward. He was a calm yet inspiring battle commander, with a remarkable ability to gain and maintain the tactical initiative. In camp, he was considerate of his officers and men. When the tide of war turned against the Confederacy, Lee was never outwardly disheartened. Small wonder that he was a hero to the South; a North Carolina woman called the Lee of 1864 "the idol, the point of trust, of confidence & repose of thousands! How nobly has he won the confidence, the admiration of the nation."[1]

Few men have been more admired during their lifetime and in the decades immediately after than Lee. Then a reaction set in. Just as George Washington became a target for debunking biographies, Lee came to "pay" for the veneration in which he had been held in the defeated South. Some critics have charged that his victories on the battlefield had been achieved at such high cost that they eventually contributed to the defeat of the Confederacy.

My argument for this volume is that we still have not got it quite "right" on Robert E. Lee. We may have passed through the period of debunking Lee, but his personality remains elusive. What turned the ebullient, good-humored Lee of the 1830s into the somber Lee of the 1850s? Why did Lee remain in the U.S. Army when so many of his comrades turned to civil pursuits? Why did Lee allow key decisions in his life, including some military matters, to be determined by others? Although there has been some fine writing in defense of Lee, there appears to be room for a fresh study. In his farewell to the Army of Northern Virginia, Lee praised his soldiers for "duty faithfully performed." I have taken these words for my title, for they epitomize Lee as much as they do his men.

In writing *Duty Faithfully Performed* I have made extensive use of secondary sources; such value as the book may have derives from my interpretations rather than fresh research. And any new interpretation can be perilous; Carol Reardon, associate professor of history at Pennsylvania State University, summed up my problem in a letter: "No matter what you write or how well you write it," she warns, "somebody is going to HATE it."

A number of able historians read all or portions of this book in manuscript, sharing their insights. Robert K. Krick, chief historian at the Fredericksburg and Spotsylvania National Military Park, not only reviewed the chapters concerning the battles of Fredericksburg and the Wilderness, but also made available his personal file of Lee-related material. D. Scott Hartwig, supervisory historian at the Gettysburg National Military Park, reviewed the two chapters on Gettysburg. Michael Parrish, a Lee scholar and the biographer of Gen. Richard Taylor, was good enough to review the manuscript in its entirety, making a number of suggestions and directing me to pertinent sources.

At the National Defense University, the chief of special collections, Susan Lemke, and her assistant, Robert Montgomery, helped locate or made available scarce Lee-related volumes. E. Lee Shepard of the Virginia Historical Society and John M. Coski of the Museum of the Confederacy in Richmond assisted with the Lee aphorisms collated in the appendix to this volume.

This book, like my earlier efforts, has benefited immeasurably from repeated readings by my wife, Priscilla, a professional editor whose publications include Phi Beta Kappa's quarterly *Key Reporter.* Repeatedly she put aside her own work to resolve some thorny organizational problem in my manuscript. Our daughter, Kathy Shaibani, also an editorial professional, offered additional suggestions, including observations on Lee's religious perspective.

I would like to express my thanks for permission to quote from the following volumes: Gary W. Gallagher, *The Confederate War* (Harvard University Press), and Thomas L. Connelly, *The Marble Man* (Louisiana State University Press). In addition, I wish to thank the Virginia Historical Society for authorization to print the Lee aphorisms that constitute the appendix to this volume.

John M. Taylor
McLean, Virginia

CHAPTER ONE

THE GENERAL AND THE HISTORIANS

ON SEPTEMBER 28, 1870, ROBERT E. LEE suffered the stroke that would carry him away two weeks later. The South's most illustrious soldier, then president of Washington College in Lexington, Virginia, had just returned home from an evening vestry meeting when he was stricken. In a letter, Mrs. Lee wrote that the general had come home later than expected and that dinner had been delayed. When she asked her husband where he had been, "He stood up at the foot of the table without replying . . . & sank back in his chair. . . . He tried to speak but muttered something unintelligible."[1]

Lee's illness puzzled his doctors, for there was no evidence of paralysis, only a general weakness and an impaired ability to speak. A bed was moved down from the second floor of the residence, and family and close friends maintained a constant vigil. Lee ate little and rarely spoke, but occasionally acknowledged the presence of family members with a squeeze of his hand.

Word spread through Lexington that "the General" was gravely ill. For many, it could not be mere coincidence that for much of the period of Lee's last illness western Virginia was buffeted by storms. William P.

Johnston, the son of Lee's fellow officer Gen. Albert Sidney Johnston, was with the Lee family during the general's illness, and his recollection of Lee's final days is appropriately reverential:

> As the old hero lay in the darkened room, or with the lamp and hearth fire casting shadows upon his calm, noble front, all the massive grandeur of his form, and face, and brow remained; and death seemed to lose its terrors, and to borrow a grace and dignity in sublime keeping with the life that was ebbing away.[2]

Lee, 63, never left his bed. On October 10 he experienced a chill, and his pulse speeded up alarmingly. The next day his mind began to wander; in his delirium he was heard to say, "Tell Hill he *must* come up." For most of that night, Mrs. Lee, herself wheelchair bound, sat holding his hand. The following morning, about nine o'clock, Lee spoke his last intelligible words. "Strike the tent," he murmured.

On the morning of October 15, a procession of townspeople, local dignitaries, and old soldiers formed in front of the residence and accompanied the hearse on a route through town and back to the college chapel. Behind the hearse a groom led Lee's famous mount, Traveller. Guns at the nearby Virginia Military Institute fired minute guns as the procession moved through the streets of Lexington.

At the chapel, mourners overflowed onto a lawn made soggy by the recent rains. The service was brief, probably in accordance with Lee's wishes. The Rev. William Pendleton read the Episcopal burial service, but there was no sermon. The service closed with one of the general's favorite hymns, "How Firm a Foundation."

In the days and weeks that followed, the South held memorial services for its most respected soldier. In Richmond the crowd grew so large that the ceremony had to be moved to Monument Square. In Atlanta an estimated 10,000 people gathered at City Hall to hear a memorial address by Gen. John B. Gordon that left many of the audience in tears.[3] The tributes that poured into Lexington were not all from the South. The *Montreal Telegraph* editorialized, "Posterity will rank Lee above Wellington or Napoleon, before Saxe or Turene, above Marlborough or Frederick, before Alexander or Caesar. . . . He has made his own name, and the Confederacy he served, immortal."[4] Field Marshal Garnet Wolseley, a British officer who had visited the Army of Northern Virginia in 1862, recalled Lee as "the ablest general, and to me . . . the greatest man I had ever conversed with, and yet I have had the privilege of meeting von Molke and Prince Bismarck."[5]

Some of Lee's admirers went further, infusing a spiritual quality to Lee's refusal of the command of a great Federal army in 1861. At the dedication of a monument to Lee in 1883, the principal orator recalled how Gen. Winfield Scott had offered Lee the command of an army to conquer the South. Acceptance of Scott's offer meant honor, glory, and power. But Lee could not be tempted: "Since the Son of Man stood upon the Mount, and saw 'all the kingdoms of the world and the glory of them' stretched before him, and turned away . . . no follower of the meek and lowly Savior can have undergone [a] more trying ordeal."[6]

Predictably, some of Lee's erstwhile enemies found such cloying praise irritating.* Ulysses S. Grant, during his trip around the world in the late 1870s, told a journalist that he had never had the same regard for Lee as for Gen. Joseph E. Johnston:

> Lee was a good man, a fair commander, who had everything in his favor. . . . Lee was of a slow, cautious nature, without imagination, or humor, always the same, with grave dignity. . . . Lee was a good deal of a headquarters general, from what I can hear and from what his officers say.[7]

A few years later, in 1887, Gen. William T. Sherman took exception to an article by the British general Wolseley in *McMillan's Magazine*. Whereas Wolseley had argued that Lee was far more capable than his Federal opponents in the late war, Sherman contended in the *North American Review* that Lee's horizon never extended beyond Virginia. "He never rose to the grand problem which involved a continent and future generations." Indeed, Sherman charged, had Lee "stood firm in 1861, and used his personal influence, he could have stayed the Civil War."[8]

Such views were very much in the minority at that time. A succession of chroniclers of the Lost Cause published books extolling Lee and his gallant army. Paradoxically, a running dispute over Lee's worst battle, Gettysburg, had the effect of further burnishing his reputation.

---

* When, in 1886, Gen. Alfred H. Terry was invited to purchase a document penned by Lee, the Federal officer replied with some annoyance that his correspondent would be better advised to seek a purchaser among those who had participated "in the same evil cause with General Lee," and had "participated in his errors." Alfred H. Terry to Darvin C. Pavy, Sept. 25, 1886. Author's collection.

In the postwar years, Gen. James Longstreet came under heavy criticism from former Confederates for his alleged slowness on the second, critical day of the battle. In an attempt to rebut his critics, Longstreet wrote a number of magazine articles that mixed praise for Lee with a portrayal of him as a rigid and unimaginative strategist. Lee, according to Longstreet, had agreed before the Gettysburg campaign that any battle in Pennsylvania should be fought defensively. Longstreet told how he had suggested to Lee, after the first day at Gettysburg, that the Confederates forgo a frontal attack in favor of a move around Gen. George G. Meade's left, only to be overruled. On the morning of the third day, Longstreet wrote, he had urged Lee as strongly as he could to abandon what became known as Pickett's Charge in favor of a flanking movement.

Longstreet, who allied himself with the despised Republicans after the war, proved an inviting target for Lee's admirers, and Gen. Jubal A. Early, another of Lee's corps commanders, led the counterattack. Charging Longstreet with having repeatedly placed obstacles in the way of Lee's plans in Pennsylvania, Early said, of the mishandled Confederate attacks on the second day at Gettysburg, that "either General Lee or General Longstreet was responsible for the remarkable delay that took place. . . . I choose to believe that it was not General Lee." [9] So did most of Early's readers.

The war of words continued, but by the turn of the century Lee was receiving praise from the North as well as from the South. Theodore Roosevelt wrote that, as a military commander, not even George Washington ranked with "the wonderful war-chief who for four years led the Army of Northern Virginia." Woodrow Wilson, then a history professor, called Lee "unapproachable in the history of our country." [10] The centennial of Lee's birth occurred during 1907, and for decades thereafter his birthday, January 19, would be a holiday in most states of the Old Confederacy.

In 1912, Gamaliel Bradford, a popular historian of the early twentieth century, published a widely acclaimed biography, *Lee the American*, which enshrined Lee as a national, as well as a Southern, hero. Bradford sought to analyze all his subjects in terms of their character traits, and he found in Lee the finest qualities of the Old South—courage, dignity, and devotion to duty. When a national hall of fame was established at New York University in 1901, Lee was one of the first to be inducted.

This honor by the hall of fame was seconded by Charles Francis Adams, a descendant of two Yankee presidents, who had himself served in a Federal cavalry regiment during the Civil War. Speaking before the Massachusetts Historical Society in 1902, Adams recalled the statue of Oliver Cromwell in front of the Houses of Parliament in London and asked rhetorically whether it was not time for a national monument to Robert E. Lee. If Lee was a traitor, Adams observed, so too were Cromwell and George Washington.

The near-universal praise for Lee as a man and a soldier reached its zenith in the 1930s with the publication of Douglas Southall Freeman's epic, four-volume biography, *R. E. Lee*. A journalist by profession, Freeman was also a meticulous scholar and an unapologetic admirer of Lee. At first under contract for a 75,000-word book on Lee, Freeman undertook instead a definitive biography. In 1934, nineteen years after his work was commissioned, the first two volumes were published. The final two volumes followed a year later.

From the day they appeared, Freeman's volumes were greeted with extravagant praise. Historian Dumas Malone wrote that, as great as his expectations had been, "the reality surpassed them." The *New York Times* called the work "Lee complete for all time." Historian Henry Steele Commager wrote that Freeman "has so combined scholarship and art that every line is fact and every page interpretation, and from this fusion has come a figure of indubitable authority and of moving beauty." [11] In 1935, Freeman was awarded the Pulitzer Prize for Biography.

Freeman viewed Lee as a master of strategy who excelled at getting the most from his subordinate commanders and from his soldiers. In the spring of 1862, Lee alone had seen how Stonewall Jackson's small army in the Shenandoah Valley could be the key to saving Richmond. In the Seven Days' campaign that followed, Lee had sought to seize the initiative wherever possible, and force the enemy to react. He had made the most of the intelligence sources available to him and routinely uncovered and exploited the weaknesses of enemy commanders. Lee's great victories—the Seven Days' campaign before Richmond, Second Manassas, and Chancellorsville—had been achieved in the face of great numerical odds. Five qualities, Freeman believed, made Lee a great commander: his interpretation of military intelligence, commitment to the offensive, careful choice of position, exact logistics, and daring.

Freeman did not claim that Lee was perfect. He acknowledged the failure of his 1861 campaign to reclaim western Virginia and the fact that early in the war Lee had made demands of his staff that were beyond their capabilities. Freeman believed that Lee had erred in promoting Gen. Richard S. Ewell to corps command and that Lee had been guilty of occasional tactical lapses in the Wilderness campaign of 1864. At Gettysburg, however, Lee had been betrayed by Longstreet.

Freeman reserved his greatest admiration for Lee's personal qualities. He had respect bordering on awe for Lee's modesty, piety, consideration for his soldiers, and above all for his devotion to duty. What was the key to his subject's personality? Lee, Freeman wrote, was one of a small number of people "in whom there is no inconsistency to be explained, no enigma to be solved. What he seemed he was—a wholly human gentleman, the essential elements of whose positive character were two and only two, simplicity and spirituality." [12]

Freeman was a tough act to follow. Nevertheless, Burke Davis published a flattering single-volume biography in 1956. Nine years later, Virginia historian Clifford Dowdey, noting the appearance of several thousand Lee documents not available to Freeman, published a comprehensive single-volume biography. Soon after, however, the tide began to turn.

In 1977, Thomas L. Connelly published a landmark study, *The Marble Man* (Louisiana State University Press, 1977), which is really two books in one. The first relates the growth of the "Lee legend" in the South; the second presents the author's personal insights into Lee's character. These insights, although heavily reliant on pop psychology, reflect a close examination of his subject.

Connelly insists that the Lee cult was largely a postwar phenomenon. During the first years of the Civil War, most Southerners viewed Stonewall Jackson as the resident military genius; Lee had to overcome the onus of his early setbacks in West Virginia. Connelly, who downplays the intense devotion that Lee inspired in his soldiers as army commander, views the Lee legend in part as a response to the South's need to explain defeat on the battlefield. Many Christians believed that there was a direct link between God's grace and one's success in earthly endeavors. Lee's sterling character was held up after Appomattox as proof that good men do not always succeed.

In Connelly's view, the Lee legend was also a by-product of a concerted campaign to discredit his controversial lieutenant, Longstreet.

Connelly chronicles the efforts of various admirers of Lee, led by Early, to portray Longstreet as responsible for the debacle at Gettysburg and to hold Lee blameless. The author calls this campaign by Lee's admirers "the most cynical manipulation" ever attempted in the writing of Civil War history.[13]

And what of Lee himself? In contrast to Freeman's view—that Lee was a model of simplicity and devoid of personality flaws—Connelly found his subject to be extraordinarily complex. Lee's life was replete with "frustration, self-doubt, and a feeling of failure." He suffered from the effects of an unsatisfactory marriage and protracted absences from his family. As for Lee's legendary self-control, Connelly sees it as "an almost mechanical device that suppressed his naturally strong temper and vibrant personality."[14]

Five years after publication of *The Marble Man*, Lee's standing as a commander came under fire from authors with a different perspective, Grady McWhiney and Perry D. Jamieson. Their *Attack and Die* (University of Alabama Press, 1982) took most of the South's military leaders to task for their aggressive battlefield tactics. Using official casualty reports, the authors note that the Confederates were the attackers in eight of the first twelve major battles of the war, and that in these eight battles the Confederates lost 20,000 more men than the Union. The authors argue that the Confederate commitment to the tactical offensive, based on U.S. Army successes in the Mexican War, destroyed the South's armies. According to McWhiney and Jamieson, Lee favored the tactical offensive and assumed it whenever he could. It brought him victories at Second Manassas and Chancellorsville, but terrible defeats at Malvern Hill and Gettysburg. The authors marvel that Lee, on the brink of being overwhelmed by George B. McClellan's great army at Antietam, was still looking for a place in the enemy line to attack.[15]

Meanwhile, military historians were assessing the outcome of the Vietnam War, and retrofitting some of its "lessons" to the Civil War. Why did the South, with its limited resources, attempt to fight a conventional war when it could have organized local guerrilla units as the Vietnamese had done? Had not George Washington demonstrated against the British the feasibility of harrying operations to wear down a stronger enemy?

For the most part, early British writers on the American Civil War had written admiringly of Lee. In 1987, however, a prominent British military historian, John Keegan, published *The Mask of Command* (Viking Books, 1987), a study of military leadership, in which he lavished praise on Ulysses S. Grant while generally ignoring Lee. In Keegan's view, both Lee and Stonewall Jackson were men of "limited imagination" who "thought in terms of defending the South's frontiers rather than exhausting the enemy."[16]

In 1991, Alan T. Nolan took up where Keegan left off. In *Lee Considered* (University of North Carolina Press, 1991), Nolan contended that, despite the biographies and other works that had dealt with Lee, the general had been the subject of little critical analysis. Nolan, while conceding perfunctorily that Lee was a "great man," devotes his book to an unrelenting search for flaws in Lee as a man and as a soldier.

Nolan points out that although Lee had expressed distaste for slavery, he had owned slaves and in at least one instance had been directly involved in selling them.[17] Nolan questions Lee's veracity in matters relating to his resignation from the U.S. Army in 1861. Noting that only forty-eight hours passed between Lee's resignation from the U.S. Army and his acceptance of a commission from Virginia, Nolan asks rhetorically whether Lee—contrary to statements that he was loyal to the United States until the moment of his resignation—may have negotiated with Confederate authorities in Richmond before resigning from Federal service.[18]

Nolan is equally tough on Lee as a strategist. In his view, the South should have concentrated on keeping armies in the field long enough to force the North to come to terms. Lee's aggressiveness, in Nolan's view, resulted in such heavy casualties to the Army of Northern Virginia as to negate this strategy. Like McWhiney and Jamieson, Nolan views Lee's preoccupation with engaging and defeating Union forces in battle as counterproductive. His favorite contemporary commentator on Lee is Gen. Edward P. Alexander, who maintained that Lee gave battle unnecessarily at both Antietam and Gettysburg.[19]

The revisionist scholarship of the 1980s and 1990s was hard on Lee, and he fared little better in the popular media. In the 1993 movie extravaganza *Gettysburg*, Longstreet emerged as a tough, realistic soldier far too experienced to take on the Federals in a frontal attack. Lee, in contrast, was portrayed as pious yet befuddled, and mindlessly committed to offensive tactics. On screen, the charismatic victor of the Seven Days' campaign, Second Manassas, Fredericksburg, and Chancellorsville was transformed into a character reminiscent of an over-worked accountant who had misplaced his hat.

IT IS DIFFICULT TO RECONCILE THE VIEW OF LEE HELD BY Freeman with the portrayals of his critics. Either Lee had a confident, vibrant personality or he was tortured by self-doubt. Either he was a brilliant strategist who carried his cause to the brink of victory or he was a mediocre tactician who needlessly dissipated his resources.

Lee has defenders among modern scholars. Authors such as Albert Castel, William C. Davis, and Gary W. Gallagher, among others, have sought to put Lee's achievements in proper perspective. A volume edited by Gallagher, *Lee the Soldier* (University of Nebraska Press, 1996), draws on a wide range of writing about Lee and his campaigns. The discovery of the "real" Robert E. Lee remains a challenge, how-ever, because the general was a private person—reticent in conversa-tion and cautious in correspondence. More than a century after his death there are still unanswered questions.

CHAPTER TWO

SON OF THE OLD DOMINION

ON A GRAY WINTER AFTERNOON IN 1806, A CAR-
riage turned into the curving driveway leading to Stratford Hall, a
stately home on Virginia's Northern Neck. The mud-splattered vehi-
cle, which showed the signs of a long day's journey from the James
River, carried a single passenger and her servant. The passenger was
Ann Carter Lee, returning from burying her father, Charles Carter, to
whom she had been devoted. Her carriage, open to the elements, was
ill suited to the rutted country roads of Tidewater Virginia, but her
husband could provide nothing better.

Ann Carter Lee was the second wife of Col. Henry Lee, who had
served in the American Revolution as a commander of cavalry, and
had earned the nickname "Light-Horse Harry." Lee's wartime dash had
brought him a degree of fame but had proved of little use after the war,
and disastrous land speculations had brought him to the brink of
bankruptcy. To be sure, debt was no stranger to the gentry of the cash-
poor Tidewater. To a remarkable extent, however, Lee had alienated
even friends by his fiscal irresponsibility. When he attempted to foist off
a bad note to George Washington in settlement of a debt, Lee had

Robert E. Lee's father, "Light-Horse Harry" Lee, at the height of his Revolutionary War fame. AUTHOR'S COLLECTION.

drawn a sharp rebuke from his wartime commander.[1] Subsequently he had sold off vast tracts of his first wife's Stratford estate, yet still could not keep his creditors at bay.

Harry Lee's political loyalties wavered from time to time, but he eventually embraced the Federalists, and in 1791 his wartime fame was sufficient for the Virginia legislature to elect him governor for the first of three one-year terms. Notwithstanding his business ineptitude, Lee gave considerable thought to political issues, and was convinced that the country required a strong central government.

Lee's first wife, Matilda, died in 1790. After a period of mourning, Harry, without money but with some political standing, sought a new bride. After one well-to-do young woman turned him down he directed his attention to Ann Carter, one of twenty-one children of Charles Carter, one of the wealthiest men in the state. At the age of 50, Lee was seventeen years older than his intended, but Ann appears to have been truly impressed with her suitor. Charles Carter at first opposed the marriage, then relented, and Harry and Ann were married on June 18, 1793. The *Virginia Gazette*, reporting the wedding, referred to Harry Lee as "Virginia's favorite Young Soldier."[2]

The Stratford Hall to which Ann returned that afternoon in 1806 had been constructed by earlier Lees, beginning in about 1740. Built in the shape of a great H, with two clusters of four great chimneys, the hall recalled the stately homes of England. It evoked, in the words of one historian, "a feeling of austerity, solidity, integrity, seriousness and permanence—a suitable symbol of the family who lived there for two centuries."[3] The lawn in front of the mansion was dotted with oaks and poplars.

At the house, however, chains were now strung across the central steps to discourage sheriff's deputies and bill collectors. Toward the Potomac River were open fields, barren and uninviting in the winter gloom. Fires were kept in only two rooms, and the great hall, warmed by a single brazier, was a frigid passageway connecting the two wings. It was in this gloomy setting that Ann Carter Lee delivered her fourth child on January 19, 1807. The parents named him Robert Edward Lee, after two of Ann's cousins.

Robert was only two when, in April 1809, his father was jailed for debt. Harry had seen it coming. From jail he corresponded with his companions of the Revolutionary War and began a memoir of the war in the southern theater. He was released from prison after a year, his most pressing debts having been satisfied by relatives. But Harry Lee was then forced to leave Stratford, for under the terms of Matilda's will the estate now belonged to her oldest son. While her husband completed his memoirs, Ann Carter Lee set about finding a new home. That summer, Harry, Ann, and their four children left Stratford and moved into a small house in Alexandria while they waited for a house owned by one of Ann's relatives, William Henry Fitzhugh, to become available. According to family legend, 3-year-old Robert returned one last time to the ground-floor bedroom at Stratford where he had been born to say good-bye to two angels portrayed in the ironwork about the fireplace.

ALEXANDRIA, ON THE WEST BANK OF THE POTOMAC SOUTH of Washington, D.C., was an important port in the early nineteenth century. Ships from many countries lay at its wharfs to take on board hogsheads of tobacco from Virginia and Maryland. The community of 7,500 was home to thirty-four taverns, but it also boasted churches, street lamps, and a public library. Its redbrick houses and cobblestone streets conveyed an air of permanence and prosperity, and Alexandria would be Robert E. Lee's home during his formative years.

For his mother, the move from Stratford was a substantial, but not especially painful, change in circumstances. Her house on Oronoco Street was tiny compared with Stratford, but there were no drafty halls, no bill collectors, and no painful memories. Her inheritance initially brought in about $1,200 per year, and while this was not a princely sum, she was soon able to purchase a new carriage.

In July 1812 Harry Lee was in Baltimore when a Federalist friend, publisher Alexander Hanson, attracted the ire of the Jeffersonians with editorials attacking U.S. involvement in the War of 1812. Lee was sympathetic to Hanson's plight, and one evening he joined the editor and a handful of friends in downtown Baltimore where they confronted an angry mob. When the crowd grew vicious, Hanson and Lee led their followers to the jail, viewing it as a sanctuary. The mayor and the local militia commander were friendly toward the mob, however, and when rioters stormed the jail on the night of July 28 the authorities did nothing to stop them. The rampaging mob attacked the Federalists by candlelight, killing one and seriously wounding the others. Harry Lee

Lee's boyhood home on Oronoco Street in Alexandria, Virginia. PHOTO BY AUTHOR.

suffered cuts to his face and a severe wound to his head. Left for dead by his assailants, he was smuggled to safety by friends the following morning.

Lee returned to Alexandria with his face disfigured and his health broken; he never fully recovered from his ordeal. With financial assistance from sympathetic friends, including James Monroe, he sailed for the Caribbean in 1813 in hopes that a tropical climate would help restore his health. For Robert and his siblings, Harry Lee would be an absentee father.

The years of Robert's boyhood are known only through family lore, viewed through the prism of his later fame. His mother taught him piety, and he is said to have learned the Episcopal catechism before he could read. Several of the Lee children, including Robert, attended family schools sponsored by the Carters, one of which was the plantation home of Ann's sister, Elizabeth Randolph. At this time we have a rare glimpse of Robert as an active, spirited boy. When his mother made some critical reference concerning Robert's behavior, Elizabeth replied that she had found him a charming child, but if he was proving difficult at home Ann should follow her own prescription: "Whip and pray, and pray and whip."[4]

As much as anything he studied in school, Lee learned in Alexandria of George Washington. The spirit of the Father of His Country was pervasive in northern Virginia. To Robert, Washington was never a remote figure; he was his father's wartime commander and friend. At Christ Church he admired the first president's pew. George Washington Parke Custis, Martha Washington's grandson, was an Alexandria neighbor; he would later become Lee's father-in-law.

Harry Lee had been away for four years when, desperately ill, he boarded a schooner whose captain agreed to return him to the mainland. At Cumberland Island, Georgia, he was sheltered by Mrs. James Shaw, daughter of Gen. Nathanael Greene, under whom Lee had served in the Revolution. Harry was treated by a surgeon from the frigate *John Adams*, on patrol nearby, but to no avail. Death came as a relief to the cancer-stricken soldier on March 24, 1818.

Robert E. Lee was only 11 when his father died. At that age he was doubtless spared the details of his father's financial ruin, and although Robert may have learned the reasons for his mother's modest circumstances, Ann Carter Lee made sure that Robert remembered his father for his wartime heroics. Twice in later life Robert would visit his father's grave in Georgia, and after the Civil War he would write the introduction for a new edition of Harry Lee's memoirs. In Robert's biographical sketch there would be no mention of financial reverses or of time in jail for debt, and the move from Stratford to Alexandria would be for the purpose of educating his children.

Thomas L. Connelly contends that Lee "never forgot his father's disgrace," and other authors have speculated that Robert's lifelong preoccupation with ethical behavior may have grown out of embarrassment at his father's reputation. Nothing in Robert's writings, however, supports such a hypothesis. Whatever he may have heard, Robert accepted his father as Harry saw himself: as a war hero who fell victim to hard times. But even as Robert sought to keep alive the memory of his father's military exploits, his personal hero was George Washington— the same Washington to whom Light-Horse Harry Lee had passed a bad note.

⋆⇒ ⇐⋆

A GERMAN TRAVELER TO NINETEENTH-CENTURY VIRGINIA was impressed at how sons of the well-to-do were indulged. "At fifteen," he wrote, "his father gives him a horse and a negro, with which he riots around the country, attends every fox-hunt, horse-race and cockfight, and does nothing else whatever."[5] There was no such carefree youth for Robert E. Lee. His older brother, Carter, was at college, and he was soon followed by Ann's second son, Smith Lee, who received a naval appointment that took him away from home in 1819. Ann herself was not well, manifesting early symptoms of the tuberculosis that in time would kill her.

Young Robert became the man of the house. No longer at boarding school, he handled many of the household chores, from caring for the horses to assisting with shopping. About 1820, however, he entered Alexandria Academy, which had begun as a private school but was free to Alexandria residents. There he studied the classics, along with mathematics, at which he excelled.

When Ann Carter Lee felt up to it she visited friends and relations at their plantation homes, doubtless taking Robert. They went often to Ravensworth, the home of William Fitzhugh, who owned the Alexandria house where the Lees now lived. They also went to Arlington to visit the home of Fitzhugh's sister Mary, who was married to Martha Washington's grandson and who had a daughter almost Robert E. Lee's age.

Meanwhile, what was Robert to do about a profession? There was no "Lee plantation" for him to manage, and in any case Robert was the youngest of three sons. He had no incentive to go into business, for upper-class Virginians were uniformly contemptuous of the trades. And for all his later piety, Lee had not been confirmed in the Episcopal Church, and probably never considered a career in the ministry. Whatever his inclinations, finances were a consideration. Ann Lee had been able to send Carter Lee to Harvard, but his four years there had depleted her resources.

Smith Lee had chosen a career in the navy. Might not his younger brother find a similar vocation in the army? As a son of Light-Horse Harry Lee, Robert had no trouble generating the necessary letters of recommendation, and in 1824 he received an appointment to West Point.

⋆⟞⟝ ⟞⟝⋆

THE U.S. MILITARY ACADEMY HAD BEEN FOUNDED IN 1802 AS a school of engineering. Situated on a rocky promontory on the west bank of the Hudson River, some forty miles north of New York City, West Point boasted a majestic natural setting. The physical appearance of the academy was less impressive. The academy in Lee's time consisted of four gray stone buildings set on a plain. Two of the buildings were barracks, one was a mess hall, and one was a two-story multipurpose building that housed a chapel, the library, classrooms, and a laboratory.

Lee quickly mastered the course of study. At West Point, engineering encompassed fortifications, the "science" of artillery, tactics, and military architecture. The study of artillery educated the cadets with respect to various types of guns and projectiles, including rangefinding and ballistics. "Grand tactics" considered strategy as well as tactics— military organization, the conduct of marches, battlefield formations, and consideration of the maxims of war. Military architecture included civil engineering—the construction of canals and bridges as well as forts. Rote learning was much in vogue, but for Lee and his classmates West Point offered an education in civil engineering that was as good as any in the United States.

Quite a few cadets went stir-crazy in the academy's monastic environment. Some smuggled liquor, tobacco, and even prostitutes into the barracks. Jefferson Davis, class of 1828, was a chronic disciplinary problem, and was nearly expelled on several occasions. Just before Christmas in 1826, Davis and several others invited selected cadets to an illegal eggnog party in Davis's quarters. Cadet Robert E. Lee was invited but declined.[6]

Lee made friends at the academy and continued to gain admirers. His closest companion was probably Jack Mackay, a Georgian with whom Lee would keep up a warm correspondence until Mackay's death in 1848. Another friend was a fellow Virginian, Joseph E. Johnston. Late in life Johnston would say of Lee,

> No other youth or man so united the qualities that win
> warm friendship and command high respect [as did Lee].
> For he was full of sympathy and kindness, genial and fond
> of gay conversation, and even of fun, while his correctness
> of demeanor and attention to all duties . . . gave him a
> superiority that every one acknowledged in his heart.[7]

Johnston's opinion was widely shared. Erasmus D. Keyes, later a Federal general, recalled, "All [Lee's] accomplishments and alluring virtues appeared natural to him, and he was free from the anxiety, distrust and awkwardness that attend a sense of inferiority."[8] These early impressions of Lee are of interest because they strike a recurring theme: his lack of pretense, his naturalness. Nothing about him was artificial or contrived.

When Lee returned to West Point for his final two years, his studies were more challenging than before. Military studies included advanced work on fortifications and readings on the science of war. On entering his first class (senior) year, Lee was appointed corps adjutant, the highest rank to which a cadet could aspire. He graduated second in his class academically—one Charles Mason of New York was first—but no one questioned that Lee stood first in general excellence.

The Lee legend began at West Point. Remarkably, he attended the academy for four years without accumulating a single demerit. He would not be the only cadet to achieve such a distinction—a few others also kept their slates clean—but it tells something of Robert E. Lee. His was an orderly universe. Regulations were to be obeyed. Above all, he had the self-assurance necessary to maintain a perfect disciplinary record in a macho environment where demerits were viewed by many cadets as a badge of honor.

Lee was 22 when he graduated. He stood slightly more than 5 feet 10 inches in height, with a square jaw, brown eyes, and curly brown hair. Broad-shouldered and erect, his physique and appearance were those of a model soldier. His manner was outgoing, with none of the reserve so characteristic of his later years. Yet even as a cadet there was something about Lee that seemed in search of a pedestal. His classmates referred to him as "the Marble Model."[9]

LEE HAD LITTLE OPPORTUNITY TO CELEBRATE AFTER GRADUATION. His mother, who had moved from Alexandria to the Fitzhugh plantation at Ravensworth, was terminally ill. Lee, who had not yet received orders, became a full-time nurse, mixing his mother's medicines and preparing her meals.

Ann Carter Lee was 56 when she died on July 10, 1829. She had lived as a widow for eleven years, nearly all that time under a cloud of financial worry. Without question she played the greatest role in shaping Robert's character as a young man. From his father Robert had

The first known portrait of Lee, by William E. West, shows him in the uniform of a lieutenant of engineers. LIBRARY OF CONGRESS.

inherited an interest in a military career. From his mother he appears to have inherited the twin virtues of self-control and uncomplaining courage, virtues that Light-Horse Harry Lee had given her many opportunities to display.

Ann Lee did not die poor. She left a trust fund worth about $20,000, which under the terms of her will was to be divided between her two daughters. To her sons, who were deemed capable of making their own way, she left thirty slaves and a 20,000-acre tract of land in southwestern Virginia. Carter would prove unable to make the land a paying proposition, but the three brothers—Carter, Smith, and Robert—appear to have netted about $3,000 each from their mother's estate.[10] Robert spent the remainder of his graduation leave visiting his numerous relatives in Virginia. He may have called on Mary Custis at Arlington, but there was nothing in the nature of formal courting at this stage.

In August, Lee received his first orders from the Chief of Engineers. Within the army the Engineers were an elite group. Not only did they receive extra pay, but their assignments were often close to urban areas and their amenities. The successful defense of Fort McHenry during the War of 1812 had provided an impetus for the construction of forts along the East Coast. As part of this program Lee was ordered to Cockspur Island, near Savannah, to assist in constructing a new fort.

The work on Fort Pulaski was carried on in wretched conditions. Cockspur Island was scarcely an island at all, and the work crews, white and black, worked in a sea of mud and amid clouds of mosquitoes. The assignment was made bearable for young Lee by the presence in Savannah of the Mackay family, the mother and daughters of his West Point friend Jack Mackay. Young Lee was "adopted" by the Mackay family, and spent as much time in Savannah as his duties permitted. He courted one of the Mackay daughters for a time, but Margaret Mackay eventually became engaged to a Harvard classmate of Carter Lee.

Meanwhile, Robert was turning his attention to Mary Custis. He had known her for several years, but not until Lee had completed his tour at Cockspur Island does he appear to have given her his full attention. Mary was the spoiled daughter of the squire of Arlington, George Washington Parke Custis, who was Martha Washington's grandson by her first marriage. When Martha Washington died, Custis inherited four tracts of land, one of which, overlooking the Potomac south of Washington, D.C., he made the site of his manor house, Arlington. Custis's great pride was his connection with George Washington, and he delighted in showing visitors the president's four-poster bed and the punch bowl from which he had served guests.

Mary Custis's mother was a Fitzhugh, and probably had good reports on Robert from her sister Anna, the mistress of Ravensworth. She quickly approved of Robert, but her husband was a different matter. While the squire of Arlington could find no fault with Robert person-

Mary Custis Lee at about the time of her marriage. LIBRARY OF CONGRESS.

ally, the fact remained that he was dependent for his livelihood on the salary of a second lieutenant.

Mary Custis was a year younger than Robert E. Lee. Slight of figure and not renowned for her beauty, Mary had a reputation as a conversationalist and appears to have been genuinely smitten by the handsome young officer who came courting. Robert proposed in the summer of 1830 and was accepted subject to Mary's parents' approval. On September 30 Lee wrote to his brother Carter, "I am engaged to Miss Mary C. . . . That is, she & her mother have given their consent. But the Father has not yet made up his mind, though it is supposed [he] will not object."[11] As Lee predicted, George Custis's reservations were eventually overcome.

Mary Lee was intelligent, pious, and well read in English literature. Many years later she related how she had undergone a religious conversion just before her wedding. She had been aware of her own sinfulness, but had been unwilling to "give up *all* for God." Now, about to wed one of the handsomest young men in Virginia, Mary felt born again. Thereafter came "joy and peace," or so Mary recalled.[12]

Robert E. Lee and Mary Custis were married at Arlington on June 30, 1831, with Smith Lee acting as best man. Their honeymoon consisted of two weeks at Ravensworth, and already there was good news: The happy couple would not have to set up housekeeping amid the mud and mosquitoes of Cockspur Island. That summer, Robert and Mary reported to Lee's new posting, Fortress Monroe, overlooking Hampton Roads at the tip of the York Peninsula.

Fortress Monroe was an improvement over Cockspur Island, but a considerable step down from Arlington. Mary Lee was accustomed to a life of luxury. In contrast to her punctual husband, she had been brought up in a society where it was fashionable to keep others waiting. When the Lees arrived at Fortress Monroe, Mary had with her two "servants," only to find that her and Robert's living quarters consisted of two rooms in a brick barracks.

Mary made few friends around the post. Whereas her husband enjoyed the company of his fellow officers and their wives, Mary did not, finding them "rather stupid." When the Lees returned to Arlington that Christmas, Mrs. Custis prevailed on Robert to return to his post alone. Mary was expecting their first child, and she would be more comfortable at Arlington than at Fortress Monroe.

During the spring of 1832 Lee wrote cajoling letters to his wife, urging her to return. "I don't know that I shall ever overcome my propensity for order & method," he wrote, "but I will try."[13] To tempt her, he managed to find more spacious quarters and to engage a housekeeper. Mary agreed to return, and the summer months passed with Mary doing needlework "while Robert reads to me."[14] Nevertheless, Mary Lee had begun a pattern of frequent absences from her husband that would be characteristic of the first three decades of their marriage.

NEARLY TWO CENTURIES AFTER ROBERT E. LEE WAS A LIEU-tenant in the U.S. Army, it is difficult to recall how strong regional loyalties were in the United States. Whereas states' rights were an issue only in the South, regional pride was found everywhere. Lee was a cit-izen of the United States and an officer in its army, but he thought of himself first as a Virginian. The nullification controversy of 1832–33, in which President Andrew Jackson threatened to use force if South Car-olina failed to comply with federal revenue laws, drew a very Southern response from the 26-year-old Lee. To a friend, Andrew Talcott, he wrote, "The South has had to bear some hard kicks from all sides."[15]

Politics aside, Lee had a strong sentimental attachment to the Vir-ginia homes that he had known since boyhood. Lee's returns to Virginia after various postings often evoked bursts of nostalgia; in 1838 he wrote to a cousin that such was his delight at returning home that "I nodded to all the old trees as I passed, chatted with all the drivers and stable boys, shook hands with the landlords, and in the fullness of my heart—don't tell Cousin Mary—wanted to kiss all the pretty girls."[16]

Lee probably saw no conflict between his potentially divided loyal-ties. If he had been educated at federal expense, it was because each state was entitled to send a certain number of cadets to West Point. If he reflected on the right of secession he may have had doubts about it; his father, after all, had believed in a strong central government. But whereas the Union in its present form had existed only a few decades, Virginia had existed as a political entity for two centuries. Robert E. Lee had been born in Virginia, owned property in Virginia, and had married a daughter of the Old Dominion. Virginia would always have first call on his loyalties.

CHAPTER THREE

THE YOUNG SOLDIER

THE U.S. ARMY THAT LEE JOINED IN 1829 WAS small—about 4,000 men—but the requirements of the Seminole War would soon cause it to treble in size. The army was primarily an Indian-fighting organization and would remain such even after the war with Mexico.

Lee was probably grateful to have been in Georgia rather than Virginia in 1830, for that year saw a new scandal in the Lee family. Henry Lee was the third child of Light-Horse Harry Lee by his first wife, Matilda, and thus was a half-brother of Robert. It was Henry who inherited Stratford after Matilda's death in 1790. In 1817 he married Ann McCarty, the orphaned daughter of a prosperous Westmoreland County planter. Now able to enjoy the life of a country gentleman, Henry neglected his estate and ran up heavy debts.

Not long after Henry and Ann married, the courts made Henry the guardian of Ann's younger sister, Elizabeth "Betsy" McCarty, who had been living with her grandparents. There were now two wealthy, attractive women at Stratford, and according to persistent rumor Henry fathered a stillborn child by Betsy. In any case, in 1821 the Westmoreland County court responded to a complaint from Betsy asking that she be taken from Stratford and restored to the care of her stepfather,

Richard Stuart. The court complied, concluding that Henry Lee had abused his trust in his guardianship of Betsy McCarty.[1]

Henry Lee was called "Black-Horse Harry" behind his back, but the scandal might have died a natural death had he not aspired to a diplomatic career. Black-Horse Harry campaigned for Andrew Jackson in the presidential election of 1828, and shortly after his inauguration the new president submitted Lee's name to the Senate for confirmation as U.S. consul to Morocco. Henry had numerous enemies, and they used the confirmation hearing to revive the McCarty scandal. The nomination was rejected amid a wave of outrage that led Henry Lee to spend the remainder of his life in France. Had Robert E. Lee needed a reminder of the perils inherent in extramarital affairs, his half-brother's ruin would have served that purpose.

At Fortress Monroe, Lee was responsible for constructing a moat around the outer works, and for building the foundations for a smaller fort at the Rip Raps, in the bay itself. Mary did not care for his long workdays. She complained in one letter that she did not walk much because Robert was rarely available to escort her. However, her husband did have admirable qualities. Robert was "tender and affectionate," and he spent his evenings at home "instead of frequenting the card games which attract so many."[2]

Indeed, young Lee had little interest in the dissipation for which the army was notorious. Not only did he not play cards, he also did not drink except for an occasional glass of wine. Teetotalers were rare in the Old Army, and in staying away from whiskey Lee set himself apart from his peers. Lee found drunkenness disturbing. He never commented on his own aversion to alcohol, but he probably looked with distrust on any activity that threatened his self-control.

Robert, handsome and accomplished, was always in demand at post entertainments. During his wife's frequent absences he served as an escort to many young belles, and managed to do so without a whiff of scandal. He maintained a lively correspondence with Eliza Mackay, the sister of his good friend Jack, and with the wife of another army chum, Andrew Talcott, whom he was fond of addressing as "my beautiful Talcott." To Jack Mackay he confessed a weakness for pretty girls, "for I have met them in no place, in no garb, in no situation that I did not feel my heart open to them, like the flower to the sun."[3]

Despite Mary's absences, the Lees managed to add to their family with regularity. Their first child, whom they named George Washington Custis, was born in 1832; their first daughter, Mary, arrived three years later. The third child and second son, William Henry Fitzhugh Lee, called Rooney, was born in 1837. He was followed by Ann in 1839 and Agnes in 1841. Not until their sixth child did they give the name Robert E. Lee Jr. The seventh and last child, a daughter born in 1845, was named Mildred.

Long before the last children were born Mary Lee's health had become a problem. After young Mary's birth in 1835, her mother was taken ill and developed an abdominal infection that kept her bedridden for more than two months. The next year she came down with mumps. Lee wrote to Andrew Talcott in June that the mumps had been accompanied by a fever "which fell upon the brain, and seemed to overthrow her entire nervous system."[4]

If Lee had second thoughts about his choice of a bride, he kept them to himself. He may have been intrigued by the thought of marrying into a family so closely associated with his hero, George Washington. But a Lee, in any case, did not simply marry the girl next door; he married a Fitzhugh, a Carter, or a Custis. Lee would never have considered marriage outside the world of his Virginia "cousins," and his union with Mary Custis, unsatisfying though it may seem to have been at times, survived many trials, in part because Lee would not permit it to fail. But Lee was not, as some have suggested, the victim of a loveless marriage. In 1864, with the army he commanded facing defeat in the Civil War, Lee wrote to Mary one of his warmest letters on the occasion of their wedding anniversary:

> I was glad to receive your letter yesterday and to hear that you were better. . . . Do you recollect what a happy day thirty-three years ago this was? How many hopes and pleasures it gave birth to! God has been very merciful and kind to us, and . . . I pray that He may continue His mercies and blessings.[5]

⊷═◗ ◖═⊶

IN FEBRUARY 1846, A 4,000-MAN FORCE AT CORPUS CHRISTI, Texas, commanded by Col. Zachary Taylor, represented more than half of the existing U.S. Army. The reason it was stationed on the Texas-Mexico border was the continuing dispute between the United States and Mexico over a strip of land claimed by Texas before its annexation by the United States. After diplomatic efforts to resolve the dispute failed, Taylor received orders on February 4 to take his force into the disputed land lying between the Nueces River and the Rio Grande. This action provoked an attack on Taylor's force that led President James K. Polk to request a declaration of war.

The first actions of the war occurred along the Texas-Mexico border. Taylor won several minor engagements but refused to go on the offensive until he received reinforcements and supplies. In October, Gen. Winfield Scott presented a plan to Secretary of War William Marcy in which he argued that the key to the war was the capture of Mexico City, and that the means by which the city could be taken was a campaign from Mexico's east coast. What Scott was proposing was the largest amphibious operation known to have been attempted up to that time. And one of the officers he wanted on his staff was Robert E. Lee.

Lee had been at Fort Hamilton, New York, in 1841, when Scott became commanding general of the U.S. Army. Their paths first crossed three years later when both served on the Board of Visitors at West Point. At first glance the two men seemed to have little in common. Lee was a modest junior officer who had yet to hear a shot fired in anger. Scott, one of the heroes of the War of 1812, was 58 years old and addicted to show in both dress and prose. Yet there were similarities as well. Both were Virginians and each was a serious student of military affairs.

On March 9, 1847, the U.S. Navy landed Scott's army near Veracruz. Scott laid siege to the city, having at his disposal some eighteen army artillery pieces and six 32-pounders provided by the navy. When the Mexican commander refused Scott's surrender demand, the Americans opened fire on March 24. The city capitulated the following day, prompting Lt. Thomas J. Jackson, the Stonewall Jackson of later years, to call Scott's victory the equal of any military operation in U.S. history.[6]

After Veracruz capitulated, Scott prepared his 13,000-man force to move against Mexico City, some 250 mountainous miles inland. Lee accompanied Gen. David Twiggs's division in the advance. About twenty miles east of Jalapa, at Cerro Gordo, the Americans encountered the enemy in force for the first time. Scott arrived on the scene on April 14 and was told that although the Mexican position was strong, one of his engineers, Lt. P. G. T. Beauregard, had found a path that might permit an advance without using the main road.

The next morning Scott ordered Lee to make a further reconnaissance. Accompanied by a guide, Lee worked his way around the Mexican left until he reached a point where he could see a good portion of the enemy force. He was making his way alone through heavy undergrowth when he came upon a spring being used by Mexican soldiers to refill their canteens. He froze, then slowly crawled over to a fallen log. He lay behind it all day, not moving even when enemy soldiers used it as a bench. The sun rose higher and the flies arrived; Lee did not move. When darkness fell he returned to the American camp, telling Scott that he had discovered a trail that led around the Mexicans' left.[7]

On the morning of April 17 Lee accompanied Twiggs's division as it attempted to outflank the Mexicans in terrain that was nearly impassable. While Lee was leading Twiggs's skirmishers through ravines and around great boulders, the American column was finally discovered and Lee came under fire for the first time. As Cerro Gordo was overrun, Lee directed artillery fire against Antonio López de Santa Anna's camp. Unlike the Mexican artillery, which could fire only solid shot, the Americans had canister and grape as well, which were more effective against unfortified troops.[8] With the American artillery taking a heavy toll, and with the Mexicans' avenue of retreat threatened, Santa Anna's line disintegrated.

Despite this series of successes, Scott's army was not yet assured of taking Mexico City. Santa Anna was determined to defend the capital, and the invading Americans would have to advance along three or four roads that could be readily defended. The American supply line from Veracruz was now 200 miles long. Although the Mexican soldiers were inexperienced and badly led, they outnumbered the Americans more than two to one and could be expected to give a good account of themselves in defense of their capital.

In San Agustin, Scott again ordered his engineers to find the best route for his army. The Americans were obliged to cope with the *pedregal*, a lava-strewn wilderness of some ten square miles, which tended to channel any attacking force into easily defended roads on either side. Lee and Beauregard, with a small escort, set out on August 18 to investigate a wagon road that led northwest across the western edge of the *pedregal*.

Scott held a council of war that evening. There, Lee and Beauregard told the general and his staff that they had found a trail to the west, one that could be widened to accommodate artillery. The next morning Lee led about 500 men of Gen. Gideon Pillow's division along the trail that he and Beauregard had scouted. The Americans pressed past Mount Zacatepec through the lava field until they had hacked out a path to a point overlooking the towns of Padierna and Contreras. Lee supervised the placement of artillery, then spent the night crossing and recrossing the lava field with information for headquarters. The rain came in torrents, and Lee relied on his sense of direction, aided by occasional lightning flashes, to find his way. Scott would call Lee's repeated trips across the *pedregal* "the greatest feat of physical and moral courage" in the campaign.[9]

Fortunately for the Americans, the Mexicans had divided their forces. On August 20 the Americans routed the enemy at Contreras, and then won a more contested clash at Churubusco. The twin victories should have brought the speedy collapse of the Mexican capital, but they did not. Santa Anna requested an armistice, and for two weeks Scott's representatives engaged in unproductive negotiations with their Mexican counterparts. Finally recognizing the talks as a delaying tactic, Scott resumed his advance. On September 13, Chapultepec, the last redoubt protecting Mexico City, fell to the Americans in a dawn attack. Once again Lee was everywhere. At some time during the battle he sustained a wound that, though not serious, involved considerable loss of blood. When Scott directed him to take one more order to Gen. William Worth, Lee made the run, returned, and promptly fell out of his saddle in a faint.[10]

IN THE UNITED STATES, THE WAR WITH MEXICO HAD BEEN controversial from the start. Antislavery leaders in the North viewed it as a veiled attempt to acquire more territory for slave states. Others believed Polk had not tried hard enough to avoid bloodshed. Henry Clay, whose opposition to the annexation of Texas had cost him the presidency, deplored a war between two neighboring republics. Ulysses S. Grant, who, like Lee, had served with distinction in Mexico, was equally critical, characterizing it in his memoirs as one of the most unjust wars ever waged against a weaker nation.[11]

Robert E. Lee apparently held no such misgivings. If he reflected on the justice of America's cause, he left no record. His experience in Mexico had not coarsened him or made him a lover of war, but it had matured him as a professional soldier. He wrote to Mary,

Fighting is the easiest part of a Soldier's duty. It is the watching, labouring, starving, freezing, willing exposure & privation that is so wearing to the body & trying to the mind. It is in this state that discipline tells, & attention night & day on the part of the Officer so necessary. His eye & thoughts must be continually on his men.[12]

Lee's own performance in the war with Mexico is often overlooked because of his far more conspicuous role in the Civil War fourteen years later. Nevertheless, no U.S. soldier below the rank of general came out of Mexico with more prestige than Lee, who garnered no fewer than three brevet promotions. Erasmus D. Keyes, later a Federal corps commander, recalled that Scott had an "almost idolatrous fancy for Lee, whose military ability he estimated far beyond that of any other officer of the army."[13] Lesser generals who could not abide one another vied in their praise for the intrepid captain of Engineers.

And what did Lee bring away from his only war before 1861? Despite his penchant for self-criticism, Lee must have recognized that he had performed extraordinarily well. He had endured the toughest campaigning, and had come repeatedly under fire, yet he not only had accomplished what was expected of him but also had become one of the army's most admired officers. For all his modesty, Lee conceded to Mary that he had demonstrated considerable stamina in the field.

As a member of Scott's inner circle, Lee had been able to view the war in strategic as well as tactical terms. From Scott he had learned that a small force, effectively led, can defeat a numerically stronger opponent. He had also learned the importance of reconnaissance; indeed, it was aggressive reconnaissance by Lee and his engineer colleagues that had paved the way for Scott's most successful moves. Lee had also learned from Scott the value of audacity. Having decided that the enemy was badly trained and badly led, Scott refused to be intimidated by numbers. Invariably outmanned, "Old Fuss and Feathers" had succeeded by seizing the initiative and taking risks. Lee had learned from Scott to ignore timid counsel and to act decisively.

Lee appears also to have concluded, from observing Scott, that the main responsibility of an army commander is to plan an operation, brief his subordinates as to what is required of them, and see to it that various components of his army are in the right place at the right time. It is not his responsibility to "lead the charge." This was Scott's theory, and in the Civil War Lee would make it his for as long as circumstances permitted him to do so.

The Americans had won in Mexico by attacking, and for Lee this may have been a lesson to be unlearned. The principal infantry weapon in the Mexican War was the smoothbore musket, a weapon that required at least thirty seconds to load and had a maximum effective range of about 100 yards. Against Santa Anna's conscripts, a determined charge invariably brought victory. In the American Civil War, however, infantry tactics would have to be changed as a result of the introduction of the repeating rifle.

Lee could not have helped noticing the burden to Scott posed by incompetent officers in key positions. To Lee, Gen. Gideon Pillow came to personify the "political general" who owed his position to his influence in Washington and who could not be trusted to carry out any mission unsupervised. To a considerable extent Scott had worked around these incompetents by using young professionals such as Lee. After the fighting was over, however, Scott had sought to court-martial Pillow, Gen. William Worth, and others. Lee thought that his commander demeaned himself by quarreling over the laurels of victory.

Because of the conspicuous role that junior, West Point–trained officers played in Mexico, it is sometimes assumed that Lee had a chance to study many of his future opponents while in Mexico, and to assess their strengths and weaknesses. In fact, Lee's dealings with officers such as Grant, Joseph Hooker, and George G. Meade appear to have been brief and perfunctory. George B. McClellan was an exception. Lee worked closely with McClellan on engineering problems and may well have gained some insight into McClellan's mode of thought.

In February 1848 the United States and Mexico brought a formal end to the war with the signing of the Treaty of Guadalupe Hidalgo. Two months later Lee was on his way home, accompanied by his servant, Jim Donnally, and two horses that he had acquired in Mexico. For all of Lee's considerable accomplishments, his return was to the monotony of the peacetime U.S. Army.

CHAPTER FOUR
DUTY, GOD, AND SLAVERY

HERE I AM AGAIN, MY DEAR SMITH," LEE wrote to his brother from Arlington in June 1848, "surrounded by Mary and her precious children, who seem to devote themselves to staring at the furrows in my face and the white hairs in my head."[1] It had been a warm homecoming. All of Lee's homecomings were warm; it was only when Mary was obliged to choose between Arlington and her husband's next posting that strain appeared.

In the autumn of 1849 the Chief of Engineers assigned Lee to Baltimore to supervise the construction of another fort, this time in Baltimore harbor. Mary divided her time between the redbrick row house Lee rented in Baltimore and her spiritual home, Arlington. As the wife of the handsome Colonel Lee she led an active social life when in Baltimore, but she appears to have had little interest in the local society.

It seems that it never occurred to Lee to be unfaithful to his wife, even when he was in Mexico, but there was something missing in his marriage, and presumably both parties knew it. Perhaps Lee felt a conflict between fidelity to the marriage bond and his then-sociable, outgoing nature. In any case, part of the Lee legacy is his warm, decades-long correspondence with a number of younger women, all ladies of probity, and all from the best families.

Martha "Markie" Williams was Mary Lee's first cousin and a distant relative of Robert as well. She grew up in Maryland, not far from Arlington, and was a friend of the Lee's oldest daughter, Mary. In 1844, when Markie was 18, Lee began a correspondence with her that continued for the rest of his life. In some of these letters Lee struck a note never found in his other correspondence:

> You have not written to me in nearly three months. And I believe it is equally long since I have written to you. On paper Markie, I mean, on paper. But Oh, what lengthy epistles I have indited to you in my mind! Had I any means to send them, you would see how constantly I think of you. I have followed you in your pleasures, & your duties, in the house & in the streets, & accompanied you in your walks to Arlington, & in your search after flowers.[2]

For Lee, a cautious flirtation by mail was unlikely to promote gossip, and therefore less dangerous than for him to escort young ladies to the post hop. There was no threat to Lee's self-control, which was already an integral part of his personality. There would be no repetition of the Black-Horse Harry Lee scandal as far as he was concerned.

Lee's correspondence with younger women also says something about Mary Lee. Although Mary could be a scold on occasion, there is no evidence that she ever chided him about his correspondence with Eliza Mackay or Markie Williams. Perhaps she recognized that there was a side to her husband that craved companionship of a type she herself was unable to provide.

In Baltimore, Lee may have experienced a period of psychological depression. He had lost his best friend in 1848, when Jack Mackay had succumbed to tuberculosis, and he continued to have reservations about the army as a career. During this time, when Mary was in Arlington, some of his letters to her took on a melancholy tone. In May 1849 he chided his wife, "You have borne with my faults so long, bear with them for the little remaining space to which perhaps my life is doomed." Nevertheless, a tour of several southern posts later that year offers a final glimpse of the youthful, outgoing Lee. He wrote to Mary,

> You have often heard me say that the cordiality & friendship in the Army, was the greatest attraction in the Service. It is that I believe has kept me in it so long, & it is that

which makes me now fear to leave it. I do not know where
I should meet with so much friendship out of it.[3]

His loyalty to the army notwithstanding, Lee was critical of its slow
promotions, mindless bureaucratic routine, and long separations from
family. Years later, while in Washington, Lee came to know Capt.
Winfield S. Hancock, who had just been posted to California. When
he heard that Hancock's wife, Almira, was planning to remain in the
East, Lee took her aside and suggested that her place was at her husband's side. When people live apart, he warned, they cease to be essential to each other.[4] Was Lee concerned about his own marriage?*

THE MOST IMPORTANT DEVELOPMENT IN LEE'S LIFE DURING
his three years in Baltimore was an intense religious experience. By
most standards, Lee was already a good Christian. He had been surrounded by deeply religious people from his youth and had worked
hard to live a good life. He had not always measured up to his wife's
piety, however, and she had periodically prayed for his "conversion."
In Baltimore, Lee heard a sermon that at long last gave him "blessed
assurance."

It would be interesting to know what sermon or sermons so influenced Lee, because they stirred in him a religious intensity that would
henceforth be an essential part of his personality. Lee appears to have
absorbed the doctrine of original sin, and to have seen himself as an
egregious sinner. "Man's nature is so Selfish, so weak," he wrote Mary.
"Every feeling, every passion urging him to folly, excess & sin that I
am disgusted with myself & sometimes with all the world."[5] Good
Christians, Lee believed, should attempt to make selflessness an instinc-
tive response. But even with the best intentions they will fail because
of the inherent evil in human nature. The theological point of Christ's
having atoned for man's sin does not appear to have impressed itself
on Lee. Surrounded by a loving family and admired by his friends and
professional colleagues, Lee was nevertheless prone to periods of

* Mrs. Hancock accompanied her husband to California as Lee had urged. During
the Civil War, Hancock was one of the most capable of the Federal corps commanders
and opposed Lee on many battlefields. His wife remembered Lee as "the beau ideal of
a soldier and a gentleman."

depression. Some of his family letters in the 1850s indicate that he found the prospect of the tomb appealing.

Considering Lee's relentless piety, it is curious that he was not confirmed in the Episcopal Church until 1853. Why Lee waited so long is unclear, but the passing of the years was making him more conscious of his own mortality. He had seen death in Mexico, and mourned with Mary the death of her mother in April 1853. In July of that year, Lee, together with daughters Mary and Annie, were confirmed at Christ Church in Alexandria by the bishop of Virginia, John Johns.

Some of Lee's critics have treated his spiritual self-flagellation as indicative of a general insecurity. This appears to be a serious miscalculation. Lee undoubtedly regarded himself as a good husband and a competent soldier. He aspired to a degree of perfection rarely achieved on earth, and sought it for his children as well; but by contemporary standards, he was already what most people would regard as a Good Man.

Where Lee found comfort was in doing his duty. For Lee, duty became a secular manifestation of his religion. In 1861 he would conclude that, notwithstanding his personal opposition to secession, it was his duty to offer his services to Virginia. Similarly, Lee's refusal to consider surrender until April 1865—well after any realistic hope of victory had evaporated—grew out of a belief that it was his duty to fight on. In 1870, while away from his home in Lexington, Virginia, Lee received word that the family cow had died. "Her troubles are all over now," Lee wrote, "and I am grateful to her for what she has done for us. I hope that we did our duty to her."[6]

For Lee, duty led inexorably to self-denial. Thus, the austere mess that Lee maintained throughout the war represented more than a sharing of the privation of his soldiers; it was a manifestation of Lee's secular creed. After the war, when he had an adequate salary as president of Washington College, Lee's study was so spartan in its furnishings as to recall the austerity of his years in the field.

--*≡◎ ◎≡*--

FROM SEPTEMBER 1852 UNTIL APRIL 1855 LEE SERVED AS superintendent of West Point, one of the most prestigious assignments in the peacetime army and one usually reserved for an officer of Engineers. Most officers would have found immense satisfaction in leading

Lee as he appeared in the early 1850s. LIBRARY OF CONGRESS.

the institution where they had once been a lowly cadet, but not Robert E. Lee. The harsh winters made him long for Virginia, and his administrative load—Lee was responsible for everything from approving faculty leaves to buying fodder for the horses—proved irksome. The War Department ignored Lee's requests for funds for physical improvements to the academy, and the Academic Board resisted any changes in the curriculum.

Yet the greatest pressure on Lee he brought on himself. He considered himself personally responsible for the physical and moral well-being of the cadets in his charge. He fretted over cadets who had academic or disciplinary problems, and wrote long letters to their parents. He took satisfaction in the performance of his oldest son, Custis, who graduated first in his class in 1854, but worried over the case of Fitzhugh Lee, Smith Lee's son, who was nearly dismissed for being absent without leave.

Among Lee's children, the one who caused the greatest concern was his second son, Rooney. When he was 16 and his father was superintendent of West Point, Rooney had decided that he wanted to attend the academy. Rooney was no scholar, and Lee suspected that his son's interest in West Point grew out of a belief that he would have an easier time there than in college. Lee urged him to improve in his studies. "Do not suppose that general intelligence or intellectual acquirement is unnecessary for an Officer of the Army," he warned.[7] In the end Rooney attended Harvard, where he charmed his classmates but not his professors. Lee confided to Mary that he would never have confidence in his second son unless he developed "self-control."[8]*

On April 9, 1855—exactly ten years before the Army of Northern Virginia would surrender at Appomattox—the Lee family left West Point. The most important decision Lee had made there concerned his own future. After two decades in the Corps of Engineers, he had initiated a career change from the Engineers to line duty. Congress was about to authorize four new cavalry regiments, and Lee had been assured that at a minimum he would be second in command of one of the new units.

Field duty would be quite a change from the punctilio of West Point. Most of the 14,000-man U.S. Army was scattered in outposts across the West, attempting to defend the frontier against the Indians. Virtually all units were understrength; a regiment that theoretically comprised about 900 men usually varied in strength between 300 and 400. Lee's new regiment, the 2nd Cavalry, was still recruiting.

Service in the field meant abominable living conditions, long separations from family and friends, and extended periods of monotony interspersed with weeks of hard service. Indian warriors posed less of a threat than did disease, exposure, and poor diet. Pay was low, prospects for advancement poor, and, for enlisted men, discipline was harsh. Pop-

---

* Rooney never graduated from Harvard but followed his father into Confederate service, where he served with distinction as one of Lee's cavalry commanders.

ular respect and appreciation were notably lacking. "Although unfair to many able officers and soldiers," writes military historian Robert Utley, "there was still a kernel of truth to the common charge that the Army formed a haven for men who could not succeed in any other pursuit."[9]

Lee's four years on the frontier were marked by extended periods of court-martial duty, interspersed with occasional forays against predatory Indians. This period—the least rewarding of his career—gave Lee ample opportunity to reflect on whether he wished to continue in the army or put his engineering skills to work in a civil capacity. His ruminations along this line were interrupted by the call to return east and serve as trustee for the tangled estate of his father-in-law, George Washington Parke Custis.

FOR AS LONG AS HE HAD BEEN AN ARMY OFFICER, ROBERT E. Lee had been a slaveholder, for he had inherited several house servants from his mother. At the same time, Lee's boyhood in Alexandria may have insulated him from the hard lot of black field hands; the house slaves with whom he came into contact in plantation society were generally well looked after. As for Mary's parents, both were active in the American Colonization Society, an organization dedicated to resettling free blacks in Africa.

While at Fortress Monroe, however, Lee had had a brush with a dark side of slavery: the underlying fear of a slave insurrection that made sleep uneasy for many a wealthy planter. In August 1831 a band of slaves in Southampton County, led by Nat Turner, had instigated the bloodiest slave uprising in American history. In twenty-four hours, before order was restored by Virginia militia and army regulars, rioting slaves killed more than fifty whites. Lee was not involved in the slave roundup, but because Turner was at large for two months the insurrection spread fear and alarm across much of Virginia. Lee, in a letter on August 31, 1831, assured the Custises that the revolt had been put down, and deplored the hysteria found in so much of southern Virginia.[10]

Lee is not known ever to have purchased a slave. Most army officers in his day had servants, either slaves or hirelings, but Lee preferred to hire those who served him. When he had set out for Mexico he had taken a free Irishman rather than a slave. In 1860, in a letter to Rooney

Lee from Texas, he regretted that he might have to purchase a servant, having found it almost impossible to hire one.[11]

After leaving Stratford as a child, Lee had few dealings with slavery until 1857, when his father-in-law died, leaving Lee as principal trustee for his estate. Custis bequeathed Arlington to Mary Lee—his only child—for her lifetime; thereafter it would go to her oldest son, Custis. Custis Lee's two brothers, Rooney and Rob, were bequeathed 4,000-acre estates in Tidewater Virginia. Each of Robert and Mary's four daughters was to receive $10,000 in cash, but the Custis will did not indicate the source of this money. Robert E. Lee figured in the will hardly at all; for his services as executor he was given title to an undeveloped lot in Washington, D.C.

Lee's father-in-law had died heavily in debt. The Arlington estate had not turned a profit for years, and at the time of its master's death it was more run down than Stratford had been in Lee's boyhood. A visitor to Arlington in the early 1850s noted in his diary that the plantation was in "a most neglected condition." The house itself, never finished, was "hastening to premature decay."[12]

For Lee, administering his father-in-law's estate would involve not only two years of administrative drudgery but also exposure to slavery in a form that he had previously been spared. His attempts to restore the manor and to make the estate profitable were complicated by the fact that Arlington was home to between sixty and seventy slaves, many past working age. Those on Custis's two other plantations brought the total number of slaves to nearly two hundred. According to Custis's will, all were to be emancipated by the end of the five-year period stipulated for settling the estate. However, word soon spread that the Custis workers were "free," and work in the fields came to a virtual halt. Mary Custis wrote to an acquaintance that her father had scarcely been laid to rest when two men were found to be "lurking about here tampering with the servants & telling them that they had a right to their freedom *immediately*." Robert acknowledged in a letter to Rooney that he had been obliged to jail three male slaves who had run away.[13]

Managing Arlington tended to confirm Lee in his attitudes regarding the South's "peculiar institution." He was opposed to slavery on both moral and practical grounds, but, in common with most Southerners of his day, he could not imagine how blacks could prosper in a free economy. In one of his few extended comments on slavery he wrote to Mary in 1856,

> In this enlightened age there are few, I believe, but what
> will acknowledge that slavery, as an institution, is a moral
> & political evil. . . . I think it, however, a greater evil to the
> white than to the black race, & while my sympathies are
> strongly enlisted in behalf of the latter, my sympathies are
> more strong for the former.

Writing as a white man at a time when whites and blacks alike led an
uncertain, hardscrabble existence, Lee continued;

> The blacks are immeasurably better off here than in Africa,
> morally, socially, & physically. The painful discipline they
> are undergoing is necessary for their instruction as a race, &
> I hope will prepare & lead them to better things. How long
> their subjugation may be necessary is known & ordered by a
> wise Merciful Providence. Their emancipation will sooner
> result from the mild & melting influence of Christianity,
> than the storms & tempests of fiery Controversy.[14]

Meanwhile, it was a measure of the growing sectional bitterness that
Lee found himself accused of abusing slaves in his charge. In June
1859, two anonymous letters to the *New York Tribune* accused Lee of
whipping slaves who had attempted to escape from Arlington. No
sources were given for these allegations, and it was not unusual for
newspapers of the day to print unverified charges if they were consistent with the journal's political orientation. Lee refused to respond to
the *Tribune*.

Lee gradually brought order to the Custis estate, supervising badly
needed repairs to the roof of the manor. When he was unable to use all
the field hands, he rented them out to other plantations. He paid off
Custis's debts and had all three farms—Arlington, as well as Rooney's
and Rob's near Richmond—in reasonably good order. Proceeds from
the farms went into a fund designated for Lee's daughters. Lee used
his influence and connections to have his son Custis assigned to Engineers' headquarters in Washington so that Custis could help take care
of his mother and her home.

Lee's problems in administering George Custis's will would in a few
years be eclipsed by those involved in organizing the Confederate
army. Nevertheless, in 1861 Custis's slaves were freed in accordance
with his will, and even in the midst of war Lee would be concerned for

their welfare. On December 21, 1861, he wrote to Mary that he would issue "free papers" to workers on the farms "as soon as I can see that they can get a support." Those who wished to remain could do so, but they would have to work. Lee would devote the proceeds of their labor "to their future establishment."[15]

An impartial observer, reflecting on Lee's role in administering the Custis will, would probably conclude that he had carried out his duties in a humane and responsible fashion. Some "historians" believe otherwise. Quoting a letter in which Lee arranges the hiring out of three plantation workers, Alan Nolan concludes that "Lee was personally involved in certain of the unseemly corollaries of the slave system, including trafficking in slaves." And what of Lee's professed desire for gradual emancipation? Nolan contends that "there is no evidence to support the acceptance of Lee's self-serving characterization of himself as one who had always been in favor of gradual emancipation."[16]

This is a curious line of argument, for if Lee was not in favor of gradual emancipation, he must have favored either immediate emancipation—which is unlikely—or perpetual slavery. Most fair-minded people will accept Lee's commitment to eventual emancipation at face value, but to one who believes Lee to have been a slave trader, with all that the term connotes, any conclusion is possible.

Lee's statements on slavery put him among a broad spectrum of enlightened Americans who deplored slavery but who could see no immediate solution. Abraham Lincoln sought an end to slavery, but had grave doubts as to whether whites and blacks could live harmoniously together. Lee's approach, typically, had a religious element: Slavery would end when Providence so decreed. For Lee, Providence served two functions. On one hand, it was the great dispenser of gifts, including military victories. But Providence also served as a back burner on which to place problems that defied easy resolution. Thus, how long slavery must endure was known only to "a wise and merciful Providence."

However stereotypical his views on race, Lee believed that all men were equal before God. In the months immediately after the surrender at Appomattox, Lee, in Richmond, attended services at St. Paul's Episcopal Church, as he often had during the war. Although it was not unusual for a "white" church to have black communicants, segregated seating was then the rule. On this day in Richmond, however, a well-dressed black man was one of the first to accept the minister's invitation to come forward and receive communion. As the man reached the communion rail, a murmur passed through the congregation and the service seemed to freeze in place. Then Lee rose from his pew, walked to the communion rail, and knelt next to the black man. Immediately, the rest of the congregation followed his example.[17]

FROM ARLINGTON, LEE WAS A CONCERNED OBSERVER AT THE collapse of the Union. The Compromise of 1850 was proving an illusion, in part because of the North's unwillingness to enforce the provision that called for the return of runaway slaves. The opening of Kansas to rival groups of proslavery and antislavery settlers led to the establishment of rival territorial governments and to a breakdown in order.

In December 1856 Lee was reconciled to James Buchanan's election as president, writing home, "I hope he will be able to extinguish fanaticism North and South, cultivate love for the country and Union, and restore harmony between the different sections."[18] At the same time there were hints that Lee considered the Union a voluntary association. In January 1857 he wrote to an army colleague, "I know no other Country . . . than the *United States* and their Constitution."[19] In retrospect, Lee's use of the plural *their* is significant.

On the morning of October 17, 1859, Lee was in his study at Arlington when a rider clattered up to the house. Lt. "Jeb" Stuart, whom Lee had known since Stuart's years as a cadet at West Point, informed Lee that he was to report to the War Department immediately. Young Stuart had been in Washington when he heard rumors that a mob that included blacks had seized the government armory at Harpers Ferry. Could this be a new slave revolt? When Secretary of War John Floyd decided to send for Lee, Stuart volunteered to act as a courier. Lee left Arlington immediately, not even taking time to put on his uniform.

Floyd had proposed that an armed force be sent to Harpers Ferry, and President Buchanan had approved. Lee would be in charge, commanding two companies of marines who were already en route to Harpers Ferry. It was nearly midnight when Lee and Stuart arrived, and no one seemed sure what was going on. Lee was told that a man named Smith and a band of his followers had crossed the railroad bridge from Maryland and seized the arsenal and engine house. By then they had concentrated in the arsenal and were holding several hostages.

Lee decided that he had more than enough marines to handle the situation; he telegraphed the War Department that additional troops would not be necessary. He then ordered Stuart to approach the arsenal at dawn, under a flag of truce, and to demand its surrender. If the occupants refused, Stuart was to wave his hat and the marines would move in.

At first light on October 18, Stuart made his way under a flag of truce to the stone building that housed John Brown, seventeen of his followers, and an unknown number of hostages. The door opened a crack to Stuart's knock, and several minutes passed in conversation. Then Stuart stepped back, the door slammed shut, and Stuart signaled to Lee. The marines swept forward and smashed through the door. Two insurgents were killed, Brown and the others were captured, and the hostages were freed unharmed.

Brown was tried, found guilty, and quickly hanged. But the South was not placated so easily, for Brown's stated intent to spark a slave uprising was viewed as abolitionist rhetoric carried to its logical conclusion. Although no slaves had joined Brown, Southerners remembered a recent, bloody slave uprising on Haiti and shuddered. In the words of one proslavery paper, it was not Brown who was responsible for Harpers Ferry but radical Northerners such as Joshua Giddings, Gerrit Smith, and William Henry Seward.[20]

Lee put the episode behind him. If he recognized in John Brown a Christian who was unable to leave slavery to the vagueries of Providence, he left no record of his feelings. The raid, he reported, was the work of a fanatic or a madman. Lee's dismissive tone suggests that he was a poor political prophet. Madman or not, John Brown was on his way to martyrdom in the North, and the abortive insurrection at Harpers Ferry would widen the chasm between the sections.

CHAPTER FIVE

"I SHALL SHARE THE MISERIES OF MY PEOPLE"

I N FEBRUARY 1860 LEE LEFT ARLINGTON TO return to army duty in Texas. He must have had very mixed feelings as he made his way west, for he was no more satisfied with his career than he had been before, and he was needed more than ever at Arlington. Previously, Mary Lee, when her husband was away, had passed the time visiting her many "cousins" in northern Virginia. Now her poor health kept her largely housebound.

There was little that Lee could look forward to in the U.S. Army. Having performed brilliantly in virtually every assignment, having distinguished himself in Mexico, and having been designated by Gen. Winfield Scott as the army's most promising officer, Lee was en route to yet another dusty frontier post. He was 53 years old and had taken twenty-two years to advance from captain to lieutenant colonel. After thirty-one years in the service he had a base salary of only $1,200 per year, although perks such as quarters and rations brought the total to slightly more than $4,000.[1] Young George B. McClellan, who had graduated from West Point just before the Mexican War, had left the service in 1857 to work for a railroad and was said to be making $10,000 per year.[2] Lee could almost certainly have done as well or better, yet he seemed unable to separate himself from the service.

In San Antonio, Lee deployed the meager resources of the 2nd Cavalry against marauding Comanches, Kiowas, and Mexican outlaws. He led a company of cavalry to the Rio Grande in pursuit of one bandit, Juan Cortinas, but to no avail. When not in the field Lee tried to follow political developments from newspapers that were often weeks old. Aware that much would depend on the outcome of the presidential election of 1860, Lee watched with concern as the Democrats, meeting in Charleston, South Carolina, split over the party platform. When Southern delegates judged the plank guaranteeing slavery in the territories too weak, eight state delegations walked out and the convention adjourned. The presidential election that fall was contested by four parties: the Republicans, with Abraham Lincoln as their candidate; the "regular" Democrats, led by Stephen A. Douglas; Southern Democrats led by Vice President John C. Breckinridge; and conservative Unionists led by John Bell of Tennessee.

Lee at first thought that Douglas should withdraw in favor of Breckinridge and work to defeat Lincoln. (He may have been influenced by sentiment in Texas, which favored Breckinridge in the election.) Four days after Lincoln's election the South Carolina legislature called a convention to take that state out of the Union. Within weeks, six other states of the lower South had followed suit, and there was strong secessionist sentiment in Texas as well.

Lee was saddened by the political turmoil and not at all impressed by the bellicose threats from Southern fire-eaters. On December 14 he wrote to his oldest son, Custis,

> My only hope [is] for the preservation of the Union, and I will cling to it to the last. Feeling the aggressions of the North, resenting their denial of the equal rights of our citizens to the common territory of the commonwealth, etc., I am not pleased with the course of the "Cotton States" as they term themselves, [with their] selfish, dictatorial bearing.[3]

Lee rarely discussed politics, but he was a Southern Whig in sentiment even after the Whigs had disappeared as a national party. He disliked extremists of all types, and the most visible of these were the Northern abolitionists. Ultimately, he sought to deal with political issues much as he did with individual conduct: All problems could be resolved if people would behave toward one another in a charitable, Christian manner. Harmony was important to Lee. He felt no obligation to act on his belief that slavery was evil. Believing as he did that Providence decreed one's station in life, it was up to each person to accept his lot without complaint.

Five days after writing to Custis, Lee left San Antonio for the 2nd Cavalry headquarters at Fort Mason, where he was even more isolated from political developments. On January 9, 1861, South Carolina troops fired on the steamer *Star of the West* when it attempted to reprovision the Federal garrison at Fort Sumter. Lee may not even have known of this development when he wrote an oft-quoted letter to Rooney Lee on January 23:

> I can anticipate no greater calamity for the country than a dissolution of the Union. It would be an accumulation of all the evils we complain of, and I am willing to sacrifice everything but honor for its preservation. . . . Still, a Union that can only be maintained by swords and bayonets, and in which strife and civil war are to take the place of brotherly love and kindness, has no charm for me. . . . If the Union is dissolved, and the Government disrupted, I shall return to my native State and share the miseries of my people, and save in defense will draw my sword on none.[4]

This letter, perhaps the most anguished that Lee ever penned, is important in that it demonstrates that he had made up his mind about his future course well before the events at Fort Sumter.

Whatever Lee thought of frontier duty, he had not been forgotten in official Washington. Early in February he received orders to return east and report to General Scott. Lee left Fort Mason on February 13, riding with his goods in an army ambulance shortly after Texas joined the list of seceded states. In San Antonio he discovered that Gen. David Twiggs, commanding the military department, had surrendered to Texas authorities and gone home to Georgia. San Antonio was now controlled by boisterous Texas militia, who were not sure what to make of the tight-lipped army colonel who had checked into a local hotel. When Lee, in civilian clothes, walked over to the local army headquarters, he found it occupied by a three-man Committee of Public Safety. The three Texans received Lee coolly, reminding him that their state had seceded and saying that Lee must declare himself for the Confederacy. If he failed to do so, they threatened, his baggage would be seized.

Lee prided himself on his self-control, but on this occasion he may have vented his considerable temper. He told the Committee of Public Safety that he was an officer of the U.S. Army and a Virginian, not a Texan, and stormed out of the room. Fortunately, he then encountered a friend—the Unionist brother of Maj. Robert Anderson, soon to be the defender of Fort Sumter—who volunteered to take care of his baggage.

Lee arrived at Arlington on March 1 after a twelve-day journey from San Antonio by stage, steamer, and railroad. Within a few days of his arrival he called on General Scott, and the two met privately for three hours. Neither participant ever recounted their conversation, but the two soldiers undoubtedly discussed the critical political situation, and Lee probably told Scott what he had been telling others: that his actions would be governed by those of Virginia.

On March 4, only days before Lee's meeting with Scott, Abraham Lincoln had been inaugurated president. The new president's inaugural address was conciliatory in tone, but in it he pledged to defend Federal property, which included Fort Sumter. Tension was high in the capital, and Scott congratulated himself for having posted sharpshooters along Pennsylvania Avenue to ensure that Lincoln's inauguration would not be marred by violence.

On April 4, Lincoln decided to resupply Fort Sumter and Fort Pickens in Florida. He made this decision even though his cabinet was sharply divided, and in the face of a memorandum from Scott urging the evacuation of both forts as a conciliatory gesture. Three supply ships were sent to Fort Sumter, but foul weather delayed their arrival until April 12. By then Jefferson Davis, provisional president of the fledgling Confederacy, had agreed with militant South Carolinians that the continued Federal presence in Fort Sumter was an affront to Southern independence. On April 10, Davis instructed Gen. P. G. T. Beauregard to demand the fort's surrender and, if his demand was refused, to attack it. War came on April 12 when Confederate batteries opened fire on the lightly manned fort, forcing its surrender the next day.

Robert E. Lee's future was determined by developments in Virginia in the days immediately following the attack on Fort Sumter. News of Sumter's fall reached Richmond on April 13, and jubilant crowds there celebrated the South's great "victory." Marchers lowered the American flag from the capitol dome and ran up the Stars and Bars of the Confederacy. Heretofore there had been a strong Unionist faction in

Virginia, men who had urged Lincoln to do nothing to antagonize the border states. What little chance these conditional Unionists had of keeping Virginia in the Union vanished with Lincoln's call, on April 15, for 75,000 volunteers to put down the rebellion. On April 17, a special convention in Richmond passed an ordinance of secession by a vote of 88 to 55.[5]

Lee was at Arlington that day when he received word that Francis P. Blair Sr. wished to see him in Washington. The wizened, 70-year-old Blair was a one-time associate of Andrew Jackson who had long been a power broker in the capital. Blair was close to Lincoln, and one of his sons was Lincoln's postmaster general. In a meeting on April 18, Blair, speaking for the administration, offered Lee command of the great Federal army now in formation. For Lee—whose career had been so lackluster since the Mexican War—the moment was filled with irony. But he had long since determined where his duty lay, and felt he had no choice other than to decline Blair's offer. No one has credibly challenged the version of this meeting that Lee wrote after the war:

> I never intimated to any one that I desired the command of the United States Army, nor did I have a conversation but with one gentleman, Mr. Francis Preston Blair, on the subject, which was at his invitation, and, as I understood, at the instance of President Lincoln.
>
> After listening to his remarks, I declined the offer he made to me, to take command of the army that was to be brought into the field, stating, as candidly and as courteously as I could, that, although opposed to secession and deprecating war, I could take no part in an invasion of the Southern States.[6]

Later that day Lee met again with Scott and recounted the meeting with Blair. Both men realized that Lee was spurning a promotion from colonel to the command of a mighty army. "Lee," the aged Scott sighed, "you have made the greatest mistake of your life; but I feared it would be so."[7]

In 1866, nearly a year after the close of the Civil War, Lee would be called on to testify before a congressional subcommittee dealing with issues of reconstruction. Asked why he had chosen to side with the Confederacy, Lee replied that "the act of Virginia, in withdrawing from the United States, carried me along as a citizen of Virginia, and . . . her laws and act were binding on me."[8]

Lee returned to Arlington and the next day rode into Alexandria on some errands. There the newspapers were full of news from Richmond: Virginia had seceded! In his only recorded comment on this development, Lee told a pharmacist to whom he was paying a bill, "I must say that I am one of those dull creatures that cannot see the good of secession."[9] But Lee remained convinced that he had no choice other than to follow his state. The next day, April 20, he wrote two letters, one to Secretary of War Simon Cameron resigning from the U.S. Army, the other to Scott. After alluding to the struggle that it had been "to separate myself from a service to which I have devoted the best years of my life," Lee added a warm tribute to his mentor:

> During the whole of that time—more than a quarter of a century—I have experienced nothing but kindness from my superiors and a most cordial friendship from my comrades. . . . I shall carry to the grave the most grateful recollections of your kind consideration, and your name and fame will always be dear to me.
>
> Save in defense of my native State, I never desire again to draw my sword.[10]

Lee's resignation from the U.S. Army was as wrenching for Mary Lee as for her husband. In early May she wrote a letter to Scott that reflected both her concern for her abandoned home at Arlington and her distress for the country:

> Nothing can ever make me forget your kind appreciation of Mr. Lee [*sic*]. . . . Were it not that I would not add one feather to his load of care, nothing would induce me to abandon my home. Oh, that you could command peace to our distracted country.[11]

⋆⇒ ⇐⋆

TO MOST READERS, THE STORY OF LEE'S RESIGNATION FROM the U.S. Army is poignant yet straightforward. With respect to the most difficult decision of his career, Lee indicated to virtually everyone to whom he spoke in the early months of 1861 that his conduct would be governed by that of his state. This position is open to criticism—Lee had little respect for those who sought to destroy the Union, yet he put his future in their hands. Other Virginians, including Scott, would remain loyal to the Union. Yet Lee took care to do nothing inimical to the Federal cause while still wearing the army blue.*

Some critics, however, have been intrigued by the speed with which Lee transferred his allegiance to Richmond. Noting that he was commanding Virginia forces within a week of resigning his Federal commission, Thomas L. Connelly calls his switch in loyalties "abrupt." [12] Alan Nolan goes further, hinting at chicanery:

> Approximately forty-eight hours passed between Lee's posting of his resignation on April 20 and his acceptance of the Virginia commission on April 22. Had Lee, in fact, been in communication with Virginia authorities before he resigned? Had he been negotiating with them before April 20? [13]

Nolan acknowledges that there is no documentary evidence that answers this question, but concludes that there must have been contact because Virginia would not have offered Lee command of its forces had there been a possibility that he would decline. Never mind that Francis Blair had made a similar cold approach, one that Lee had rejected.

The record indicates that Lee acted with scrupulous correctness in his dealings with Scott and Blair. The abruptness with which he entered Virginia's service did not result from any "deal"—had there been any such arrangement, it would almost certainly have come to light over the years. The promptness with which Lee was offered a Virginia commission grew out of the desire of Virginia authorities to recruit one of the most respected officers of the Old Army. As for the speed with which Lee switched his allegiance and began preparing Virginia to resist the United States, his action was a logical outgrowth of his concept of duty. Once Lee had resigned from the U.S. Army, his dedication to the cause that now commanded his loyalty was total.

---

* Lee's punctiliousness with respect to his resignation contrasts with the actions of James Longstreet, who accepted a Confederate commission eight days before resigning from the U.S. Army, and accepted pay from both the U.S. and Confederate governments for this brief period. See Wert, *General James Longstreet*, 53–54.

If we absolve Lee of any improper behavior, what can we say, given Lee's opposition to secession, of his inflexible loyalty to Virginia? The fact is that Lee had been brought up more as a Virginian than as a citizen of the United States.* Indeed, Virginia had been a political entity for more than two centuries; the United States had been in existence for about eighty years. Lee was more than a *resident* of Virginia; the extended Lee clan had a proprietary interest in the state. Men such as Scott and Gen. George H. Thomas, both of whom were Virginia-born, could ponder and conclude that their loyalty to the Union was paramount. Their roots in the state did not go back to 1640.

Connelly, among others, has asked why Lee did not attempt to use his influence in Virginia to squelch the secession movement.[14] The question credits Lee with far more influence than he actually possessed. Lee was known throughout the U.S. Army as one of its ablest officers, but in much of Tidewater Virginia he was no more than Mary Custis's handsome husband. In any case, Lee had none of the politician's gifts. He was comfortable in a vertical military hierarchy, where orders were given and obeyed; he was not accustomed to political give-and-take and despised confrontation. It is difficult to picture the soft-spoken Lee having any influence on the rabid secessionists with whom he would have been negotiating in Richmond.

ON APRIL 21 LEE ATTENDED SERVICES AT CHRIST CHURCH IN Alexandria. There were crowds all over town—at the church, the railroad station, the Athenaeum—discussing the latest news from across the river. According to some, Lee was headed for great things and would soon be named commander of Virginia's forces. Most Alexandrians hoped that story was true. Another rumor had it that a messenger from Richmond had asked Lee to report to Governor John Letcher at his early convenience. This *was* true.

The following morning, Lee, alone and wearing a black suit, said farewell to Mary and to the staff at Arlington. Although he viewed the

---

* It can be argued that states'-rights thinking was paramount in the antebellum U.S. Army. For instance, in the oath Lee executed on accepting his commission as a lieutenant colonel in 1855 he swore that he would "bear true allegiance to the United States of America, and that I will serve *them* honestly and faithfully. . . ." (Emphasis added.)

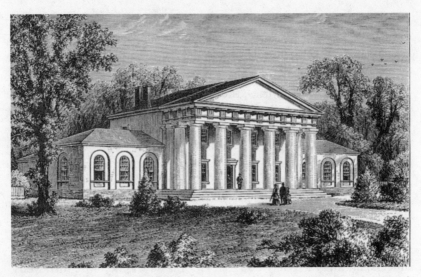

Arlington, the Lees' home overlooking the Potomac across from Washington. AUTHOR'S
COLLECTION.

future with foreboding, Lee could hardly have realized that he was
leaving Arlington for the last time. He boarded a train at Alexandria
and made his way to Richmond through whistlestops and junctions
that would soon become famous: Manassas Gap, Centreville, and
Culpeper. Twice—at the Orange and Louisa stations—he was called
on to greet wellwishers, but Lee, never comfortable before crowds,
merely bowed an acknowledgment.

At Richmond, Lee found that he was in fact commander of Virginia's forces, so appointed by Governor Letcher on the recommendation of the Secession Convention. Four days later he was in the
rotunda of the state capitol, standing alongside a statue of his idol,
George Washington. Lee could not have helped being impressed with
the moment. In these halls his father had served as governor. Now,
"Light-Horse Harry" Lee's son was about to serve his state in a far
more difficult time.

Lee was led into the Chamber of Delegates where he was intro-
duced with his new rank of major general. The president of the convention, John Janney, bade him welcome to the hall "in which we may
almost yet hear the echo of the voices of the statesmen, the soldiers
and sages of bygone days, who have borne your name, and whose
blood now flows in your veins." Warming to his task, Janney spoke in

rolling prose of Lee's service in Mexico, his gallantry and modesty, and his devotion to liberty. Virginia had placed her sword in his hand, Janney said, knowing that Lee would fall with it in his hand "rather than that the object for which it was placed there shall fail."[15]

Lee probably winced at the bombast. He accepted his appointment with a few pro forma words in which he dedicated himself to the service of his native state, "in whose behalf alone will I ever again draw my sword." Lee's sober demeanor probably seemed out of place in festive Richmond, but he knew that much was expected of him. He also knew the awesome force that the North would bring to any war.

CHAPTER SIX
WAR

RICHMOND, VIRGINIA, WITH A POPULATION OF about 38,000, was the third-largest city in the South—slightly smaller than Charleston and about one-quarter the size of New Orleans. It was, however, the fastest-growing urban area in the largely agricultural Confederacy. Mule-drawn canal boats brought tobacco and grain to Richmond via the James River and Kanawha Canal. Seagoing vessels sailed and steamed up the James River to Richmond's busy docks. Nearby, the belching smokestacks of the Tredegar Iron Works were testimony that the industrial revolution had not passed Virginia by.

Businesses and homes spread out from the river across the city's seven hills. Although one-third of the city's population was black, and another third foreign born, the city took its tone from the stately homes of the gentry, the Greek revival state capitol, and St. Paul's Episcopal Church.

Residents of the capital, rich and poor, had confidence in their new defender, Robert E. Lee. His dark hair was flecked with gray, but his strong neck, broad shoulders, and erect carriage conveyed a sense of strength and endurance. A Richmond native, seeing Lee for the first time, thought him "the noblest-looking man I had ever gazed upon. . . . handsome beyond all men I had ever seen."[1] Moxley Sorrel, an aide to Gen. James Longstreet, was most impressed with Lee's eyes, which he called "sad eyes! The saddest it seems to me of all men."[2] Young Walter Taylor, who would serve on Lee's staff throughout the war, remembered his first sight of the general:

> I was at breakfast at the Spotswood Hotel when he entered the room, and was at once greatly . . . impressed by his appearance. [He had] strikingly handsome features, bright and penetrating eyes, his iron-gray hair closely cut, his face cleanly shaved except a mustache, [and] he appeared every inch a soldier and a man born to command.[3]

Lee's good looks and handsome carriage had a special meaning for his contemporaries, for nineteenth-century Americans saw the face as a mirror to the soul. But in Lee's case it was more than appearance; there was something about him that impressed people whatever their station. In time, Lee's aides would find him demanding and even difficult. But another of his staff officers, Armistead Long, would write of his chief's "ease and grace of . . . bearing." Most of all, Long recalled Lee's courtesy and lack of pretension.[4]

For seven weeks Lee was busy with paperwork, processing volunteer regiments, procuring arms, and locating camp sites. In June 1861, Virginia's forces were integrated into those of the Confederacy, and, as expected, Lee was named one of the Confederacy's five full generals. With one exception they were a talented group: Albert Sidney Johnston, whom Jefferson Davis regarded as the South's ablest soldier; Joe Johnston, Lee's companion as a junior officer; and P. G. T. Beauregard, the Louisianan with whom Lee had reconnoitered enemy lines outside Mexico City. The one exception was Samuel Cooper, a Northern-born army bureaucrat who would play no important role in the war.

Jefferson Davis knew that he had an asset in Robert E. Lee. Indeed, the Confederate president's acquaintance with senior army officers was one advantage he had over his Yankee counterpart. But affairs were still disorganized in Richmond, and Davis was unsure how to use the talent available to him. When, on July 21, Confederate forces under Johnston and Beauregard won the first important battle at Manassas, Lee was doing paperwork in his small office on the fourth floor of the Mechanics Institute. In a letter to his wife he applauded the "glorious victory," adding a sentiment that helps explain how a humanitarian like

Lee could devote himself to war. "Do not grieve for the brave dead," he wrote. "Sorrow for those who are left behind—friends, relatives, and families. The former are at rest. The latter must suffer."[5] Although his organizational efforts had been a major factor in the Confederate victory, Lee was "mortified" that he had not been able to serve in the field. He did not intend to fight the war from behind a desk.

One week after the victory at Manassas, Davis found a place for Lee in the field. Federal forces under George B. McClellan had invaded western Virginia from Ohio, and threatened key railroad lines. In the last week of July, Davis asked Lee to go to western Virginia to bring order to a deteriorating front where local Confederate commanders were more combative with one another than with the Union forces. Davis appears to have assumed that Lee's prestige and his title as commander of Confederate forces in Virginia would convey whatever authority he required. He carried no official orders, however, and it was widely assumed that his role was that of an adviser rather than a commander.[6]

Lee faced the formidable task of "coordinating" the operations of three small forces whose commanders were mutually antagonistic. The main Confederate force in western Virginia was camped at Huntersville and numbered perhaps 10,000 men under Gen. William W. Loring, a competent, but prickly, veteran of the Old Army. To the north were small, ill-disciplined bands commanded by two long-time political rivals, Generals John B. Floyd and Henry A. Wise.

Lee received a cool reception from Loring when he arrived in the camp at Huntersville on August 3. Some commanders would have promptly pulled rank on Loring, or even demanded that he be replaced. Instead, Lee worked with Loring on a complicated plan for bringing several Confederate columns to bear against a Federal force entrenched at Cheat Mountain.

Both officers would have been wiser if they had put the campaign on hold. Western Virginia was experiencing some of the heaviest rains in recent memory, and the Confederate soldiers were not only badly trained, but also sick, hungry, and poorly supplied. But Lee persevered, and developed a plan for Loring's five brigades to attack at Cheat Mountain on September 12.

Rain fell heavily on the night of September 11, and on the following morning the unit designated to lead the attack never moved. Lee's ambitious campaign floundered in a sea of mud, and the Confederates pulled back to Huntersville. His first campaign had been an embarrassing failure, and Lee probably wondered if he would ever again be asked to serve in the field. Lee's frankest assessment of the debacle was in response to a sympathetic letter from Governor Letcher of Virginia:

> I was very sanguine of taking the enemy's works on last Thursday morning. I had considered the subject well. With great effort the troops intended for the surprise had reached their destination. . . . When morning broke, I could see the enemy's tents on Valley River, at the point on the Huttonsville road just below me. It was a tempting sight. We waited for the attack on Cheat Mountain, which was to be the signal. Till 10 A.M. the men were cleaning their unserviceable arms. But the signal did not come. . . . The attack to come off from the east side failed from the difficulties in the way; the opportunity was lost, and our plan discovered. . . . But for the rain, I have no doubt it would have succeeded.[7]

Lee would not have many defeats to explain, and his letter to Letcher is of interest. Rather than criticize the command arrangements or the behavior of particular commanders, he put much of the blame on a factor beyond anyone's control: the weather.

ALTHOUGH THE CAMPAIGN HE HAD DEVISED WAS IN SHAMbles, Lee left some admirers behind in western Virginia. He had a way with soldiers. Once, while Lee and his staff were making some observations, a group of volunteers crowded around him, curious about Lee and about his plans. Lee turned on the most inquisitive of the group.

"What regiment do you belong to?" he asked.

"First Tennessee, Maury Grays," the soldier replied.

"Are you well drilled?"

"Yes, indeed," the soldier replied.

"Take the position of a soldier," said Lee.

Lee ran him through some drill movements until the soldier was pointed toward his camp, then ordered "Double-quick, march!" He and his companions got the message without a voice being raised, and the officers continued their reconnaissance.[8]

Lee stayed in western Virginia for another three weeks, then returned to Richmond. The same newspapers that had hailed him as the reincarnation of "Light-Horse Harry" Lee were now patronizing, if not hostile. Edward Pollard, an editor with the *Richmond Examiner*, characterized Lee's stint in western Virginia as remarkable mainly for having been conducted by a general "who had never fought a battle, who had a pious horror of guerrillas, and whose extreme tenderness of blood induced him to depend exclusively upon the resources of strategy, to essay the achievement of victories without the cost of life."[9]

At about the time Lee returned to Richmond the Federals launched an amphibious offensive against the North Carolina coast. The governors of the South's East Coast states bombarded Davis with demands for assistance, and on November 5 the president responded by sending Lee to see what could be done to strengthen the defenses there. In contrast to Lee's earlier mission to western Virginia, there was no confusion as to his authority; Davis named Lee commander of a new Department of South Carolina, Georgia, and East Florida.

His mission got off to an inauspicious start when the Federals successfully landed 12,000 men around Port Royal and occupied a portion of the South Carolina coast near Savannah, Georgia. Governor Francis Pickens of South Carolina was not certain that Lee was the best man available to deal with the Federal threat; Davis assured Pickens that he was.

Two weeks after his return from western Virginia, Lee, accompanied by Armistead Long, took the train south for Charleston and Savannah. He spent four months examining coastal fortifications, including Fort Pulaski, where he had worked as a young engineer. He strengthened weak positions, fortified harbors, and constructed earthworks where needed.* What could have been drudgery became a useful exercise for Lee: He had to decide if the Confederacy was capable of protecting itself at all points. It was not, and Lee abandoned small forts on St. Simon and Jekyll islands off the Georgia coast.

During this trip, Lee made time to visit Cumberland Island, Georgia, where his father was buried. He wrote to Mary of the visit—his

---

* The Confederates hoped to defend Fort Pulaski, with its seven-foot-thick walls, to keep Federal warships away from the Savannah channel. However, not even Lee's ministrations could make the old fort resistant to rifled cannon. In April 1862 the fort surrendered after a thirty-hour bombardment from Federal batteries on a nearby island.

first—and of his father's grave, "marked by a plain marble slab." The Shaw family had moved, he said, leaving only a few servants to tend the house, but the garden was beautiful, "inclosed by the finest [wild olive] hedge I have ever seen."[10]

It was during this period outside Virginia that Lee acquired the mount that would be associated with him for the rest of his life. For $200 in gold, Lee bought a horse that he named Traveller. Responding after the war to Markie Williams, who wanted to paint the famous steed, Lee wrote a letter that reflected his warm feelings for the horse that had carried him through the war:

> If I were an artist like you I would draw a true picture of Traveller—representing his fine proportions, muscular figure, deep chest and short back, strong haunches . . . quick eye, small feet, and black mane and tail. Such a picture would inspire a poet, whose genius could then depict his worth and describe his endurance of toil, hunger, thirst, heat, cold, and the dangers and sufferings through which he passed. He could dilate upon his sagacity and affection, and his invariable response to every wish of his rider. He might even imagine his thoughts, through the long night marches and days of battle through which he has passed. But I am no artist; I can say only that he is a Confederate gray.[11]

ON MARCH 2, 1862, LEE RECEIVED A TELEGRAM FROM PRESIdent Davis ordering him to return to Richmond. He boarded a train three days later, amid rumors that he was to be the new secretary of war. But when Davis issued the announcement it was to appoint Lee to a position analogous to chief of staff to the president.

Davis needed the best advice he could get, for Confederate prospects were now looking very doubtful. No longer were young Southerners rushing to the colors, and the Federals' capture of Forts Henry and Donelson had opened much of the Mississippi Valley to the Federal forces. Western Virginia had been lost and the U.S. Navy was preparing to attack New Orleans. A Federal enclave at Port Royal, South Carolina, posed a threat to Savannah. But the most serious threat was to the Confederate capital. McClellan had persuaded a

Maj. Gen. George B. McClellan strikes a characteristically Napoleonic pose. NATIONAL ARCHIVES.

reluctant Lincoln that the most advantageous route for an advance on Richmond was via the York Peninsula, and during the latter half of March a stream of vessels carried men and equipment from Alexandria to the peninsula. By early April, Federal ships had delivered more than 120,000 men, 15,000 animals, and huge amounts of equipment to the Federal enclave at Fortress Monroe.[12]

In Richmond, Lee handled whatever assignments Davis gave him. His day began with a two-block walk from his rooms at the Spotswood Hotel to his office in Mechanics Hall. Rarely did a day pass when he was not called to confer with President Davis in his offices in the old Customs House. For the midday meal Lee usually returned to his hotel, occasionally dining with members of his staff. Although he had horses stabled in Richmond, he appears to have had few opportunities for his principal recreation, riding.[13] In Walter Taylor's recollection,

> His correspondence, necessarily heavy, was constantly a source of worry and annoyance to him. He did not enjoy writing; indeed, he wrote with labor, and nothing seemed to tax his amiability so much as the necessity for writing a lengthy official communication; but he was not satisfied unless at the close of his office hours every matter requiring prompt attention had been disposed of.[14]

The first and perhaps the most important matter that Davis asked Lee to look into was that of military conscription. Joe Johnston, defending Richmond, had no more than 60,000 men with which to confront McClellan. Conscription, for a government based on states' rights, was an act of desperation; yet with terms of enlistment for volunteers expiring and few volunteers coming forward, it could not be avoided. Lee, aided by a new addition to his staff, Virginia lawyer Charles Marshall, drafted the first conscription law in U.S. history. By the time it was enacted by the Confederate congress on April 16 there were far more loopholes than Lee would have liked. Exempted categories included state officials, telegraph operators, railway workers, apothecaries, and teachers. Otherwise, it provided for three years' military service for all white males between the ages of 18 and 35, and required that one-year volunteers serve for another two years.

Lee's brief stint as Davis's military adviser receives little attention in most biographies, but it represented excellent preparation for his later service as army commander. There was virtually no aspect of the Confederate war effort that escaped his scrutiny. And he had words of reassurance for his friend Sidney Johnston, who in March 1862 was widely criticized for Confederate setbacks in the West. "I have watched your every movement & know the difficulties with which you have had to contend," Lee wrote. "I hope your cares will be diminished if not removed when your junction with the other lines of your Army has been completed."[15]

Meanwhile, McClellan was advancing slowly on Yorktown, sixty miles from Richmond, complaining as he went of the rutted Virginia roads. Johnston had evacuated his lines along the Rappahannock River, moving his troops to positions where they could better defend the capital. Unfortunately for the Confederates, the enemy threat was not limited to the peninsula, for the Federals had a second army, commanded by Gen. Irvin McDowell, in position to advance on Richmond from the north. Tension increased in the Confederate capital. Martial law was declared, furloughs were canceled, and the sale of liquor was prohibited.

Lee cast about for means of dealing with McClellan. The first Confederate line was a force of about 34,000 at Yorktown, commanded by Gen. John Magruder, who expected shortly to be overwhelmed by the advancing Federals. It was clear that McClellan was a cautious commander, but he commanded so overwhelming a force that the fall of Richmond seemed only a matter of time.

When Davis arrived at his office early on the morning of April 14 he found Johnston waiting. During an extended conversation, Johnston presented a pessimistic assessment of the Confederates' situation on the peninsula, then outlined his own plan. Instead of trying to defend the peninsula, he urged, the Confederacy should strip the defenses of South Carolina and Georgia and assemble the greatest force possible just outside Richmond. With such a force, Johnston predicted, the Confederacy could defeat McClellan in the decisive battle of the war.[16]

Davis's initial session with Johnston began a day of meetings that would influence the outcome of the war. Davis was noncommittal regarding Johnston's proposal, but asked him to return at ten o'clock when they would be joined by Lee and Secretary of War George W. Randolph. Johnston returned as requested, bringing with him two of his subordinates, Gen. James Longstreet and Gen. Gustavus W. Smith, and bearing a memorandum that summarized his recommendation that the Confederacy not defend the peninsula.

Davis asked each person present to comment on Johnston's proposal. General Smith, Johnston's deputy, supported his chief. Next to speak was Secretary of War Randolph, who opposed retreat. Abandonment of the peninsula, he pointed out, would jeopardize Norfolk, and with it the ironclad *Virginia* that was the most potent warship in the Confederate navy.

When Lee's turn came, he spoke out strongly against Johnston's proposal, urging an all-out defense of the peninsula. The conference continued into the afternoon and became a contest of wills between Lee and Joe Johnston. Lee pointed out that if coastal defenses were abandoned the Federals would be free to launch amphibious operations, such as the one against North Carolina, and might easily sever Richmond's railroad links to the south.[17] He probably raised questions of logistics as well. How were the Confederates to feed an army of nearly 100,000 in an enclave around Richmond?

Davis recessed the meeting at six o'clock, directing that it resume an hour later at his residence. There, Lee and Johnston continued to pit argument and rebuttal. If the Confederates in fact lost portions of the coast, Johnston maintained, these could easily be reclaimed after McClellan was defeated in front of Richmond. But why give up the peninsula, Lee asked, when it offered "great advantages to a smaller force?" Johnston responded that the peninsula was unhealthy, subjecting its defenders to a high incidence of disease. Lee may have made the point that health problems would not be limited to the defenders.[18]

Finally, Lee insisted that Johnston's plan allowed the Federals to come too close to the Confederate capital too easily. What if McClellan did not attack a strongly defended Richmond as Johnston assumed? Lee preferred to fight the enemy at a distance from Richmond, to isolate a portion of the enemy army and attack it. His philosophy as a soldier was fundamentally different from that of his friend Johnston, who believed that he could surrender the initiative and still achieve a decisive victory.

In the end it was Davis's aversion to risk that carried the day. Johnston's plan offered the hope of a smashing victory, but it ran counter to Davis's reluctance to yield any Confederate territory to the invader. Johnston returned to Yorktown with instructions to hold the line there, but he remained convinced that the Davis-Lee strategy was folly.

MEANWHILE, LEE WAS MAKING PLANS OF HIS OWN. STUDYing Northern newspapers that made their way into Confederate hands, he noted the inflated figures of Confederate strength that emanated from McClellan's headquarters. Could he not play on McClellan's inferiority complex? In early June Lee sent an entire division to the Shenandoah Valley, dispatching it in so obvious a manner that

McClellan's spies could not help noticing. As Lee expected, McClellan wired Lincoln on June 18 that if Lee felt able to send Jackson 10,000 or 15,000 men, "it illustrates their strength and confidence."[19]

Lee sought a way to discourage any move by General McDowell to assist McClellan. Lee scarcely knew Thomas J. "Stonewall" Jackson, who was then commanding a small army in the Shenandoah Valley. However, some letters from Jackson to Longstreet showed that Jackson was eager to take the offensive in the valley. Lee wrote encouragingly to Jackson and sought to build up his force; on April 21 he invited Jackson to use Gen. Richard Ewell's division, then at Culpeper, but warned that any offensive must be a quick strike. In the famous Valley campaign that followed, Jackson aroused such concern in Washington that Lincoln, on May 24, suspended orders for McDowell to move toward Richmond, and ordered him instead to send two of his divisions to Gen. Nathaniel P. Banks at Winchester.[20]

Jackson's success in the valley, however, did not ensure Richmond's survival. On May 3 Johnston pulled out of his lines at Yorktown, leaving McClellan to proclaim a brilliant success. Johnston had only 55,000 men with which to confront McClellan's 100,000, but the Federal commander was by then so convinced that he faced superior numbers that he continued to advance at a snail's pace. But even at that pace McClellan would arrive at Richmond eventually, and Davis was losing confidence in the secretive Johnston. On May 9, with McClellan some twenty miles from Richmond, President Davis evacuated his wife to Raleigh, North Carolina, and Secretary of War Randolph began loading government records onto railroad cars.

At a cabinet meeting on May 14, Davis and his advisers considered their options if Richmond were abandoned. Lee, when asked for his advice, stated that the next logical defense line would be along the Staunton River, nearly 100 miles to the southwest. "But," said Lee, "Richmond must not be given up; it shall not be given up!" Lee had tears in his eyes, and Postmaster General John Reagan later wrote that he had never seen Lee show such deep emotion.[21]

So it was that Lee himself endorsed the decision that confirmed Richmond to be the great prize of the war. This need not have been the case. When Confederate authorities decided that Montgomery, Alabama, was far too provincial to serve as capital of the Confederacy, they could have chosen a central, inland city such as Atlanta, Columbia, or Raleigh. In the spring of 1861, however, Confederate delegates had been courting the border states, especially Virginia. And Richmond was vital to the Confederate war effort, if only because the Tredegar Iron Works there was the only facility in the South capable of producing heavy ordnance. By locating their capital just 120 miles from Washington, D.C., however, the Confederates virtually guaranteed that Virginia would be the principal battleground of the war.

In the spring of 1862 Richmond was in danger of attack from every direction except the southwest. Given the city's geographic vulnerability, Davis and Lee were fortunate that McClellan had committed himself to a campaign along a peninsula that did not lend itself to creative maneuvering. Eventually, however, the requirement to defend Richmond would limit the ability of its defenders to maneuver. The commitment to defend Richmond would preclude a strategy such as the one George Washington had pursued against the British—avoiding major battles while keeping an army in the field.

THE PAST YEAR HAD WROUGHT IMPORTANT CHANGES IN LEE. The tepid secessionist, who deplored Virginia's withdrawal from the Union, had lately seen friends killed, his wife's home occupied, and measures by the Federals, such as the naval blockade of Charleston, that he considered barbaric.

Meanwhile, Lee tried to mediate between Davis and Johnston. The latter continued to be secretive about his plans—a virtue in some respects, but a problem when it extended to President Davis. In March, when Johnston had retired from his Manassas line in favor of one along the Rappahannock, he had not even informed the president. Davis believed Johnston was insubordinate, while Johnston considered the president an incompetent meddler in military affairs. Now, in front of Richmond, Johnston's tone was increasingly pessimistic.

Lee assumed the role of intermediary. On May 18 he wrote to Johnston that "as you are now so convenient to the city"—a sense of irony was not Lee's strong point—the president desired Johnston to confer about his plans. Three days later Lee wrote again, noting that "the President desires to know the number of troops around Richmond, how they are posted, and the organization of the divisions and brigades."[22]

By late May, Federal advance units were within three or four miles of the city, and McClellan was awaiting his siege artillery. Even Johnston recognized that he could not retreat forever. East of the city, the Confederates noted, McClellan had moved his forces into an awkward position. He had two corps, those of Erasmus Keyes and Samuel Heintzelman, south of the normally sluggish Chickahominy River. The remainder of his army, comprising the corps of Fitz John Porter, William Franklin, and Edwin Sumner, was north of the river. A heavy rain on the night of May 30 gave Johnston his opportunity, for the swollen river promised to isolate the two wings of McClellan's army, or at least make it difficult for one to support the other.

Johnston initially planned to attack north of the Chickahominy. When he learned that McDowell was no longer approaching, however, he chose to attack the weaker Federal lines south of the river. Alas, little went right for Johnston on May 31. Longstreet's division went down the wrong road, and another division never got into the action. At Fair Oaks, what was to have been a pulverizing attack degenerated into a brawl. Much of the fighting took place in swampy ground, where soldiers fought in knee-deep water and where the wounded were propped against trees to prevent them from drowning.

By evening the Confederates had gained some ground but the outcome was in doubt. Johnston, with two aides, was observing the fighting from a small rise when he was wounded, first by a rifle bullet in the shoulder and then by a shell fragment. For a time his wounds appeared fatal. Johnston was taken to the rear on a stretcher and the Battle of Fair Oaks sputtered to a close.

Both Davis and Lee had observed the battle. After Johnston was wounded, Lee gave instructions to Gen. Gustavus Smith, Johnston's deputy, and helped stabilize the Confederate line. Dusk fell, and the sound of firing gave way to the moans of the wounded and the calls of those attempting to locate their units. Davis and Lee made their way back to Richmond, arriving there about nine thirty in the evening. They talked far into the night, and by early morning there was a consensus that Smith was not qualified to command an army.

The next morning Davis and Lee rode back to the battlefield. At some point the president told Lee that the Army of Northern Virginia was now his. Johnston, in Richmond, would tell a caller, "The shot that struck me down is the best that has been fired for the Southern cause yet, for I possess in no degree the confidence of our government, and now they have in place one who does."[23]

CHAPTER SEVEN

SAVING RICHMOND

R OBERT E. LEE BROUGHT BOTH ASSETS AND
liabilities to his new role as commander of the Army of Northern Virginia.* While serving under Scott in Mexico he had seen what an inferior force, skillfully led, could accomplish against much greater numbers. He himself had demonstrated in Mexico three vital qualities in a soldier: bravery, judgment, and endurance. Later, his tour as superintendent of West Point had allowed him to study the military literature of his day. Over the years he had developed the kind of analytical mind that could visualize a battlefield in its entirety, and determine how best to bring firepower to bear in a crucial place.

In the Civil War to this point, Lee had demonstrated, in his dealings with Jackson, an ability to see opportunities in a secondary theater of operations where others could not. He had served so long in the U.S. Army that he knew, either personally or by reputation, many of the senior commanders on both sides. Lee also had a remarkable ability to

---

* Lee is sometimes credited with having coined the name *Army of Northern Virginia* to reflect his intention to take the war to the enemy. Although Lee appears to have been among the first to use this term, he did so months before it became his command. In March 1862, at a time when Gen. Joe Johnston's responsibilities embraced the Department of Northern Virginia, Lee, in correspondence, referred to Johnston's force as the Army of Northern Virginia. See Freeman, *R. E. Lee*, II, 78.

win the loyalty of those around him, be they generals or privates in the ranks. Courteous by nature, he was always prepared to soothe fragile egos. Patriarchal in manner, he was constantly concerned for the welfare of his men. And, although the man in the street regarded Lee's performance to date as disappointing, he retained the confidence of President Davis. Lee had every intention of justifying this confidence, and to this end he would never repeat Johnston's error of keeping Davis out of the loop.

At the same time, most of Lee's career had been with the engineers, building or repairing forts. Although he had been in the front lines before Mexico City, the only time Lee had commanded troops in even a skirmish was the brief peacetime action to capture John Brown's insurgents. The largest force he had commanded was a cavalry regiment in Texas, and he had no experience dealing with the raw militia on which the Confederacy now depended.

The enthusiasm with which Richmond had first greeted Lee had long since cooled. His unsuccessful campaign in western Virginia, followed by his offstage service in South Carolina and Georgia, did nothing to inspire confidence in Lee as a combat commander. The *Richmond Examiner* greeted Lee's appointment to command the Army of Northern Virginia with the observation that henceforth the army would never be allowed to fight, only to dig, "spades & shovels being the only implements Gen. Lee knew anything about."[1]

Outside Richmond, McClellan had no qualms about his new opponent. Several weeks earlier he had been informed, prematurely, that Lee was commanding Confederate forces on the peninsula, and McClellan had seen the appointment as a good sign. He wrote to President Lincoln, "I prefer Lee to Johnston—the former is *too* cautious & weak under grave responsibility—personally brave & energetic to a fault, he yet is wanting in moral firmness when pressed by heavy responsibility & is likely to be timid & irresolute in action."[2]

However strange such a judgment may appear today, Lee was an unknown quantity even in the army he now commanded. Col. Edward P. Alexander, later Longstreet's chief of artillery, wondered to a colleague, Col. Joseph Ives, whether Lee had the audacity necessary to command an army. Ives was reassuring. "Alexander," he replied, "if there is one man in either army, Federal or Confederate, who is head and shoulders far above every other one . . . in audacity, that man is General Lee."[3]

Among all the professions, the military is unique in that only the catastrophe of war allows a soldier to practice the skills he has often spent decades acquiring. For all of his outward humility, Lee never doubted that he was equal to his responsibilities as army commander. His modesty—a reflection of his piety—effectively disguised a soldier who at last faced a challenge consistent with his abilities.

Later in the war Lee would offer a somewhat simplistic explanation for his success. "I plan and work with all my might to bring the troops to the right place at the right time," he said. "With that I have done my duty. As soon as I order the troops forward into battle, I lay the fate of my army in the hands of God."[4]

The situation was in fact more complex. Lee brought with him a commitment to the offensive, which could prove either an asset or a liability. Although wars were not won by entrenchments, the introduction of accurate rifles had increased the range at which battles could be fought, and effectively moved artillery from the front of the line, as in Napoleon's day, to positions in the rear. Rifles had sharply reduced the effectiveness of cavalry; unless the battle was won and the enemy routed, the cost of a cavalry charge against infantry could be prohibitive. In terms of manpower, the Civil War was already awesome in its scale. The numbers on both sides were virtually inconceivable to officers of the peacetime U.S. Army.

Only weeks after taking command of his army Lee was planning his first offensive. On June 22 he held a conference of all his generals—perhaps forty in all—at a house known as The Chimneys, not far from the front lines. It was the largest council of war he would call, and was intended primarily to give Lee insight into the thinking of his subordinates. He posed a key question: Should the army retire closer to Richmond and await a Federal attack, or go on the offensive? Two division commanders, John Magruder and Chase Whiting, favored retreat, on the grounds that Confederate lines were already within range of Federal artillery and likely to become untenable. Longstreet was impressed with the fact that Lee said little; he later recalled how "The brigadiers talked freely, but only of the parts of the line occupied by their brigades." Longstreet was relieved that Lee confided nothing of importance to so large and talkative a group.[5]

Lee remarked after the conference that if his army were to withdraw simply because they were within artillery range, he did not see how they could stop east of Richmond. Two days later Lee wrote to President Davis spelling out his own thinking. He wanted to "change the character of the war," perhaps to allow Jackson to invade Maryland and Pennsylvania.[6] Any move into the Northern states would have to wait, but it is interesting that Lee, manning Richmond's last defensive line, was already thinking offensively. Meanwhile, he had a plan with which to break the iron vise on Richmond:

> It will require 100,000 men to resist the regular siege of Richmond, which perhaps would only prolong not save it. I am preparing a line that I can hold with part of our forces in front, while with the rest I will endeavor to make a diversion to bring McClellan out.[7]

Davis, too, was a soldier, and although he appreciated the audacity of Lee's plan he was wary of the attendant risks. In a conversation after the war, Lee recalled that Davis hesitated, visited Lee's headquarters to discuss the plan, and only reluctantly gave his approval.[8]

The first phase of Lee's plan involved strengthening Confederate defenses south of the Chickahominy River. This phase emphasized entrenching, work that did not sit well with the men, and Lee became known, again, as the "King of Spades." Lee also required accurate intelligence on Federal dispositions. On June 10 Lee ordered "Jeb" Stuart, his newly minted cavalry commander, to make a scouting movement toward the enemy's right and discover McClellan's dispositions. Stuart suggested to Lee that he might ride around the entire Federal army in carrying out this mission, and Lee appears to have given him broad discretion so long as he did not unnecessarily hazard his command.

Two days later, Stuart, with 1,200 troopers, rode off on one of the most spectacular missions of the war. He first took his command north to the South Anna River. From there he turned east, moving behind the Federal right flank and ascertaining that there were no entrenchments there to anchor Porter's corps. Stuart then rode around McClellan's entire army, crossing the Chickahominy southeast of Richmond. He was able to inform Lee that McClellan's right was in fact "in the air," and by making his raid so conspicuous he was able to disguise the fact that his main objective had been to gather intelligence.[9]

This enabled Lee to make final plans. The Army of Northern Virginia comprised eight infantry divisions plus Stuart's cavalry brigade. Jackson had three divisions, which, if added to Lee's, would bring Confederate numbers to about 86,000. Lee sought to bring Jackson's army from the Shenandoah Valley to strike Porter on the Federal right, while three of Lee's own divisions would cross the Chickahominy and attack McClellan from the front. This would give Lee a two-to-one numerical superiority north of the river, but at a price of stripping almost bare his defenses south of the Chickahominy, where only 27,000 Confederates would face some 70,000 Federals. It was a good plan but it would require exact timing, especially from Jackson.

On Monday, June 23, Lee called a conference of his principal subordinates at his headquarters at Dabb's House. Joining him that afternoon were Stonewall Jackson, who had ridden more than fifty miles to attend the meeting; A. P. Hill, who had distinguished himself at Williamsburg and who already had a reputation as a hard fighter; James Longstreet, who had received mixed reviews for his performance at Seven Pines; and the acerbic D. H. Hill, a one-time mathematics professor who had served under Johnston on the York Peninsula.

In contrast with the heavily attended, wide-ranging meeting at The Chimneys, this was a true council of war. Lee was counting on Longstreet and the two Hills to drive the Federals down the north bank of the Chickahominy, and on Jackson to strike the enemy rear from the north. But after outlining his objectives Lee did a curious thing: He left the room, leaving his subordinates to determine the timing of attacks and routes of march. It was dark before the meeting ended, and Jackson began a long ride back to his headquarters. Lee's plans called for Jackson to participate in an attack at Mechanicsville on June 26, and Jackson had only two days to get ready.

Fortunately for Lee, the Federals did little to interfere with his preparations. Much of McClellan's time was occupied in appealing for more reinforcements and spinning excuses for his inaction. When he learned of Jackson's approach from the valley, McClellan wired Secretary of War Stanton that he now faced a total force of 200,000—an estimate that was more than 100 percent wrong.

On June 25, in the first action in what became known as the Seven Days' campaign, Federal forces reconnoitering on the south side of the river triggered heavy skirmishing at Oak Grove. The next day Lee took the initiative. His plan called for three Confederate divisions to attack Mechanicsville from the west, while Jackson came in from the north. Lee's ambitious plans went awry, however. Jackson, who had been fifteen miles north of Richmond the previous day, was unable to bring his forces up to make the key flank attack on Porter. Much of the day passed in nervous speculation about Jackson's location, for it was the sound of his guns that was to initiate the Confederate frontal attack.

Some time after three o'clock in the afternoon, tired of waiting for Jackson, A. P. Hill attacked the Federals at Beaverdam Creek, near Mechanicsville. After some early success, the Confederates suffered heavy casualties as a result of Hill's unsupported attack. Lee attempted to maintain his usual calm demeanor at his command post outside Mechanicsville, but one officer noted that "his eyes were restless with the look of a man with fever."[10]

Lee, as he wondered what had become of Jackson, knew that his plans had come unraveled and that he had not been able to deliver a heavy blow against the enemy. He could not know that the ferocity of his attack had shaken McClellan, who that night ordered Porter to withdraw in the direction of Gaines's Mill. Early the next day Lee sent a staff officer to find Jackson, and the two conferred late that morning. No record of their meeting survives, and Lee probably accepted Jackson's explanation that he had encountered unexpected problems en route. Still hopeful of attacking Porter's flank, Lee doubtless urged Jackson to hurry his march toward the next Federal line at Powhite Creek.

Meanwhile, the Federals were active. Porter had objected to McClellan's order to pull back, but the morning of June 27 found him entrenching in a strong position behind Boatswain's Swamp near Gaines's Mill. Lee's revised plan called for Longstreet to threaten Porter's left, while A. P. Hill attacked the Federal center and Jackson fell upon the Federal right with his three fresh divisions. If Porter shifted his troops to meet Jackson, Longstreet was to join the attack. A journalist recalled the scene at Lee's headquarters:

> While General Lee waited to get all his divisions in hand, he made his temporary headquarters at a farmhouse near the battlefield. . . . He sat entirely alone on the rear portico . . . while the foreground and adjoining orchard were occupied by general officers, aides, couriers, and prisoners, making an animated scene of war.[11]

Gaines's Mill, on June 27, was in some respects a repeat of the previous day's fighting at Mechanicsville. When one o'clock came and went without any sign of Jackson, Hill attacked unsupported and suffered heavy casualties. Not until about five o'clock did Jackson make his

Federal troops at the Battle of Gaines's Mill. LIBRARY OF CONGRESS.

appearance. "Ah, General, I am very glad to see you," Lee greeted him, with just a hint of reproach. "I had hoped to be with you before." [12] Jackson was to have marched against Porter by way of a crossroads known as Old Cold Harbor. His staff was operating in unfamiliar territory with inadequate maps, however, and Jackson's corps lost three hours when it took a wrong road.

Lee briefed Jackson on the battlefield before them, and at some time after six o'clock the Confederates finally launched the attack that should have taken place hours before. By then Porter had a well-manned convex line with strong artillery support. Only after heavy fighting did Hood's Texans and Pickett's Virginians break through, and Porter withdraw across the Chickahominy.

> As the roar of battle died away an insistent crying filled the air; thousands of wounded men were calling for help, and all about there were unwounded Confederates trying to get their fragmented battalions together, chanting regimental numbers endlessly so that stragglers would know where their comrades were. . . . The darkness was flecked with shifting lights as stretcher bearers with lanterns probed the splintered underbrush.[13]

Much had gone awry in Lee's campaign to date, but much had gone well, not all of it immediately evident. Lee's gamble—leaving the defense of Richmond to John Magruder and 27,000 men—had gone splendidly, with Magruder demonstrating so realistically that the Federals feared an attack south of the Chickahominy. Lee's greatest success, however, was in preying on the mind of George McClellan. Although the Federals had inflicted more casualties at Mechanicsville and Gaines's Mill than they had incurred, McClellan was whipped. In the early hours of June 28 he telegraphed Stanton that he had lost at Gaines's Mill because of inferior numbers, adding bitterly, "If I save this army now, I tell you plainly that I owe no thanks to you or to any other persons in Washington. You have done your best to sacrifice this army." [14] *

Saturday, June 28, saw a lull in the fighting. McClellan's great army, with its artillery and wagon trains, began to withdraw from near Rich-

---

* That McClellan was not immediately removed for sending this insolent telegram probably resulted from the fact that a horrified War Department telegrapher deleted these two sentences from his message.

mond toward the James River. Reconnaissance on the peninsula was difficult because the roads were narrow and the woods often impenetrable. The Federals had used observation balloons on several occasions, and Lee, curious, had ordered one from Richmond. During the fighting at Gaines's Mill he sent up one of his artillery officers in the balloon to detect enemy movements. The officer, Col. Porter Alexander, recalled that although the smoke provided some idea of the action, he could seldom see troops.[15]

Lee required more precise information. He suspected that McClellan was about to pull back, and sent Stuart to confirm his suspicions. Stuart was soon able to advise Lee that the Federals were recrossing the Chickahominy in the direction of the James River.

THE CAMPAIGN HAD ENTERED A NEW PHASE, THAT OF PURsuit. Lee sent his freshest troops, Magruder's and Huger's divisions, to attack from the west while Jackson and D. H. Hill struck from the north. But Jackson once again disappointed Lee, taking time to construct a bridge when his men might easily have forded the now-quiescent Chickahominy. When Magruder attacked the Federal rear guard at Savage Station, the Confederates had slightly the better of a two-hour clash that ended when night fell. But little had been done to impede McClellan's retreat, and Lee's patience was wearing thin. Although Jackson was responsible for most of the lost opportunities, Magruder was the one who came in for a scolding. "I regret very much that you have made so little progress in the pursuit of the enemy," Lee wrote him on the evening of June 28. "In order to reap the fruits of our victory the pursuit should be most vigorous."[16]

The following day brought more disappointment as Lee's very complex plan for assaults by seven divisions foundered, in part because of poor communications and inept leadership. Only Longstreet and Hill were able to get their divisions into action, fighting an afternoon engagement against McClellan's rear guard near Glendale. For yet another day Jackson, approaching from the north, was not a factor. While Longstreet's and Hill's men fought elements of five Union divisions near White Oak Swamp, Jackson took a nap. Lee remarked after the war that he never had known why Jackson did not cross White Oak Swamp, "and I don't know now after having studied it for years."[17]

On both June 29 and 30 Lee had perceived opportunities to assault an enemy in retreat, but in neither instance had he been able to mount a coordinated attack. When, after the fighting at White Oak Swamp, Gen. Jubal Early expressed concern that McClellan would escape, Lee replied tartly, "Yes, he will get away because I cannot have my orders carried out!" [18]

By July 1 the head of McClellan's column had reached Harrison's Landing, where it was under the protective fire of Federal gunboats. Porter deployed four divisions and 100 pieces of artillery on Malvern Hill, high ground overlooking the James River. In the late morning Lee and Longstreet reconnoitered the Federal position, and Lee agreed that it was too strong to assault. Then, as the day wore on, the Confederates succeeded in placing some artillery on a rise on their right, and the situation appeared to change. Lee ordered an artillery barrage, adding that if the artillery fire appeared to be taking effect—a subjective judgment—the infantry should attack.

Lee then rode off to the Confederate left to investigate a possible flanking movement. About four o'clock a courier brought word that the Federals appeared to be retreating, and that Confederate infantry on the right had successfully advanced. Lee, without confirming this information, ordered a general attack. Elements of three Confederate divisions advanced against the entrenched enemy, resulting in a disaster for the Army of Northern Virginia. The Confederate attack was uncoordinated, which gave the Federal artillery an opportunity to mow down the advancing columns. Magruder's and D. H. Hill's divisions were badly mauled; Hill remarked after the battle that it was not war but murder. The 5,500 Confederate casualties at Malvern Hill were more than double the Federal losses.

For days Lee had sought not merely to defeat McClellan but to destroy him. Repeatedly frustrated, he had interpreted the trail of abandoned equipment in the wake of the retreating Federals as evidence of demoralization. Would not one more attack drive "those people" into the river? It would not, and at Malvern Hill the Federals demonstrated the marked superiority in artillery that they would enjoy throughout the war.

As for Lee, only at Gettysburg would he allow his aggressiveness to overcome his judgment to the degree that it had at Malvern Hill. But never again would he have as promising an opportunity to annihilate an opposing army as had presented itself during the Seven Days' campaign. In a general order, Lee sought to gain the maximum psycholog-ical advantage from a campaign that had, after all, saved Richmond:

> On Thursday, June 26th, the powerful and thoroughly equipped army of the enemy was entrenched in works vast in extent and formidable in character within sight of our capital.
>
> Today the remains of that confident and threatening host lie upon the banks of the James River, seeking to recover, under the protection of his gunboats, from the effects of a series of disastrous defeats.[19]

In his official reports Lee was rarely critical of even the most egregious lapses by his lieutenants. In his report on the Seven Days' campaign, he wrote ambiguously, "Under ordinary circumstance the Federal Army should have been destroyed." He went on to deplore the absence of timely tactical intelligence, but did not elaborate on what other circumstances in the campaign had not been "ordinary." Privately, Lee was bitterly disappointed, especially with Jackson. He and his "foot cavalry" alike appear to have suffered from the cumulative fatigue that results from extended campaigns and long, hard marches. Jackson might have intimated some of this to Lee, but Jackson was not one to acknowledge weakness.

Lee's success in maneuvering McClellan away from Richmond was a remarkable achievement. He recognized immediately that the rain-swollen Chickahominy presented a unique opportunity. Lee's skillful use of defensive works south of the Chickahominy had permitted him to use his best troops on the offensive and in some instances to achieve numerical superiority. His strategy had been sound, but Lee had not taken into account the inexperience of his staff and the difficulties in coordinating attacking units that rarely were in sight of one another.

Lee's greatest success was in wresting the initiative from the enemy. Just hours after the initial Confederate success at Mechanicsville, McClellan was planning to retreat. Although Lee had nowhere near the 200,000 men with which the enemy credited him, he had acted so boldly that McClellan cannot be blamed for assuming that the Confederates were defending their capital with a mighty host.

The most serious criticism of Lee by recent students of the Civil War relates to the casualties that he and other commanders accepted in the course of their victories. McWhiney and Jamieson, in their criticism of the Confederate penchant for the offensive, contend that Confederate aggressiveness "brought them no decisive victories and [entailed] unbearable losses."[20] For the Seven Days' campaign casualties were extremely heavy. From Oak Grove to Malvern Hill, the Army of Northern Virginia suffered 19,700 casualties, including 950 missing, for a casualty rate of 20.7 percent. Federal losses totaled 15,850, including 6,000 missing, for a casualty rate of 16.7 percent.[21] Considering that the Confederates were the attackers everywhere except at Oak Grove, however, it is remarkable that the statistical gap is not greater.

But could Richmond have been saved by passive measures? Assuredly not, for even Joe Johnston conceded that the city would fall if McClellan brought it under siege.

Except for his lapse at Malvern Hill, Lee had waged a brilliant campaign, and the erstwhile "King of Spades" was now a Southern hero. Newspapers that only weeks earlier had been writing of "Granny" Lee now were fulsome in their praise. "No captain that ever lived," wrote the *Richmond Dispatch*, "could have planned or executed a better plan."[22] The editor of the *Richmond Examiner*, who early in 1862 had concluded that Lee was good only for digging, wrote after the war that the Seven Days' campaign had set Lee on a course where he "might have had the Dictatorship of the entire Southern Confederacy."[23]

In a campaign in which nearly all his plans had gone awry, Lee had won a stunning victory. A week earlier, McClellan's soldiers were in sight of the spires of Richmond and could hear their clocks strike the hours. Now, the Federals were thirty-five miles away and McClellan and the authorities in Washington were exchanging bitter reproaches. Meanwhile, the hard fighting of the Seven Days' campaign had confirmed what everyone suspected: The Confederate capital would be the great prize of the war.

CHAPTER EIGHT

SUPPRESSING POPE

DESPITE THE PRESTIGE THAT ACCRUED TO LEE as a result of the Seven Days' campaign, Confederate strategy was being determined in Richmond, and President Davis was obliged to listen to many voices. The governors of the various states were vocal in demanding that their states be defended, with the result that during the first year of the war various small forces were dispersed around the perimeter of the Confederacy in such a manner that they invited attack. The surrender of Forts Henry and Donelson in Tennessee in February 1862 brought changes, but demands for "total security" continued.

One factor that influenced the South's strategy was the temperament of its people. Many Southerners were outraged by the idea that Lincoln and his "abolitionist hordes" would wage war against the South, and they were not inclined to fight in a defensive mode. "The idea of waiting for blows, instead of inflicting them, is altogether unsuited to the genius of our people," thundered the *Richmond Examiner* in September 1861. "A column pushed forward into Ohio or Pennsylvania is worth more to us, as a defensive measure, than a whole tier of seacoast batteries from Norfolk to the Rio Grande." [1]

President Davis held views that were opposed to those of the *Exam-*

iner, and not in complete agreement with Lee's. Ideally, Davis wanted to defend every inch of Confederate soil. At the same time, his greatest fear was of a military disaster that might put a sudden end to the Confederacy.

In Lee's opinion, a defensive strategy of any sort could only postpone defeat. Indeed, although Lee had little respect for armchair strategists, his own views were similar to those of the *Examiner*. Lee was eager to seize the initiative wherever he could, for he was convinced that time was not on the side of the Confederacy and that the Federals must be brought to the negotiating table quickly. In a rare comment regarding a theater other than his own, Lee wrote approvingly to Davis of Gen. John T. Morgan's July 1862 cavalry raids into Kentucky: "If the impression made by Morgan in Kentucky could be confirmed by a strong infantry force, it would have the happiest effect."[2] Even as Lee commanded the largest army he would ever have at his disposal, he was outnumbered, and he could expect the odds to worsen as the war went on.

President Lincoln had problems of his own, however, the most pressing of which was what to do with the Army of the Potomac. He visited McClellan's headquarters on July 9 and subjected the general and his subordinates to some searching questions. The good news was that the army was now "safe." The other news was that McClellan insisted that he could resume the offensive only if he received reinforcements.

Lincoln and Stanton had lost faith in the general who had promised so much and delivered so little. On June 27, with the outcome of the Seven Days' campaign still in doubt, Lincoln had consolidated the Federal forces around Washington and those in the Shenandoah Valley into a new "Army of Virginia." To command it he chose Gen. John Pope, whose experience included some minor victories along the northern Mississippi River. It was a curious choice—one that reflected Lincoln's lack of personal knowledge of army personnel—for Pope's bravado had made him a figure of ridicule among his fellow officers even before the war. At the same time, Lincoln revived the rank of general-in-chief of the Federal armies and awarded the position to Gen. Henry W. Halleck, who was widely credited with the Union's recent successes in the West. The effect of these moves was to reduce McClellan to a subordinate role.

On taking command, Pope issued a series of general orders that he had cleared with Lincoln and Stanton. In them, Pope indicated that his army would live off the countryside and would hold local residents responsible for any acts of sabotage or guerrilla activity against Federal troops. Any male who refused to take an oath of loyalty to the Union would be sent south, and any person found violating his oath would be shot. To modern readers these orders hardly smack of barbarism, but they challenged the belief, widely held in Lee's time, that wars were to be conducted by professional armies.

Lee reacted angrily to Pope's orders. Like many other soldiers, North and South, he justified his commitment to the profession of arms in terms of chivalry—the traditional association of combat with love of country and the protection of hearth and home. To fight in defense of principle was a worthy and even noble undertaking. Though war was cruel, it could call forth the noblest of impulses, such as valor and sacrifice.

Lee deplored any aspect of war that threatened noncombatants. When, in December 1861, the Federal navy had sunk the "great stone fleet" in Charleston harbor in an unsuccessful attempt to close it down, Lee called the attempted blockade an expression of "malice and revenge."[3] Lee's views with respect to noncombatants were not unlike those of McClellan, who twice had found Mrs. Lee residing in territory occupied by the Federals and twice had delivered her safely to Confederate lines. Most Federal commanders in the first year of the war had respected private property—even escaped slaves were sometimes returned to their owners—but this was beginning to change. Rooney Lee's home on the James had been capriciously burned to the ground by Federal cavalry.

Lee wrote a letter of protest to Halleck regarding Pope's pronouncements. If the Federals began killing civilians, he warned, the Confederates would retaliate. He would have no choice but to fight the war in the same manner as the Federals "until the voice of an outraged humanity shall compel a respect for the recognized usages of war."[4]

Lee, meanwhile, was reorganizing his army. He deftly rid it of generals such as John Magruder and Benjamin Huger whose performance in the Seven Days' campaign he had found unsatisfactory. Although the creation of corps as such had not yet been sanctioned by the Confederate congress, he divided the army into two corps-size wings under Jackson and Longstreet. Lee said nothing to reflect on Jackson's performance in the Seven Days' campaign, but his July 1862 reorganization left Jackson with seven brigades instead of the fourteen he had commanded earlier. Longstreet, who had led six brigades during the Seven Days, now commanded twenty-eight.[5]

Of all Lee's subordinates, James Longstreet would prove the most controversial. The 41-year-old Georgian, who had been known, inexplicably, as "Old Pete" while a cadet at West Point, was largely unknown to Lee when the war began. In the Old Army, Longstreet had been known to relish poker and to enjoy a drink. In the first weeks of the war, however, he had lost three children to scarlet fever, and it was now a stolid, serious soldier who served the Army of Northern Virginia.

Old Pete had won Lee's confidence as a division commander during the Seven Days' campaign and had gained admirers elsewhere as well. A staff officer described his chief as "a most striking figure . . . tall and well proportioned, strong and active, a superb horseman." His beard was brown and full, his eyes "steel-blue, deep and piercing."[6] Longstreet had a high opinion of his own ability, and did not hesitate to make his views known to his superiors. Thoughtful in matters concerning his profession and seemingly fearless in battle, he had the potential to be as great an asset as that idol of the Southern press, Stonewall Jackson.

It was Jackson to whom Lee wrote on July 23, raising the possibility of a new campaign. To be sure, McClellan's forces would still have to be watched, but Lee was ready to reinforce Jackson along the Rapidan River as soon as there was a good prospect for offensive action.[7] Four days later, reflecting on the "miscreant" John Pope, Lee addressed Jackson again. "I want Pope to be suppressed," he wrote. "The course indicated in his orders if the newspapers report them correctly cannot be permitted."[8]

Any campaign against Pope had a strategic dimension as well. Lee was a careful student of the Northern newspapers that found their way into the Confederate lines. Having read of differences between President Lincoln and McClellan regarding future operations, and having noted Lincoln's concern for the safety of Washington, Lee wondered if a threat to the Federal capital might not lead to McClellan's army being withdrawn from the peninsula. In a meeting with President Davis on July 13, Lee appears to have gained Davis's assent to an offensive designed to drive the Federals back to the Potomac.

The campaign that would be known as Second Manassas began modestly. To counter a Federal threat to Gordonsville, a rail junction north of Richmond, Lee sent Jackson there with two divisions on July 13.

Pope, with 55,000 men, was just to the north at Culpeper. In addition to Pope's army, Lee had to take into account 11,000 Federals at Fredericksburg who were in a position to threaten Jackson's communications. There was also McClellan's army at Harrison's Landing. Jackson could not do much against Pope with just two divisions, but when McClellan remained quiescent on the James, Lee sent Jackson reinforcements in the form of A. P. Hill's 12,000-man Light Division. Lee had the advantage of interior lines in dealing with Pope, and he moved most of his units to Gordonsville by rail. As to what Jackson should attempt with three divisions, Lee wrote, "I must now leave the matter to your reflection and good judgment. Make up your mind what is best to be done under all the circumstances . . . and let me hear the result at which you arrive."[9]

In Washington, meanwhile, Halleck responded exactly as Lee had hoped. On August 3 he ordered McClellan to withdraw his army to Aquia Creek, north of Fredericksburg, in order to unite with Pope. McClellan protested, arguing that he could still capture Richmond if reinforced, but Halleck prevailed.

By August 15, Lee had word that McClellan was evacuating his army from Harrison's Landing and that his destination appeared to be northern Virginia. Lee was annoyed with Gen. D. H. Hill for allowing McClellan to slip away unmolested, but this was water over the dam. The point was that if Lee was to deal with Pope, he must do so before Pope was reinforced by McClellan. The armies of Lee and Pope at this time each numbered about 55,000 men—20,000 of Lee's men had been held back for the defense of Richmond—but a union of Pope's army with McClellan's 90,000-man force would make the Federals unassailable.

Meanwhile, McClellan's army was moving, albeit slowly. It had to travel by water down the James River, north through the Chesapeake Bay, and up the Potomac before making a landing from which it could march to Pope's assistance. Lee saw a chance for a blow, but wrote to his wife of modest objectives: "I think we shall at least change the theater of war from the James River to north of the Rappahannock. . . . If it is effective at least for a season it will be a great gain."[10]

Much would depend on Stonewall Jackson, and Lee's handling of Jackson suggests that he retained a high degree of confidence in that eccentric officer. An army commander can issue several kinds of orders. He can issue directives that dictate every movement by a subordinate, spelling out the schedule on which they are to be made. Or he can give orders that specify only an objective, leaving his lieutenant wide latitude as to how it is to be achieved. Lee gave Jackson plenty of latitude.

By the first week of August, Jackson had concentrated his 24,000-man force at Cedar Mountain, twenty miles north of Gordonsville. There, on August 9, he turned back an attack by his old antagonist in the valley, Gen. Nathaniel Banks. While Pope awaited the reinforcements that would give him overwhelming numerical superiority, Lee sought to do what he had tried to do in the Seven Days' campaign: isolate a portion of the enemy army and punish it before reinforcements could arrive.

There were significant differences between what Lee now attempted and what he had accomplished in the Seven Days. On the positive side, he did not have to concern himself with the immediate safety of Richmond; he had room in which to operate. On the other hand, he would have to maneuver to achieve the local superiority that he had enjoyed at Mechanicsville and Gaines's Mill, where the Chickahominy had served as a barrier to Federal reinforcements. Time was running short, for the first units of McClellan's vanguard would soon be debarking north of Fredericksburg.

In the second week of August, Lee brought the remainder of his army, primarily Longstreet's corps, to Gordonsville. He himself arrived there on August 15, and was met at the station by Jackson. There, Lee spelled out his plans to Jackson, Longstreet, and Jeb Stuart. His initial proposal was for Stuart to strike Pope's communications so that Pope would fall back toward Washington. This operation was discarded, however, when one of Stuart's aides was captured carrying Lee's orders. When Lee and Longstreet climbed Clark's Mountain a few days later to examine Pope's dispositions, they were astonished to find only empty campsites. The enemy was already withdrawing to the north bank of the Rappahannock.

Lee went back to his maps and came up with an ambitious new scheme: He would send Jackson, with half the Confederate infantry and Stuart's cavalry, to cut the Orange and Alexandria Railroad between Culpeper and Washington. Jackson's corps would make a long flanking march north, then east, which would put them between Pope and Washington. Lee would follow with Longstreet's corps. Confederate thinking was that the enemy's fear of Jackson, in the context of Longstreet's advance, would cause Pope to pull back toward Washington.

If Jackson was delayed, or if Pope seized the initiative, Lee was in trouble. To divide his army in the face of an enemy of equal or greater size went against one of the most basic military maxims, but Lee appears to have had even less respect for Pope than for McClellan. On August 25, Jackson's corps began an epic fifty-mile turning movement. Pope thought that Jackson was headed for the Shenandoah Valley and failed to detect his turn to the east. The following day Jackson completed his two-day march by seizing the large Federal supply base at Manassas. After allowing his hungry soldiers a day to gorge themselves from the enemy's larder, Jackson slipped away, went to ground behind the cut of an unfinished railroad, and awaited developments.

On the evening of August 28, one of Pope's divisions stumbled onto Jackson's position, resulting in a brisk exchange. Pope concentrated his forces that evening, and the next morning began a series of frontal attacks against Jackson, who held his position in fierce fighting. That morning Pope received reinforcements from the newly arrived corps of Fitz John Porter and Irvin McDowell, but their arrival merely created a great deal of confusion without enabling Pope to put more men in the line against Jackson.

Lee, meanwhile, accompanied Longstreet's corps as it marched east to Jackson's rescue. While Jackson was pillaging Manassas on August 27, Longstreet was passing through Salem Courthouse twenty miles to the west. The pace was leisurely, and if Pope had made a determined defense of Thoroughfare Gap he might have delayed Longstreet long enough to permit Jackson to be overrun. But the Confederates marched through the pass on August 28, brushing aside light resistance. Federal intelligence was poor, and it appears that Pope never recognized the implications of Confederate infantry at Thoroughfare Gap.

By the morning of August 29, most of Longstreet's corps was east of the Bull Run mountains and some of his elements were within ten miles of Jackson's lines. West of Gainesville, Longstreet's advance units met up with Confederate cavalry, and Lee and Longstreet conferred with Stuart. That zealous cavalryman, fresh from his own raid on Federal supplies, described Jackson's defensive line and suggested how Longstreet might best link up with it. Lee, with several aides, cantered ahead of the column to get a feel for the land. When he returned his face bore a mark where a bullet had grazed his cheek; he remarked to an aide that a Yankee sharpshooter "came near killing me just now."[11] It was Lee's closest call during the war.

Jackson's corps continued to bear the brunt of savage but uncoordinated Federal onslaughts. At about eleven o'clock, Longstreet's advance units came into the Confederate line on Jackson's right, sending a ripple of cheers along the battered Confederate line. Shortly after noon Lee urged a prompt attack against the Federal left flank. Longstreet, however, declined to order an assault until he had reconnoitered the enemy lines. Lee issued no direct order, and Longstreet concluded after his reconnaissance that an attack would be unwise. Lee, according to Longstreet, was "quite disappointed."[12] He asked his corps commander to reconsider, but again Longstreet declined to order an attack.

Meanwhile, although Pope never got more than 32,000 men into action against Jackson's 22,000, the Confederates were hard pressed. A South Carolina officer recalled,

> It was now about 4 o'clock, and although wearied, we knew the struggle was yet to be renewed. They soon came, now in still greater force. . . . [The Federals] pressed on, crossed the cut, and slowly compelled us, step by step, to yield the long-coveted position. Here again our men fought the enemy at a few yards.[13]

Nearby, Confederate scouts confirmed that Pope was receiving reinforcements. There was no way Lee could know that Pope was so despised by his Federal colleagues that cooperation was difficult even on a battlefield. For a third time Lee urged an attack, and the fact that even then there was no direct order is an interesting commentary on Lee's most conspicuous weakness as a commander: his deference to subordinates. "Though more than anxious to meet [Lee's] wishes," Longstreet would write, he regarded the day as so far spent that he would undertake only a reconnaissance in force.[14]*

Saturday, August 30, dawned clear, and with an ominous quiet. Although Longstreet was at last prepared to deliver his long-delayed

---

* Lee's deference to Longstreet at Second Manassas has been the subject of considerable speculation, given Longstreet's later performance at Gettysburg. Freeman, in his analysis of Second Manassas, wrote, "The seeds of much of the disaster at Gettysburg were sown at that instant—when Lee yielded to Longstreet and Longstreet discovered that he would." Freeman, *R. E. Lee*, II, 325.

Well over a century after the Second Battle of Manassas, one can still see the railroad cut where Stonewall Jackson held off Pope's assaults. PHOTO BY AUTHOR.

assault, Lee now fretted about the swelling numbers of the enemy. After conferring with Jackson and Longstreet, Lee decided to let the enemy make the first move. The morning calm gave way to fresh attacks against Jackson, and some of his soldiers, out of ammunition, were reduced to throwing rocks at the Yankees. When Pope, who seemed to be unaware of Longstreet's presence, committed his army to yet another assault against Jackson, the Confederates smashed the enemy flank with five fresh divisions. The Federals were swept from the field.

Lee was not content with victory; he wanted to destroy the opposing army. As rain turned the countryside to mud on the night of August 30–31, Lee ordered Jackson, on the Confederate left, to make a sweep to the east in the hope of netting the retreating Federals. Accordingly, at noon on August 31, Jackson led his weary soldiers in pursuit of Pope's shattered regiments. But the rain continued, and, combined with fatigue, proved an effective deterrent to pursuit. The campaign of Second Manassas ended with an action at Chantilly in which two Federal divisions held off Jackson while rain-sodden blue-coats found refuge behind the forts ringing Washington.

Casualties in the Second Manassas campaign were heavy on both sides. The Federals had 1,700 killed, 8,400 wounded, and 6,000 missing, for a total of 16,100. Confederate casualties consisted of 1,500 killed, 7,600 wounded, and 100 missing, for a total of 9,200.[15] Because many of the Federal "missing" probably found their way back to Washington, the final casualty ratios may have been less favorable to the Southerners.

Nevertheless, the Confederate triumph was complete. In a telegram to President Davis on the evening of August 30, Lee reported "a signal victory over the combined forces of Generals McClellan and Pope."[16] The Federals, so recently on the outskirts of Richmond, were now completely on the defensive in Virginia. In Washington, hospital beds were filled with Pope's wounded, and the streets filled with stragglers and deserters. A shaken President Lincoln removed Pope and brought McClellan back to restore the Army of the Potomac as a fighting force.

The victory at Second Manassas placed Lee on a pedestal from which he would never descend. Longstreet described the campaign as "clever and brilliant," giving the credit entirely to Lee. Gen. Dorsey Pender, commanding a brigade in A. P. Hill's division, wrote, "There never was such a campaign, not even by Napoleon."[17] Stonewall Jackson remarked that he would follow Lee blindfolded.[18] For his part, Lee saw his faith in Jackson fully vindicated; in the campaign just ended, Jackson had been not the somnolent sluggard of the Seven Days, but the hard-marching "Stonewall" of the valley.

The defense of Richmond was a nonnegotiable imperative for Lee, and at the end of June, McClellan had been still within striking distance of Richmond. Had Pope moved on Richmond from the north, as Lee had feared he might, the Confederates might have been forced on a permanent defensive, and Richmond subjected to an early siege. The presence of a Federal army—even one considerably smaller than McClellan's—near Richmond would have reduced Lee's ability to maneuver. It was Halleck's order to McClellan to pull back to Aquia Creek that freed Lee to go after Pope.

Two years would pass before the Federals would be as close to Richmond as they were in July 1862. After Second Manassas, the capital in jeopardy was not Richmond but Washington.

CHAPTER NINE

DETERMINED VALOR

T HE CONFEDERACY HAD ENTERED THE WAR
outgunned but with some strategic assets. Its greatest asset was that it
had no territorial ambitions; all it asked of its adversary was that the
Confederacy be recognized as a separate nation. This modest political
objective, translated into military terms, meant that the Confederacy
did not have to conquer the North; it only had to make war so costly
that the North would accept separation.

In the American Revolution, George Washington had won America's independence largely by keeping an army in the field. Although he
rarely inflicted a defeat on the British, he managed over a period of six
years to make the war so apparently unwinnable that Britain chose
peace rather than the probable costs of victory.

Robert E. Lee had studied Washington's campaigns, but he had not
found them especially relevant to the war in which he was engaged.
Nearly a century after Yorktown, more would be required of the Confederacy than the ability to sustain an army in the field. Whereas Britain
had been forced to fight the Americans from across the Atlantic Ocean,
the United States and the Confederacy shared a long common border.
Also an expanding railroad network provided both sides with much

greater mobility than had been available to either Washington or his foes. Like Washington, Lee would have to make the war prohibitively expensive to the enemy, but to do so he would have to win battles.

Fortunately, Lee had created an army that could win battles, and the enemy knew this. In the Second Manassas campaign the Federals had suffered some 16,000 casualties out of 65,000 men engaged. In Washington the streets were filled with deserters and walking wounded. Within the Lincoln administration there was no talk of "On to Richmond," only of keeping the rebels out of Washington. The Army of the Potomac—long riven by factions—was united only in its loathing for Pope and his luckless colleague, Irvin McDowell. Pope denounced McClellan for failing to come to his aid at Manassas, and demanded that two of McClellan's corps commanders be court-martialed. New York diarist George Templeton Strong wrote, "The nation is rapidly sinking now. . . . Disgust with the present government is certainly universal."[1]

⊷⊷▭ ◖▭⊷⊷

AFTER THE WAR LEE SOMETIMES GAVE A SIMPLISTIC EXPLA-nation for what became the Antietam campaign: He went north in order to feed his army. In fact, a number of considerations led to Lee's invasion of Maryland in 1862. Although his own army was badly supported—it was at the end of a cumbersome and poorly run supply line—the Union forces were demoralized and Richmond was no longer in danger. An invasion of Maryland held intriguing possibilities. Lee wrote to Davis that he was about to enter Maryland "with a view to affording the people of that State an opportunity of liberating themselves." In any case, he hoped to "annoy and harass the enemy."[2] Although Lee was hardly a textbook general, he may have had in mind the dictum of Dennis Hart Mahan, long the resident strategist at West Point, that "carrying the war into the heart of the assailant's country . . . is the surest way of making him share its burdens and foiling his plans."[3]

In a conversation after the war, Lee reminisced with Col. William Allan about the Antietam campaign:

> Gen. Lee said . . . that especially in 1862 his object was
> not primarily to take Baltimore or to undertake any very

decided offensive movement. It was in the first place to get the enemy away from the works in front of Washington, which he tho't it folly to attack from the Manassas side, next to subsist our own army. . . . By crossing the river, and thus threatening Baltimore and Washington, he drew the enemy from their works, thus relieving Va. from their presence, and got ample supplies from Md. for his own troops.[4]

Lee's explanations, delivered at different times, have different emphases. In writing to Davis, Lee appears to have been careful not to promise more than he could deliver. He would be able to feed his army in Maryland, but more was at stake than logistics. A war that was defensive in its strategy was to be taken to the enemy. Lee did not request authorization to invade Maryland, and informed Davis of his plans only after his army was on the move. But Lee was not one to exceed his authority, and the subject of taking the war to the North had doubtless arisen in the course of Lee's many meetings with the president.

The mind of Robert E. Lee was not remarkable for its breadth, but Lee had a clear grasp of the war's dimensions, and a political motive underlay his eagerness to enter Maryland. If opinion polls had existed in 1861 and 1862, Maryland would probably have been shown to support the Confederacy. Lincoln had been able to keep the state in the Union only by drastic measures; in September 1861 the Lincoln administration, hearing that the Maryland legislature planned to take the state out of the Union, had ordered the arrest of twenty pro-Confederate legislators.

Lee initially hoped to gain recruits in Maryland, but he was warned before crossing the Potomac that he should not expect a rush to the colors in pro-Union western Maryland. However, there were other considerations. Eighteen-sixty-two was a congressional election year, and Northern Democrats were believed to endorse a negotiated peace over continued war. For Lee to execute a successful foray into Maryland would embarrass the Lincoln administration at a politically sensitive time.

There was, in addition, the international dimension. In letters and conversations Lee had reiterated that the South must win its own independence; it should not rely on assistance from abroad. Nevertheless, the South hoped desperately for recognition by Britain, France, or both—action that Southerners viewed as foreshadowing a flood of trade and assistance. Was not cotton "king," and were not the textile looms of Europe dependent on Southern cotton? Even if there were few tangible benefits, foreign recognition of the Confederacy would be a blow to the North.

The governments of Britain and France were sympathetic toward the Confederacy for sound political reasons. Napoleon III was hoping to make Mexico a French protectorate, but he knew that a French coup in Mexico would provoke the government in Washington. What the emperor desired was a Confederate victory, or a war that so weakened the North that it would not challenge a French move in Mexico. The U.S. minister in Paris, John Bigelow, reported in August 1862 that Napoleon III had dismissed the possibility of a Northern victory: "He is now hovering over us, like the carrion crow over the body of the sinking traveler."[5]

Washington's relations with London were even more sensitive than those with Paris. Not only did Britain require cotton from the American South, but its shipping interests were eager to check the growing challenge from the North's merchant marine. Indeed, the United States was widely perceived in London as an upstart republic that should be put in its place. The seizure of a British mail packet, the *Trent*, by the U.S. Navy in November 1861, had been resolved, but the memory still rankled. When news of Second Manassas reached London, Prime Minister Palmerston remarked to his foreign secretary that the Federals had received a severe smashing. Was it not time, Palmerston asked, for Britain and France to address the warring parties in America, and recommend a peace based on separation? Foreign Secretary Lord John Russell concurred, and suggested that the subject be taken up in cabinet. The U.S. consul in Liverpool warned Secretary of State Seward that if Federal armies did not win a decisive battle soon, public opinion would force the Palmerston government to recognize the Confederacy.[6]

Lee knew little of these developments, but he was convinced that the Confederacy must build on its military successes in the East. On September 8 he wrote to Davis from Maryland, suggesting that the president again urge an end to the fighting and Northern recognition of Confederate independence:

> Such a proposition coming from us at this time, could in
> no way be regarded as suing for peace, but being made
> when it is in our power to inflict injury upon our adversary,

would show conclusively to the world that our sole object
is the establishment of our independence, and the attainment of an honorable peace.[7]

Lee was not alone in recognizing that the stakes were high in Maryland. In the wake of Second Manassas, Lincoln had returned McClellan
to command of the Army of the Potomac, over the objections of Secretary of War Stanton and others. Lincoln was fully aware of McClellan's shortcomings, but he also believed that he had no one more
capable than McClellan to bring order out of the chaos of Second Manassas. Like Lee, President Lincoln had a political agenda. He was eager
to add a moral dimension to the war by issuing an emancipation proclamation. But first, as Seward reminded him, he needed a victory.

On September 4, the first units of Lee's 40,000-man army crossed
the Potomac near Leesburg. The Army of Northern Virginia was
organized into two corps, five divisions under Longstreet and four
under Jackson. They were not an impressive sight. There had been
little time to recover from the Manassas campaign; the men were hungry, weary, and in some cases barefoot. A Virginia woman living near
the Potomac could not believe that she was seeing a conquering army:

> When I say that they were hungry, I convey no impression
> of the gaunt starvation that looked from their cavernous
> eyes. All day they crowded to the doors of our houses, with
> always the same drawling complaint: "I've been a-marchin'
> and a-fightin' for six weeks stiddy, and I ain't had n-a-r-
> thin' to eat 'cept green apples and green cawn, and I wish
> you'd please to gimme a bite to eat." . . . That they could
> march or fight at all seemed incredible.[8]

In part because the Army of Northern Virginia was at the end of its
supply line, there was more straggling and desertion than in previous
campaigns. Some soldiers feigned illness while others threw away their
shoes as an excuse to fall out of ranks. Lee, alarmed, ordered brigade
commanders to sweep up stragglers and return them to their units. In
some instances the problem went beyond food and shoes—groups of
soldiers held back on the grounds that they had joined the army to
defend their homes, not to invade the North. The upshot was that the
army that invaded Maryland was numerically weaker than at any time
since Lee took command.

Nor did it find a warm reception east of the Potomac. The western portion of Maryland was indeed Unionist in its sympathies, and Lee gained few recruits. Acts of kindness were often qualified. One woman placed a bucket of water by her door for the thirsty Southerners, but she told one group of soldiers, "Remember, a *Union lady* is giving you water."[9]

On September 6, Lee set up his headquarters at Frederick. In this position, twenty-three miles north of the Potomac, his army would appear to be threatening either Baltimore or Washington. Lee would let the Federals fret about his intentions. President Davis, meanwhile, had delivered the proclamation that Lee had requested, explaining Confederate objectives in Maryland. The South, Davis proclaimed, had no design for conquest: "We are driven to protect our own country by transferring the seat of the war to that of an enemy who pursues us with a relentless and apparently aimless hostility."[10]

The campaign soon took an unexpected turn. Lee had assumed that the Federals would evacuate Harpers Ferry after the Confederates had crossed the Potomac between it and Washington. When the enemy did nothing, the 12,000-man garrison at Harpers Ferry became a tempting prize. On September 9, Lee issued General Order 191 outlining his plans. The army was to march west from Frederick the next day and then divide into four columns. Longstreet, with two divisions, would head northwest on the road to Boonsboro. Jackson, with three divisions, would recross the Potomac and move on Harpers Ferry from the west. Two divisions under Gen. Lafayette McLaws were also targeted against Harpers Ferry, but their goal was Maryland Heights, overlooking the town. Gen. John G. Walker's small division was to occupy Loudoun Heights, across the Shenandoah from Harpers Ferry.

The attention required by a single river garrison was distracting, but Harpers Ferry lay astride the Confederate supply line to the Shenandoah Valley, and for that reason it must be in Confederate hands. It was also a link in the Baltimore and Ohio Railroad, and Yankee railroads were one of the targets of the Maryland campaign. Finally, the arsenal at Harpers Ferry had a huge stock of ordnance.

In correspondence with Davis, Lee had rationalized his campaign in general terms. Now it appeared that he hoped to threaten the capital of Pennsylvania, Harrisburg, where a nervous Gov. Andrew Curtin was calling up 50,000 volunteers to defend his state.

Lee had divided his army audaciously in the Second Manassas campaign; now, in enemy country, he was subdividing his force and marching for objectives as far apart as Harrisburg and Harpers Ferry. In conference, one of Lee's division commanders, John Walker, expressed misgivings. Lee responded, acknowledging that it could be hazardous to campaign with an enemy army threatening his communications. But he asked whether Walker knew McClellan, adding, "He is an able general but a very cautious one. . . . His army is in a very demoralized and chaotic condition, and will not be prepared for offensive operations—or he will not think so—for three or four weeks. Before that I hope to be on the Susquehanna." [11]

Lee would not have a chance to implement his grand design, because on September 13 two Federal soldiers made the most remarkable find of the war—a copy of Lee's General Order 191, wrapped around two cigars, lying in a cornfield outside Frederick.* The document was passed quickly up the Federal chain of command and reached McClellan on the day it was found. Lee's order told his adversary that the Army of Northern Virginia was divided, with some twenty-five miles separating Jackson from Longstreet. McClellan had more than 70,000 men at his command, including thirteen divisions in the area of Frederick, only a fifteen-mile march from Longstreet's encampment. McClellan exulted, "Here is a paper with which if I cannot whip Bobby Lee I will be willing to go home!" [12]

Nevertheless, McClellan waited until the next day to get his army on the move. On the morning of September 14, two Federal corps eventually overcame D. H. Hill's division at South Mountain and poured westward through Turner's Gap. On the same day other Federal troops brushed past McLaws's division at nearby Crampton's Gap. Lee was puzzled and probably alarmed by Stuart's reports of these movements; either McClellan had extraordinarily good intelligence sources in Maryland or he had developed a recklessness that was totally out of character. Not until the next year would he learn of the Lost Order.

When McClellan had succeeded in forcing the South Mountain passes, Lee's first impulse was to pull back across the Potomac. On the morning of September 15, however, Lee heard from Jackson that he

---

* Few incidents in the Civil War have been more hotly debated than responsibility for the Lost Order. The copy in question was addressed to Gen. D. H. Hill, but Hill flatly denied ever having received it. Historian Stephen W. Sears, who has studied the subject in depth, concludes that the order was dropped by a Confederate courier en route to Hill. See Robert Cowley, ed., *Experience of War* (New York: W. W. Norton, 1992), 206.

expected to capture Harpers Ferry that day. Lee had second thoughts: It would take time to capture Harpers Ferry and remove the ordnance there—but might it not be possible to concentrate the army at Sharpsburg and establish a line there capable of holding off McClellan? It was one thing to abandon his campaign to the Susquehanna; it was another to return to Virginia without a victory. "We will make our stand on those hills," Lee told one of his aides, motioning in the direction of Sharpsburg as they rode toward the town.[13]

While Lee gathered his forces he attempted to keep the peace among his generals. They tended to be a fractious lot, hypersensitive in matters of rank and honor. In Maryland, Stonewall Jackson renewed a simmering feud with Powell Hill, relieved him of command, and put him under arrest. Then Longstreet arrested Gen. John B. Hood, one of Lee's best fighters. On April 14, near Boonsboro, Lee and his staff pulled off the road to let Hood's Texans march past. The men, spotting Lee, began a cry, "Give us back Hood!" "You shall have him," Lee responded, and when Hood came up at the rear of his column Lee took him aside. He did not want to give battle without one of his best commanders; if Hood would express regret for his alleged insubordination, Lee would restore him to command. Hood refused, and began to argue his case. "Well," said the exasperated Lee, "I will suspend your arrest until the impending battle is decided."[14]

Lee would need every man in the next few days. Longstreet established a defensive line northeast of Sharpsburg on September 15, but he had fewer than 15,000 men. By the afternoon of the following day the line had been reinforced by Jackson's corps, less Powell Hill's division, which had stayed in Harpers Ferry to remove captured ordnance. Jackson's arrival brought the Confederate strength to about 30,000, and Lee was able to gather up an additional 5,000 men that evening. If McClellan had moved more promptly, however, the Confederates would have had no time to construct a defense.

The Battle of Antietam began on the morning of September 17, when Hooker's Federal corps smashed into Jackson on the Confederate left. When the infantry attack stalled, Hooker put nine batteries of artillery on a low ridge and blasted Jackson's men in "The Cornfield." In some of the fiercest fighting of the war, the Federals drove Jackson's corps from The Cornfield, obliging Lee to send reinforcements from D. H. Hill's division in the center, and Longstreet's corps on the right, to stem the enemy advance. Had McClellan attacked the Confederate right simultaneously he would probably have had his long-sought victory over "Bobby" Lee. But poor timing was a bane to both sides for much of the war, and McClellan was unable to bring off the coordinated attack that would have broken the Confederates at Antietam.

Antietam saw Lee in the unaccustomed role of battlefield tactician. Contrary to his usual practice of allowing his subordinates to command on their fronts, Lee himself responded to the successive Federal attacks, moving his brigades wherever they were most needed. The battle on the Confederate left raged for five hours, resulting in some 12,000 Union and Confederate casualties.

Lee's fighting blood was up, and with it his temper. In camp the army commander was noted for his gentle reproofs, but now he was in the chaos of battle. Spotting a skulker heading for the rear carrying a squealing pig, Lee lost his vaunted self-control. Furious, he ordered the soldier arrested and sent to Jackson, who was to have him shot. Jackson would shoot many a deserter in his day, but with a battle in the balance he chose instead to send the miscreant into his line where the firing was hottest. He emerged unscathed, prompting Lee's aide, Armistead Long, to remark that the skulker had "lost his pig but saved his bacon." [15]

Midday saw the fighting shift to the center of Lee's line, around the sunken road that came to be known as Bloody Lane. The Federals brought a fresh corps to the front, and after three hours of slaughter the Federals had forced Gen. David Jones's Confederate division to the outskirts of Sharpsburg. A Northern war correspondent, Charles Coffin, reached Bloody Lane shortly after the Federals had captured it. "Confederates had gone down," he wrote, "as the grass falls before the scythe." [16]

Never had the Army of Northern Virginia been in such a desperate position. Longstreet had members of his personal staff working guns in an artillery battery, and D. H. Hill was seen with rifle in hand, attempting to rally stragglers. For all of Lee's sleight of hand, McClellan would probably have destroyed the Army of Northern Virginia if he had committed his reserves in a final assault. But Lee's confidence in his opponent's caution was vindicated. Believing that Lee was mobilizing reserves for a counterattack, McClellan concluded that a renewed attack on the Confederate center would be imprudent.

The final phase of the battle came in the afternoon, when Burnside finally attacked across the creek southeast of Sharpsburg. The Army of

Northern Virginia was closer to defeat than at any time before Appo-mattox. Lee had sent a courier to Harpers Ferry that morning, urgently ordering Powell Hill to come up with his division. At 3:30 P.M. there was no sign of Hill, however, and Lee had no reserves. The battered Confederate right braced for the enemy's onslaught.

Powell Hill was perhaps Lee's favorite division commander. He had proven himself in the Seven Days' campaign, and although he was prone to rashness, this was a quality that Lee was quick to forgive. Hill was prickly to a degree remarkable even among Confederate generals—he had running feuds with both Jackson and Longstreet—but he rec-ognized an emergency when he saw one. Hill had his division on the road within thirty minutes of receiving Lee's order. He drove his men at a killing pace toward the sound of gunfire east of Sharpsburg.

At about four o'clock, one of Lee's staff called his attention to a cloud of dust on the road from Harpers Ferry. He offered the general his glasses, but Lee could not hold them; he had traveled with both hands in splints since an accident when Traveller had reared, and Lee had fallen while attempting to gather the reins. Lee asked an artillery officer with a spy glass to identify the approaching column. After studying the road for a moment the officer replied, "They are flying the Virginia and Confederate flags, sir." Lee replied, doubtless breathing a prayer of relief, "It is A. P. Hill from Harpers Ferry." Hill had driven his four brigades seventeen miles almost without rest, and when he rode up to Lee's command post the army commander embraced him—a rare dis-play of emotion from the reserved Lee.[17] He ordered Hill to place his men along the wafer-thin Confederate right.

When Hill halted Ambrose E. Burnside's attack he helped bring an end to the bloodiest single day of the war. Federal losses totaled 12,400, including 2,100 killed. Lee's casualties exceeded 10,300, includ-ing 1,600 dead. Henry Kyd Douglas, one of Jackson's staff officers, described the "fearful" night of September 17:

> Not a soldier, I venture to say, slept half an hour. Nearly all
> of them were wandering over the field, looking for their
> wounded comrades, and some of them, doubtless, plunder-
> ing the dead bodies of the enemy left on the field.[18]

Lee's commanders expected him to order the army back to Virginia with the first light on September 18. But the morning passed with the two armies eyeing each other warily. Lee stood his ground, moving only his wounded. His delay was prompted in part by the need to remove stores from Harpers Ferry, where the Confederates had captured some 11,500 prisoners, more than seventy cannon, and a huge number of small arms. But Lee was confident that his army had salvaged a victory and that McClellan would not renew the attack. "Though still too weak to resume the offensive," he wrote dryly in his official report, "we awaited without apprehension [any] renewal of the attack." [19]

⊷⇒◉ ◉⇐⊶

WITH ITS TOTAL OF MORE THAN 23,000 KILLED AND wounded, Antietam remains the bloodiest single day in U.S. history. Casualties there were more than four times the number suffered on D-Day in World War II. If one counts only the killed and wounded among units actively engaged, the Army of Northern Virginia suffered 30 percent casualties, the Federals 24 percent. It was highly unusual for an attacking army to suffer a lower percentage of casualties than the defenders, but whereas Lee's soldiers were in line all day, Burnside's corps in particular was a latecomer to the field.

Who "won" the Battle of Antietam? Militarily, Antietam represented a Federal opportunity lost. McClellan had been presented with an opportunity to destroy the Army of Northern Virginia, yet allowed his great chance to slip away. Lee, for his part, had drawn the Army of the Potomac away from Virginia and, at Harpers Ferry, had captured valuable equipment. But his plans had gone awry; he had been unable to reach the Susquehanna, much less bring on a decisive battle.

In political terms, Antietam was a Federal victory. It would be Lincoln who found the battle's aftermath suitable for issuing the Emancipation Proclamation; the Confederate proposal calling for an end to hostilities was put aside for a more propitious time. Henry Adams would write from London that "the Emancipation Proclamation has done more for us here than all our former victories and all our diplomacy. It is creating an almost convulsive reaction in our favor all over this country." [20]

Northern voters, however, were restive. Some deplored what they perceived as the failure of the Lincoln administration to pursue the war more vigorously. Others despised the notion of turning the war into a crusade against slavery. As a result, the November 1862 elections were a disaster for the Lincoln administration. Although the Republicans, attempting to appeal to War Democrats, campaigned as the Union party in most states, the Democrats picked up thirty-one seats in the House of Representatives.

For Lee, Antietam was a flawed campaign. He had misjudged the morale of his soldiers, who wanted no part of an invasion of Maryland hard on the heels of Second Manassas. Thousands straggled and hundreds more risked the fate of deserters rather than continue. Never again would he so misjudge the temper of his soldiers.

When the Federals failed to evacuate Harpers Ferry, it came to dominate Lee's thinking. Had he not stayed in Maryland an extra day while he awaited the capture of Harpers Ferry there would have been no Battle of Antietam. Lee's decision to fight, with his back to the river, was probably an error. The odds being what they were, the best he could expect was a drawn battle, whereas a defeat might have carried the entire Confederacy with it. Antietam was a gamble that Lee "won," but one that perhaps should not have been taken, for the rewards of victory were not commensurate with the price that would be paid for a defeat.

Once the battle was joined, Lee was at his best. His timing in the deployment of his few reserves was masterful. With a weary and outnumbered army, he conducted a defense that was so aggressive that the Federals credited their enemy with far greater numbers than they possessed.

Lee would look back on Antietam with greater satisfaction than on any of his other battles. He wrote in his report that nothing could surpass the "determined valor" with which his soldiers met "the large army of the enemy, fully supplied and equipped."[21] The odds against Lee's army were greater at Antietam than in almost any other battle, yet his officers and soldiers had demonstrated the skill and tenacity that he had sought to instill in his army.

Not long after Antietam, Lee reviewed one of his divisions in the presence of an observer from the British army, Col. Garnet Wolseley, later one of Britain's most prominent soldiers. Lee's men marched by, their uniforms ragged even by Confederate standards. Wolseley remarked to Lee that the men looked like fighters, and marched well, "but my, how ragged they are in the breeches!" To which Lee is said to have replied, "Well, Colonel Wolseley, that doesn't matter very greatly because the enemy never sees their rear."[22]

CHAPTER TEN

HIGH TIDE AT FREDERICKSBURG

LEE NEITHER EXULTED IN VICTORY NOR despaired when results fell short of his hopes. So it was with the Antietam campaign; he believed he had fulfilled the design of Providence when he did the best that he could. For all that had gone amiss in Maryland, Virginia was clear of the enemy for the moment, and its farmers could harvest their rich crops. Lee rested his army in the fields west of Winchester through the early weeks of autumn.

Did Lee ask himself how America had come to such a sorry pass? He rarely revealed his inner thoughts in correspondence, but occasionally wrote memoranda on various subjects that he kept among his effects. One of these memoranda, although undated, appears to have been written shortly after the publication of Lincoln's Emancipation Proclamation:

> The purpose of the war has been perverted by the party in power. If the present policy had been announced at the time, I cannot believe that it would have been tolerated by the North, & it now seems to me so revolting to reason, & patriotism, that I cannot help wondering at its endorse-

ment by men who must possess the common attributes of pride of race & country.[1]

Lee probably viewed the Emancipation Proclamation, which freed only slaves in the Confederacy, as an attempt to incite a slave insurrection. His own inclinations, both political and social, were so conservative that he appears to have had little understanding of the moral fervor at the heart of the antislavery movement. His view of Lincoln was similarly one-dimensional. Lee had discovered that he could play on Lincoln's concern for the safety of his capital. He had also discovered that the enemy president was a novice at choosing military commanders. Lee failed to appreciate that in Lincoln he faced an adversary whose core values were as firm as his own, and who was convinced that the eradication of slavery could not be left to Providence.

Meanwhile, Lee labored at restoring his army to its earlier prowess. It had fought the Battle of Antietam with fewer men in its ranks than ever before. Once the army was back in camp near Culpeper, Virginia, however, stragglers returned and conscripts arrived from Richmond. There was good-natured bantering in the camps as the men received rations of beef and vegetables to supplement the standard fare of corn flour and bacon. Packages from home brought badly needed clothing, and gleanings from the fall harvest provided forage for the horses.

By October 10, Lee had 68,000 men in his ranks, almost the number with which he had begun the Seven Days' campaign. He believed his army was in the best condition since he had taken command, although shoes remained a problem. The small cattle herds now with Lee's army did double duty. After the animals had been slaughtered for food, their hides were tanned and made into new shoe soles and sandals.

Lee was as combative as ever. He wrote to Davis in October that he hoped McClellan would cross the Potomac; if he did, Lee would seek an opportunity to attack him. For a time Lee feared a new move against Richmond, but this did not materialize. October proved to be so quiet a month that Lee contemplated sending his army to winter quarters, or even sending troops to South Carolina and Georgia.

Lee used this quiet period to reorganize his army. He did not have a free hand either to create new units or to promote deserving officers; his actions had to conform to Confederate laws and regulations. Until September 18, 1862, for example, there was no provision for lieutenant generals in the army. In October, Lee promoted Jackson and Longstreet to that rank and formally organized his army into two corps. Elsewhere, artillery batteries that had been put out of commission at Antietam were disbanded, their cannon and horses transferred to other units. Infantry regiments improved the marching drills through which firepower was concentrated at the point where it was needed on the battlefield.

Because of the casualties incurred in the Seven Days, Second Manassas, and Antietam, the proportion of Lee's army represented by volunteers had fallen and would continue to fall. Nevertheless, the Army of Northern Virginia remained a hotbed of individualism; one officer termed it "a voluntary association of gentlemen organized and sustained to drive out the Yankees."[2] By 1862 the Army of Northern Virginia had accepted the need for discipline, but only reluctantly. Quarrels among Lee's officers were endemic, and at times the army commander seemed less a warrior than a conciliator.

The worst offender was Stonewall Jackson. Lee, while still in Richmond, had followed Jackson's valley campaign closely. He had seen in Jackson a kindred spirit, and this recognition had created a bond that had survived Stonewall's weak performance in the Seven Days' campaign. Jackson was able to goad his infantry into remarkable feats—including his fifty-mile march against Pope—but his secrecy, abrasiveness, and rigid sense of duty often antagonized his subordinates.

Longstreet was a different matter. He had little of Jackson's aggressiveness, but fought with a deliberate, sturdy competence. He had proved himself a superior tactician, albeit one with an eye for defense rather than attack. Like Jackson, Longstreet had Lee's total confidence, as was demonstrated when Lee delayed his assault on Pope out of deference to Longstreet's wishes. After Antietam, Lee had grabbed Longstreet with his bandaged hands and exclaimed, "Here is my old war-horse!" The name stuck.

Lee had quickly learned the strengths and weaknesses of most of his senior officers. By the fall of 1862 he had been in command long enough to make distinctions among units down to the brigade level, and in some instances to the regimental level. Their capabilities were not uniform, for in the Confederate army officers up to the rank of colonel were elected by the soldiers, and men who owed their position to the votes of their neighbors were not likely to be tough disciplinarians. The brigades of the Army of Northern Virginia had developed distinctive personalities, and Lee knew them. One of his favorite units was John B. Hood's Texas brigade, which Lee regarded as his best shock unit, the one to be called on when a battle reached a critical point.

At the same time, Lee's control over his army was not absolute. He had no authority to give even temporary promotions in the field; promotion was the prerogative of the Confederate congress, which was primarily concerned with equalizing honors among the states. Not until the third year of the war could Lee remove an incompetent officer other than by a time-consuming court-martial. As a result, Lee became adept at foisting off senior officers who had disappointed him in action, often to prestigious-sounding posts far from Virginia. He did not have this option for junior officers.

Meanwhile, Lee himself remained an enigma, even to close associates. Although his lieutenants called one another by their surnames, they called Lee "General," and he almost always addressed his officers by their rank. This remoteness was not surprising, for Lee was twenty years older than most of his generals. Nor did proximity breed intimacy. Lee demanded much from those around him, and although he did not subject his aides to harsh criticism he was not an avuncular figure to those who saw him every day. Lee's personal staff grumbled at his demands; behind his back they called him the Tycoon, which was also the nickname assigned to Abraham Lincoln by his secretaries.

Affection for Lee was more visible at a distance, and he enjoyed a remarkable degree of trust from his army at all levels. Stonewall Jackson was known to have declared that he would follow Lee anywhere, and Longstreet returned the esteem Lee felt for his "war-horse." But it was the men in the ranks who made Lee their own—the embodiment of Southern virtues worth fighting for. On October 9, 1862, the *Charleston Daily Courier* published an anonymous letter from a reporter with Lee's army:

> To a man the troops of this army feel an unbounded confidence in their Commander-in-Chief, and though he does fail to excite the same enthusiasm as Jackson . . . he nevertheless possesses that profound respect which places him at once above their criticism. The universal sentiment of the army in this particular instance is—"Whatever Gen. Lee does is sure to be right; time will prove it." It is probably this very thought that has enabled the men so soon to recover their disappointment in Maryland.[3]

Lee did nothing to cultivate popularity, but his willingness to stand up to McClellan at Antietam was seen as a vote of confidence in his men. Lee also had a natural courtesy, which, his soldiers learned, had nothing to do with rank. In the first days of the Antietam campaign, Lee, Powell Hill, and their staff officers had found the road to one of the Potomac crossings blocked by some of Hill's troops who were waiting to cross the river. Hill told his men to clear the road, but Lee overruled him. "We will ride around them," he said. "Lie still, men."[4] Soldiers of both armies loathed self-important staff officers who galloped past the luckless infantry, spraying dust or mud in their wake, and word of Lee's consideration doubtless fueled the legend of "Marse Robert."

Lee's family was never far from his thoughts. One morning in October his aide, Walter Taylor, left Lee's tent and then, remembering something that he had forgotten, reentered without announcement. Inside, he was shocked to find the general overcome with grief, tears coursing down his cheeks as he stared at a letter telling him that his 23-year-old daughter Annie had died in North Carolina after a brief illness.[5] Just weeks later the news was of the death of Rooney Lee's infant daughter. Lee wrote to his daughter-in-law, Charlotte,

> I heard yesterday, my dear daughter, with the deepest sorrow, of the death of your infant. I was so grateful at her birth. I felt that she would be such a comfort to you, such a pleasure to my dear Fitzhugh, and would fill so full the void still aching in your hearts. But you have now two sweet angels in heaven. What joy there is in the thought! . . . May God give you strength to bear the affliction He has imposed, and produce future joy out of your present misery, is my earnest prayer.[6]

October turned into November, and Lee watched closely as the Army of the Potomac began a slow advance across the Potomac toward Warrenton. Unknown to Lee, McClellan's advance was so deliberate, and his objectives so uncertain, that Lincoln's seemingly inexhaustible patience had reached its limit. On November 7, the president relieved McClellan, who returned to his New Jersey home to await orders that never came. Lee heard the news with a tinge of regret. "We always understood each other so well," he remarked to Longstreet. "I fear they may continue to make these changes till they find someone whom I don't understand."[7]

McClellan's successor was 38-year-old Gen. Ambrose E. Burnside, whose greatest asset was that he was totally responsive to Lincoln's desires. Tall, heavy-set, with an erect carriage, and a magnificent set of "sideburns," the Army of the Potomac's new commander was an affable soldier who had attempted to remain apart from the factionalism in the Federal officer corps. Not only had Burnside never sought command of the Army of the Potomac, he had serious doubts about his own qualifications for any command. The government in Washington wanted action, however, and Burnside would give it to them.

Burnside moved his army with commendable speed to Falmouth, across the Rappahannock River above Fredericksburg, from where he hoped to cross the river and drive for Richmond. Burnside got off to a good start; he stole a march on Lee and had two corps at Falmouth on November 17, when Lee was still a two-day march away. Unfortunately for Burnside, the pontoons he needed to bridge the river were nowhere in sight.

Stuart believed that Fredericksburg was Burnside's goal, and it appears that he persuaded Lee. Lee, however, was in no hurry to summon Jackson from the Blue Ridge, where his presence represented a threat to Washington. Lee arrived at Fredericksburg on November 20, and after a brief reconnaissance concluded that the town—which was under the guns of Federal artillery across the river—could not be defended. Instead, he would make his stand in the hills behind the town. By November 22, when Burnside received his pontoons, Longstreet's corps was dug in along the hills behind Fredericksburg.

For the first time since McClellan's threat to Richmond, the war threatened a major urban area. The Federals warned the 4,000 residents of Fredericksburg to leave or suffer the consequences. When the city fathers told Lee of this warning he agreed that it would be advisable to evacuate the city. The weather was bitter, and the stream of refugees out of the city in the final days of November symbolized the grim arrival of total war.

Burnside believed, despite the delay caused by the late arrival of his bridges, that a move against Fredericksburg could be carried out with some degree of surprise. Federal artillery had an excellent field of fire from the east side of the river, and Lee would not be expecting a direct attack on the town. Burnside's subordinates considered it madness to assault the Confederate line, but their commander was adamant. In the early hours of December 11, Federal engineers laid down three pontoon bridges at Fredericksburg and three more downstream. Later that day the bulk of Sumner's twin-corps "grand division" crossed the river at Fredericksburg, breaking step as they tramped across the bridges. Yankee soldiers, angered by sniping from rebel sharpshooters, vandalized Fredericksburg's abandoned homes. A Federal soldier from Pennsylvania recalled his first view of the town:

> The city had been rudely sacked; household furniture lined the streets. Books and battered pictures, bureaus, lounges, feather beds, clocks, and every conceivable article of goods, chattels, and apparel had been savagely torn from the houses and lay about in wanton confusion in all directions. Fires were made, both for warmth and cooking, with fragments of broken furniture.[8]

The next day Hooker's grand division, 26,000 strong, crossed the Rappahannock on Longstreet's front. The Federal left, under Gen. William B. Franklin, was unopposed as it crossed three bridges downstream from Fredericksburg. Burnside's plan called for two blows, one through the town against the Confederate center, the other against Jackson on the Confederate right. There was a heavy fog on the morning of December 13, and as dawn broke Confederate soldiers could see only the church spires of the town below. By then, Lee had every unit in place along a three-mile line behind the town. The Federals knew little of the terrain and their ignorance would cost them dearly.

About ten o'clock the fog lifted, and Lee, from his position behind the town, could see the well-dressed lines of Franklin's grand division advancing toward Jackson on his right. Artillery opened on both sides, and for once—Lee had more than 300 guns in place—the Confederates were able to give as much as they received. The plain between Fredericksburg and the hills to the west had become a mass of blue, but there was little cover for the advancing Yankees. Longstreet's artillery commander assured him that not even a chicken could survive on the Fredericksburg plain.

The enemy advance began on Jackson's front. The Federals reached his main line in midmorning, and there was heavy fighting before Franklin turned back. The main assault, however, came about noon against the Confederate center. Although carried out by some 27,000 men, the attack was so hopeless in its conception that some Federal soldiers attached name tags to their uniforms so that their bodies could be identified. Sumner's soldiers, assaulting Marye's Heights, surged uphill against Confederate defenders firing from a sunken road. By early afternoon, the base of the heights was littered with the bodies of blue-clad soldiers.

Lee viewed the slaughter from his command post on Telegraph Hill. For him there was none of the tension of Antietam, where he had been forced to make tactical dispositions to head off defeat. At Fredericksburg he watched the enemy self-destruct, and the sight prompted his best-remembered remark about war. At one point, he turned to some officers and remarked to the effect that "It is well that war is so terrible. We should grow too fond of it."[9] Lee's comment encapsulates the soldier's dilemma: The extent to which he performs well is often measured in terms of lives destroyed.

Lee thought that the enemy might renew his assault the next day, and Burnside considered doing so. His subordinates dissuaded him, however, and on the night of December 14–15 the Federals retreated across the Rappahannock. They had lost 12,700 men, of whom nearly 11,000 had been killed or wounded. Confederate casualties totaled 5,300. The ratio of enemy to Confederate casualties was the highest of any of Lee's battles.

The victory at Fredericksburg came so easily that Lee did not realize that he had come the closest he would ever come to breaking his enemy's resolve. Along the Rappahannock, Federal desertions rose sharply. Mural Halstead, editor of the influential *Cincinnati Commercial*, covered the battle; he wrote in his account, "It can hardly be in human nature for men to show more valor, or generals to manifest less judgment, than were perceptible on our side that day."[10] "The people are growing exceedingly tired of the war," concluded *Chicago Tribune* editor Joseph Medill, in a private letter written shortly after Fredericksburg. "[They] are becoming very much discouraged."[11] In Washington, a perceptive volunteer officer, Brig. Gen. James A. Garfield, wrote to a friend about the religious zeal that seemed to be motivitating the rebel armies. "Generals Lee, Jackson, and J. E. B. Stuart," he wrote, "have inspired their men with a kind of Cromwell spirit which makes their battalions almost invincible. All this time our own men have grown discouraged."[12]

Congressional Radicals took advantage of this latest military setback

A Fredericksburg street after the battle. NATIONAL ARCHIVES.

in an attempt to assert a degree of control over administration policy. A few days after Fredericksburg, Republican members of Congress caucused and appointed a committee to call on Lincoln and demand changes in both personnel and policies. That night Lincoln confided to a friend, Sen. Orville Browning, that the government was close to collapse: "It appears to me the Almighty is against us, and I can hardly see a ray of hope."[13]

Lincoln was able to turn back this challenge by demonstrating to the angry legislators that their favorite, Secretary of the Treasury Salmon P. Chase, had supported the policies to which they objected. The immediate crisis passed, but Lincoln's signing of the Emancipation Proclamation on New Year's Day, 1863—it had been announced the previous September—was not uniformly popular, and cost the administration support among Democrats and independents.

Dissension within the Union army was perhaps more serious in that it was unprecedented. Although most officers of the Army of the Potomac were prepared to serve under any commander, the officer corps included an influential cadre of McClellan loyalists, a second group who were vocally critical of Burnside, and a number of senior

officers with private agendas. At the end of the year, two general officers called on Lincoln to tell him that the army had lost all confidence
in Burnside.[14]

Burnside lacked the qualities of an army commander, but he sensed
the unhappiness around him and the seething discontent among many
of his senior subordinates. He had plans for another attempt to cross
the Rappahannock and hoped for a vote of confidence from the president, but Lincoln was understandably wary. A dreary January dragged
on, and on the 25th Burnside traveled to Washington to call on the
president. He handed Lincoln two documents: his plan for the army's
next move and his resignation, and asked Lincoln either to approve the
one or accept the other. Gravely, Lincoln accepted Burnside's resignation and the following day appointed Gen. Joseph Hooker to command the Army of the Potomac.

FOR JEFFERSON DAVIS, JANUARY 1863 WAS A TIME FOR REJOIC-
ing. In Richmond, he responded ebulliently to a crowd that had come
to greet him on his return from an inspection of the western theater.
Things were going well in the West, he insisted, in sharp contrast to
his private convictions. And closer to home,

> Our cause has had the brightest sunshine fall upon it. . . .
> Our glorious Lee, the valued son, emulating the virtues of
> the heroic Light-Horse Harry, his father, has achieved a
> victory at Fredericksburg. . . . and driven the enemy back
> from his last and greatest effort to get "On to Richmond."[15]

The only serious criticism of Lee at Fredericksburg relates to
whether the Confederates might have pursued their beaten foes and
driven them into the river. Lee, in a letter written after the war, recalled
that a disproportionate number of Confederate casualties at Fredericksburg were incurred in pursuit of the retreating enemy. "To have
advanced the whole army into the plain for the purpose of attacking
Gen. Burnside," he wrote, "would have assured its destruction by the
fire from . . . Stafford Hills."[16] James Longstreet, for one, was convinced that his corps could not have made a transition to the offensive.
"Our line was about three miles long," he later recalled, "extending
through woodland over hill and dale. An attempt at concentration to

throw the troops against the walls of the city at that hour of the night would have been little better than madness." No one could have anticipated when the Federal attacks would cease, "nor could any skill have marshaled our troops for offensive operations in time."[17]

One criticism of Lee that has some validity is that his keen eye for terrain did not always extend to the placement of artillery. At Fredericksburg, Longstreet's chief of artillery, Porter Alexander, ordered guns to be placed in a forward position overlooking the town. Lee disapproved of their location, telling Alexander that they should be situated behind the brow of the hill, where they would be able to fire from protected positions. In the heat of battle they were moved forward, however, where they employed canister effectively against the attacking Federals. In Alexander's recollection,

> A few evenings afterward, visiting Gen. Lee's camp, I took the opportunity, when the general was near enough to hear, to say loudly to [Capt. Sam] Johnston, "Sam, it was a mighty good thing those guns about Marye's were located on the brows of the hills when the Yankees charged them!" I was half afraid the general might think me impertinent, though I could not resist the temptation to have one little dig at him. But he took it in silence & never let on that he was listening to us.[18]

Lee took no personal satisfaction in the outcome at Fredericksburg, but he wrote to Mary,

> Their hosts covered the plain & hills beyond the river. . . . Still I felt a confidence we could stand the shock & was . . . prepared to meet it here. . . . This morning they were all safe on the north side of the Rappahannock. They went as they came, in the night. They suffered heavily as far as the battle went, but it did not go far enough to satisfy me. . . . The contest will have now to be renewed.[19]

CHAPTER ELEVEN

"MAY GOD HAVE MERCY ON GENERAL LEE"

WRITING HOME FROM FREDERICKSBURG IN late January 1863, one of Lee's soldiers complained of the cold: "To be on picket in such weather is perfectly awful, but we console ourselves by knowing that the Yankees have the same to endure." He had no fear of another enemy attempt to cross the Rappahannock. "If the enemy should attempt to cross in our front, I think we will finish Mr. Burnsides [*sic*] . . . to our own and the entire satisfaction of the whole South."[1]

Burnside would soon be gone, but the bitter weather would not. Lee had nothing but admiration for the residents of Fredericksburg, whose homes had been plundered and who now must endure such a severe winter. It was an austere period for Lee's army as well, for it was dependent for supplies on a single overworked rail link. Although scurvy appeared, the troops were urged to spare the fields that would produce antiscorbutic vegetables for the army come spring.

In mid-February Lee concluded that he would not be able to take his army on the offensive soon. The rivers were too deep to ford, he lacked pontoon bridges, and the roads were so muddy as to be almost impassable. His horses and mules were so run down that "the labor and exposure incident to an attack would result in their destruction and leave us destitute of the means of transportation."[2] For his soldiers, Lee instituted a system whereby two men per company—chosen by lot—were allowed furloughs. The length of the approved absence depended on the distance to be traveled.

For those left in camp, the winter of 1862–63 brought the "Great Revival" to the Army of Northern Virginia. Ministers from Southern cities joined army chaplains in preaching to men for whom familiarity with death had stimulated an interest in religion. Lee welcomed this development, as did the pious Jackson. In one account, Lee and Jackson, seated on a log, were moved to tears by a sermon in which the minister talked of the homes and hearths that Confederate soldiers had left behind.[3]

In addition to his problems of subsistence, Lee found it necessary to send two divisions south on detached duty. McClellan had evacuated the York Peninsula, but he had left behind four Federal enclaves, Fortress Monroe and Newport News on the peninsula, and Norfolk and Suffolk to the south. The Confederates were concerned about these enclaves, particularly after the enemy, in mid-February, sent a flotilla of troop-laden transports down the Potomac to Newport News. To meet this possible threat, Lee sent Longstreet, with Hood's and Pickett's divisions, to defend southeastern Virginia and North Carolina.

In the months that followed, Longstreet directed two futile operations in North Carolina, attempting to relieve towns that had been captured by the Federals early the previous year. The only benefit that Lee reaped from Longstreet's independent command was some food for his army from the largely untouched fields of North Carolina. In Longstreet's absence, however, Lee had only 60,000 troops with which to face Hooker's 135,000.[4]

⊷⊷⊷⇒ ⇐⊷⊷

LEE LIVED SIMPLY. IN CAMP HE DECLINED TO EAT OFF CHINA, insisting on tin plates and cups like those of his soldiers. In a letter to Custis Lee, in February 1863, he blamed the Confederate congress for the army's privations:

What has our Congress done to meet this exigency, I may
say *extremity*, in which we are placed? As far as I know, con-
cocted bills to excuse a certain class of men from service,
and to transfer another class . . . out of active service, where
they hope never to do service.[5]

By this time Lee had achieved such popular fame that he received
many gifts of food from local admirers. At Fredericksburg these
included a brood of chickens, which found their way one by one into
the headquarters pot. By the time it was the turn of the last hen, she
had developed a habit of going into Lee's tent each morning and laying an egg under his cot. So regular was this performance that Lee left
a tent flap open for her comings and goings. She traveled with Lee's
headquarters for two years, including the entire Gettysburg campaign.
Alas, in 1864 this noble fowl became a victim of mistaken identity and
she, too, ended up in the pot.[6]

In late March the normally robust Lee became seriously ill. He was
moved from his tent to a room in a nearby house, but his symptoms—
which included fever, an elevated pulse, and pain in his chest and
arms—continued. One of Lee's doctors wrote home of having treated
the commanding general:

I was first called to see him in consultation, then his physi-
cian was taken sick and he is now my patient. . . . I wish
you could all see him—he is so noble a specimen of man
that even if he were not so distinguished, you would be
attracted by his appearance and manner. He is a tall robust,
fine-looking man, with white beard all over his face and
white hair, always polite and agreeable, and thinking less of
himself than he ought to . . . hoping and praying for nothing but the success of our cause and the return of blessed
peace.[7]

Lee returned to work in mid-April, but conceded in a letter to Mary
that he was "feeble & worthless." His doctors concluded that he had
suffered an attack of angina pectoris, an inflammation of the mem-
brane enclosing the heart, the most visible manifestation of which was
a more florid complexion. Lee's illness of March 1863 appears to have
marked the onset of the cardiovascular problems that would be the
bane of his final years.

Spring found Lee barely convalescent, his army supplied on a subsistence level, and Longstreet's divisions still on detached duty. Nevertheless, Lee was thinking of taking the offensive once more. He wrote Mary in a tone of cautious optimism,

> I do not think our enemies are so confident of success as they used to be. If we can baffle them in their various designs this year & our people are true to our cause & not so devoted to themselves and their own aggrandisement, I think our success will be certain. . . . This year I hope will establish our supplies on a firm basis. On every other point we are strong.[8]

Lee was not unduly concerned about manpower. Outnumbered more than two to one, his concern was for civilian morale and supplies. But problems in other parts of the Confederacy were beginning to impinge on Lee's planning. In Tennessee, a Federal army commanded by Gen. William S. Rosecrans occupied a threatening position at Murfreesboro. On the Mississippi River, Ulysses S. Grant's army threatened Vicksburg. Secretary of War James A. Seddon, seeking Lee's advice, called his attention to the need to reinforce the armies in the West. Lee replied that although the logical move would be to send troops from Virginia, rail travel was so uncertain that reinforcements might not be timely. Lee believed that the best way to relieve Federal pressure in the West was to keep the enemy fully occupied in the East. On April 9 he wrote to Seddon that if Hooker remained on the defensive, "the readiest method of relieving the pressure upon Genl. Johnston & Genl. Beauregard would be for this army to cross into Maryland." Such a move, however, would be possible only if the Army of Northern Virginia received more provisions and stronger animals.[9]

Lee had problems, but so did the Federals across the river. As noted earlier, Burnside had failed to get a vote of confidence from Lincoln following the disaster at Fredericksburg. Instead, he found himself replaced by the man he despised above all others, Gen. Joseph Hooker.

Hooker, 49, was a handsome West Pointer who had followed various careers before the war. Returning to uniform, he had performed well on the peninsula, where journalists began referring to him as "Fighting Joe." Other observers spoke of his "Apollo-like presence" and fine rapport with the troops.[10] He had more than lived up to his nickname at Antietam, where his corps had been engaged in the heaviest fighting and where Hooker himself had been slightly wounded. As ambitious as he was brave, Hooker had sought to ingratiate himself with Lincoln by publicly endorsing the Emancipation Proclamation.

Hooker did not lack for detractors. He was known to have schemed for Burnside's ouster and his own promotion. He had a reputation as a drinker in an army where alcoholism was so prevalent that to be known as a drinker required some effort. He also had a reputation for sexual promiscuity, and although the term *hooker* was in the lexicon long before General Joe came along, the coincidence in names made for many a wink and nod. When William T. Sherman heard of Hooker's appointment he wrote, "I know Hooker well and tremble to think of him handling 100,000 men in the presence of Lee."[11]

Despite his weaknesses, Hooker was an able soldier who understood what his army needed. He brought about the retirement of some of the older generals, such as Sumner and Franklin. He improved the commissary, making sure that fruit and vegetables reached the lowliest picket on the front line. He insisted on proper sanitation in camp and instituted a system of furloughs more generous than what Lee was able to offer. In the words of one chronicler, "Cheerfulness, good order, and military discipline at once took the place of grumbling, depression, and want of confidence."[12]

Hooker also tackled a chronic problem, his army's cavalry. Traditionally, Federal cavalry units had been attached to the corps and divisions. Hooker, however, created a separate cavalry corps similar to that of the Confederates. Elsewhere, he abolished Burnside's grand divisions as too cumbersome. Lincoln, after a visit to the Army of the Potomac in April, was impressed with what Hooker had accomplished but worried about his brash confidence. The hen is the wisest of animals, Lincoln mused, "because she never cackles until the egg is laid."[13]

On April 12 Hooker gained the president's approval for a spring offensive. "Fighting Joe" had spent several months studying how to avoid a repetition of Burnside's disaster, and he put forth a thoughtful and innovative plan. To keep Lee's attention on the Rappahannock, Hooker would station two corps to threaten Fredericksburg. Then he would launch a large-scale cavalry raid aimed at severing Lee's communications with Richmond. Once Lee learned that his single rail link was cut, Hooker theorized, the Confederates would have to evacuate their Fredericksburg line and retreat. When the Confederates began pulling back, Hooker would cross the Rappahannock beyond Lee's left flank with three corps, march east to Chancellorsville, and there attack

"Fighting Joe" Hooker, Lee's opponent at Chancellorsville. AUTHOR'S COLLECTION.

the flank of Lee's retiring army. After the war, Porter Alexander, Lee's artillerist, would describe Hooker's plan as the best strategy conceived by the enemy against the Army of Northern Virginia.[14]

Hooker not only had a promising plan, but also had seven corps to Lee's two, and one of the Confederate corps had been weakened by the absence of Longstreet and his two divisions. Hooker told his officers, "My plans are perfect, and when I start to carry them out, may God have mercy on General Lee, for I will have none."[15]

RIDING WEST FROM FREDERICKSBURG IN 1863 A TRAVELER would start along the Orange Plank Road, passing through pleasant farming country. A few miles from the town, however, the landscape turned into a gloomy forest known locally as the Wilderness, a thinly populated seventy-square-mile area of shallow ravines and scrub growth. It was easy to get lost in such a place. One Federal soldier referred to it as a land of "grinning ghosts."[16]

A short distance into the Wilderness the turnpike passed a crossroads, shown on the maps as Chancellorsville. The name was a misnomer, for the "village" consisted of a single dwelling, the rambling redbrick residence of the George E. Chancellor family. In a rustic way Chancellorsville was something of a transportation hub; five roads converged there, three of them from nearby fords across the Rappahannock and Rapidan Rivers. If Hooker were to come after Lee, he would almost certainly pass through Chancellorsville.

The campaign began on April 13, as Federal cavalry under Gen. George Stoneman attempted to cross the Rappahannock. Stoneman's cautious crossing of the largely undefended fords underscored one of Hooker's critical decisions: He was entrusting a vital function—one on which his campaign relied—to his cavalry, the one branch of the two armies in which the Confederates excelled in all respects. Stoneman had a few troopers across the river on April 15 when a downpour turned the river into a torrent and the roads to mud, prompting him to pull back to the north side of the Rappahannock. Federal cavalry did not recross the river in force until April 29, after Hooker's infantry was already in motion.

One day later, on April 30, Hooker had approximately 50,000 men at Chancellorsville, with 22,000 more on the way. Back at Falmouth, opposite Fredericksburg, were 47,000 more under Gen. John Sedgwick. The two Federal forces were separated by about ten miles, but this situation was intended to be temporary; on May 1, according to Hooker's plan, the Federals would move east to the river and the two wings would be again in contact. Meanwhile, Sedgwick laid down pontoon bridges south of Fredericksburg, attempting to convince Lee that the Federals were again moving against the town.

Although Lee was badly outnumbered, his prospects were improving. Stoneman's troopers, if they had been aggressively led, might have threatened Lee's communications. Confederate cavalry, however, successfully contained the raiders, harassing the Federal troopers and keeping them away from the railroad. Ultimately, Stoneman's raid was only an irritant, yet the absence of Federal cavalry deprived Hooker of vital tactical intelligence.

Even so, how Lee chose to meet Hooker's main thrust was remarkable. To some degree Lee appears to have lost respect for his opponent; he never went on record with an opinion of Hooker, but he disliked braggarts, and among his aides he came to refer dryly to "Mr. F. J. Hooker." Having sent cavalry to occupy Stoneman's troopers, Lee prepared to take on Hooker's army in full knowledge that he would have to do so without Longstreet.

Lee knew that the enemy had moved Sedgwick's two corps below Fredericksburg and had their main force in motion west of Chancellorsville. Logic directed that Lee move against one of the enemy wings or retire. On April 30, he conferred with Jackson, whose first impulse was to smash Sedgwick. Although Lee was skeptical—the Federals still had artillery on Stafford Heights—he asked Jackson to look into the prospect. When Jackson agreed that Sedgwick could not be successfully attacked, Lee decided that the battle must be fought at Chancellorsville. He telegraphed the War Department that the enemy had crossed the Rapidan to his left, adding, "I determined to hold our lines in rear of Fredericksburg with part of [my] force, and endeavor with the rest to drive the enemy back to the Rapidan." [17]

Lee ordered Anderson to move his division west on the turnpike to the area of Zoan Church, and there fortify his line. "Set all your spades to work," he directed. Lee then rode to Fredericksburg, where he studied the enemy dispositions through his field glasses. After several minutes he said to aide Walter Taylor, "The main attack will come from above." He had made his first critical judgment—that the primary threat was from Hooker rather than from Sedgwick. [18]

❖

ON THE EVENING OF APRIL 30, HOOKER AND HIS STAFF RODE to the Chancellor house, where the Federals established their headquarters. In the recollection of one Federal officer it was a pleasant, moonlit evening, and the Chancellor house "became the center for hundreds of officers. . . . It was a gay and cheerful scene." Hooker marked the occasion with a general order to his army:

> It is with heartfelt satisfaction the commanding general announces to the army that the operations of the past three days have determined that our enemy must either ingloriously fly, or come out from behind his defenses and give

us battle on our own ground, where certain destruction awaits him.[19]

Already, however, there were hints that the Confederates were not where Hooker expected them to be. Three miles from the Chancellorsville crossroads the Federals had encountered Anderson's field works near Zoan Church. There was sharp fighting, and Hooker gained his first intimation that the Confederates might not be adhering to his own scenario.

The following morning, Jackson, with three divisions totaling about 26,000 men, attacked west on the turnpike. Lee and Jackson together directed a chaotic mix of gray-clad infantry up the turnpike and the nearby Orange Plank Road. "How splendidly the pair of them looked to us," wrote artillerist Porter Alexander, "& how the happy confidence of the men shone in everyone's face."[20] The Confederates were making only slow progress, however, when the fighting took an unexpected turn. After first ordering a general attack for two o'clock that afternoon, Hooker directed that the army retire to defensive positions around Chancellorsville. The Federal commander, listening to the "ghosts" of the Wilderness, was having second thoughts.

Hooker's decision to go on the defensive was unpopular with his generals, and has been the subject of considerable speculation among historians. Hooker later admitted, with unusual candor, that he had "lost faith in Joe Hooker." His loss of confidence probably stemmed from several factors. By sending off all except two brigades of cavalry Hooker had denied himself accurate information about Lee's movements. By accepting battle in the Wilderness, he had nullified much of the advantage of his superior artillery. Perhaps worst of all, the vigor of Confederate attacks on the morning of May 1 had shattered his assumption that Lee had no choice but to retreat.

While Jackson pressed the retiring Federals toward the Chancellor house, Lee undertook a personal reconnaissance to the right, where he found either enemy troops or hostile terrain. He then rode back on the Orange Plank Road, where he met Jackson. The two men dismounted and sought privacy in a nearby pine grove. There, Jackson described the Federal defenses at Chancellorsville as strong and getting stronger. Lee summarized his own reconnaissance and asked rhetorically how they were to get at "those people." Jackson thought that Hooker might now abandon his offensive, but Lee disagreed.

While Lee and Jackson shared a log, Stuart rode up. His cavalry controlled the roads, and he advised Lee that Hooker's right flank was apparently "in the air"—not anchored on any natural obstacle. Did this provide the opportunity that Lee and Jackson sought? The Confederates were almost as ignorant of the roads in the area as Hooker was, but Lee and Jackson quickly agreed on a move against the enemy's right. His own troops, Jackson promised, would move at four o'clock the following morning. Neither officer knew what route Jackson might take, but each took time out for a few hours' sleep.

When Lee awoke, he found Jackson huddled next to a fire drinking coffee. Lee joined him, and the two were joined in turn by Jackson's topographical engineer, Jed Hotchkiss, and a chaplain, the Rev. Beverly Tucker Lacy, who was familiar with the area. Hotchkiss and Lacy had created a crude map showing how Jackson's corps might make its way around Hooker's right to the enemy rear. The dialogue between Lee and Jackson that followed is one of the most famous of the war:

> "General Jackson, what do you propose to do?"
> "Go around here."
> "What do you propose to make this movement with?"
> "With my entire corps."
> "What will you leave me?"
> "The divisions of Anderson and McLaws."
> "Well, go on." [21]

The passage of time has done nothing to diminish the audacity of what Lee was attempting. He had already divided his inferior force by leaving Early to contain Sedgwick at Fredericksburg. But Sedgwick appeared passive, and Early occupied a strong line on Marye's Heights. Lee now felt justified in dividing his army again, in the face of a force nearly twice the size of his own. On May 2, Lee had about 40,000 men with which to face Hooker's 75,000.

While Jackson marched, Lee sent skirmishers toward the enemy line, attempting to give the impression of an army in great strength. Jackson marched on, not always with the secrecy his mission required. Early in his movement a gap in the woods gave the Federals a clear view of marching columns, and the Federals opened up with artillery. A little farther along, Jackson's column was again spotted, this time by elements of Gen. Daniel Sickles's corps. Sickles sent word to Hooker that Lee was retreating, but Hooker, to his credit, had doubts. [22]

Jackson's projected march was one of about fourteen miles. Cheering was forbidden, and noise was suppressed as much as possible. If Jackson's column had been able to average two miles per hour he would have been in position by noon, but the troops were confined to a single narrow lane and the Confederate column stretched for at least six miles. One officer recalled,

> No one who has ever marched with a long column can form any conception [of] how every little inequality of ground, & every mud hole, especially if the road be narrow, causes a column to string out and lose distance. So that, though the head may advance steadily, the rear has to alternately halt & start, in the most heartbreaking way, wearing out the men & consuming precious daylight.[23]

By about noon the Confederate vanguard was approaching the Orange Plank Road, where Jackson had planned to turn right and attack Hooker's flank. Before Jackson could order an attack, Gen. Fitzhugh Lee—Lee's nephew and one of his cavalry commanders—intercepted him and took him to a nearby hill to view the Federal camps. Jackson saw that the Federals had stacked their arms and were cooking, brewing coffee, and otherwise looking unready for battle. Realizing that he had not quite reached the Federal rear, however, Jackson ordered a march of another two miles along the Brock Road.

The Federals Jackson had scouted were elements of Gen. O. O. Howard's Eleventh Corps, a hard-luck organization manned to a considerable extent by German Americans—"Dutchmen" to other Federal soldiers, who found their language unintelligible. Not only was the Eleventh Corps the weakest of Hooker's corps, but also the Federals had allowed a gap to emerge between it and the rest of the army. Howard was a man of unquestioned courage—he had lost an arm in the Seven Days' campaign—but his military skills were limited.

So luck was with Jackson when, about five thirty in the afternoon, he unleashed the bulk of his 20,000 men on the unsuspecting Federal camps. Yankee soldiers got their first intimation that something was amiss when rabbits and other forest creatures came bounding out of the brush. Then bugles proclaimed the advance as the two-mile-wide Confederate line crashed through the thickets. As their attack gained momentum, Jackson's men broke into the spine-chilling, falsetto rebel yell. "The Plank road, and the woods that bordered it, presented a scene of terror and confusion," a Pennsylvania officer recalled. "Men and animals were dashing against one another in wild dismay before the line of fire that came crackling and crashing after them."[24] Although some Federal units fought bravely, there was no neighboring corps to come to Howard's rescue, and Jackson swept more than two miles toward Chancellorsville in the gathering dusk. A Federal officer recalled how "darkness was upon us, and Jackson was on us, and fear was on us."[25]

Night fell before Jackson could complete his victory, and that evening he was fatally wounded by North Carolina troops who mistook him and his staff for enemy cavalry. Command of Jackson's corps passed to Stuart, who handled his new responsibilities with a sure hand. When Porter Alexander urged that the Confederates seize Hazel Grove, which overlooked the battlefield as far as the Chancellor house, Stuart complied, and Alexander placed some thirty artillery pieces on that commanding ground.

Hooker was leaning against a pillar at the Chancellor house when one of the shells from Hazel Grove struck the column. The shell did not explode, but a fragment of the pillar struck the Federal commander and left him dazed. On the morning of May 3 the Federals at Chancellorsville greatly outnumbered the Confederates, and stood between the wings of Lee and Stuart. A vigorous Federal counterattack might yet have saved the day, but the necessary leadership was lacking. Although several of Hooker's officers believed that the battle could still be retrieved, the disoriented Hooker remained passive.

That morning saw the fiercest fighting of the three days as Lee sought to unite his army. The link was accomplished late in the morning. Through smoldering woods the Confederates pushed the Federals back to the Chancellor house, now in flames; its capture had somehow come to epitomize victory. A final rush of gray threw back the last Federal defenders and brought hoarse shouts of victory from the weary Confederates.

Robert E. Lee was totally lacking in a sense of the dramatic, but at this climactic moment he was drawn irresistibly to the Chancellor house. In the words of one officer,

> His presence was the signal for one of those outbursts of enthusiasm which none can appreciate who have not witnessed them. The fierce soldiers with their faces blackened

Lt. Gen. Thomas J. "Stonewall" Jackson just two weeks before his fatal wounding at Chancellorsville. LIBRARY OF CONGRESS.

with the smoke of battle, the wounded crawling with feeble limbs from the fury of the devouring flames, all seemed possessed with a common impulse. One long, unbroken cheer . . . rose high above the roar of battle, and hailed the presence of the victorious chief.[26]

Lee had little time to savor his triumph. From Fredericksburg came word that Sedgwick's corps, heretofore dormant, had broken Early's line and was threatening Lee's rear. Once again blue-clad troops stormed Marye's Heights as they had attempted to do the previous December; this time there was little opposition. The Federals had an opportunity to move west on the Plank Road to the Chancellor house, but a rearguard action by Cadmus Wilcox's Alabama brigade gave Lee enough time to bring McLaws's division into line at Salem Church. On the night of May 4–5, Sedgwick retired across the Rappahannock.

Lee was then able to turn his attention again to Hooker's main force. The Federals had built earthworks along their defenses between Chancellorsville and the river, but Lee still sought a means to destroy his foe. He complained to the correspondent of the London *Times:*

> True, we have driven our enemy from every field, swept away his every formation, scourged him out of works from which neither whirlwind nor hurricane could ever drive my poor ragamuffins—but what of that? I have learnt that nothing but the entire capture of a whole corps will ever produce an effect, and such a capture should unquestionably have been effected yesterday.[27]

Lee's disposition did not improve when, on the morning of May 6, Gen. Dorsey Pender advised him that, according to his skirmishers, the Yankees had recrossed the river during the night. Lee was chagrined. "This is the way that you young men are always doing," he snapped. "You have again let these people get away. I can only tell you what to do, and if you do not do it it will not be done."[28]

Others, more charitable than Lee, would call Chancellorsville his greatest victory. Yet for all his reckless brilliance, Lee had also been favored by fortune. He might never have been able to launch Jackson's stroke if Hooker had not sent the Federal cavalry on a wild-goose chase. For Sickles to have seen Jackson's marchers and not to have recognized the threat was remarkable, as was Howard's failure to place pickets around his position on Hooker's far right. The failure of the Federals to defend Hazel Grove enabled the Confederates to make good use of their artillery. For Sedgwick to remain quiescent for so long at Fredericksburg was almost too much to ask.

The triumph at Chancellorsville came at great cost. The Confederates suffered about 12,000 casualties—some 22 percent of their force—while the Federals suffered 18,000 casualties, about 15 percent of Hooker's army.[29] The most serious of the Confederate losses was Stonewall Jackson. Lee, when told that Jackson was failing, told Chaplain Lacy that he was confident that God would not take General Jackson "at such a time when his country so much needed him." Hours before Jackson died on Sunday, May 10, Lee spoke again with Lacy. "When a suitable occasion offers, tell him that I prayed for him last night, as I never prayed, I believe, for myself."[30]

Lee's prayers for Jackson went unanswered, and with Jackson's death went Lee's hopes for any future Chancellorsvilles. Indeed, the fruits of Lee's greatest victory were bittersweet. Although the Confederates captured vast quantities of Federal ordnance, the effect on Federal morale was less than they had hoped. There was no "generals' revolt" or surge in desertions, such as had followed Fredericksburg. One Federal soldier spoke for many when he wrote home, "Our boys stood like heros [*sic*]. . . . I suppose we shall make another move soon, and I hope we shall be more successful this time."[31]

⊷⊷⊜ ⊜⊶⊶

WITH RESPECT TO JACKSON'S FAMOUS FLANK ATTACK AT Chancellorsville, it is difficult to determine which required the greater daring: Jackson's march or Lee's willingness to confront Hooker's army with only two divisions. There was glory enough for both, but after the war some of Jackson's partisans attempted to claim for their hero credit for the conception as well as the execution of the May 2 attack. In one postwar biography, the Rev. Robert Dabney, who had served on Jackson's staff, maintained that Jackson had proposed the move and that Lee had acquiesced only after "profound reflection." In contrast, members of Lee's staff gave full credit for the move to the commanding general.

There is little doubt that Lee believed the plan to be his, and some of the evidence is to be found in Lee's own writings. In his reports he was meticulous in crediting acts of valor to those who committed them, and useful suggestions to those who put them forth. Where he himself took action, Lee most often used the passive voice. In his report on Chancellorsville, he devoted a single sentence to his discussions with Jackson: "It was therefore resolved to endeavor to turn [the enemy's] right flank and gain his rear, leaving a force in front to hold him in check and conceal the movement."[32]

Lee felt the loss of Jackson personally, and rarely spoke of his famous lieutenant in other than terms of highest praise. In 1867, however, he wrote to the editor of a Baltimore journal to set the record straight with respect to Chancellorsville. He had learned, Lee wrote, that certain authors were crediting Jackson with having gained successes for the Army of Northern Virginia by movements "undertaken at his own suggestion and upon his own responsibility." Lee diplomatically made it clear who had been in charge:

> I have the greatest reluctance to do anything that might be considered detracting from [Jackson's] well-deserved fame; . . . yet your knowledge of military affairs, if you have none of the events themselves, will teach you that this could not have been so. Every movement of an army must be well considered and properly ordered, and every one who knew General Jackson must know that he was too good a soldier to violate this fundamental principle.[33]

The final word on the flank march may be that of Robert Krick, chief historian at the national military park at Chancellorsville. "Based on primary sources," Krick writes, "it is clear that Lee initiated the concept and Jackson perfected and executed it."[34]

CHAPTER TWELVE

THE ROAD TO GETTYSBURG

On May 12, 1863, church bells tolled in Richmond, flags flew at half mast, and places of business closed in honor of Stonewall Jackson. Thousands stood bareheaded in the streets to see his coffin pass. The day before, Lee had issued a general order to his army. With deep regret, the commanding general announced the death of Gen. Stonewall Jackson:

> The daring, skill, and energy of this great and good soldier, by the decree of an all wise Providence, are now lost to us. But while we mourn his death, we feel that his spirit still lives, and will inspire the whole army with his indomitable courage and unshaken confidence in God as our hope and our strength.[1]

Lee knew full well the extent of his loss. In his most candid assessment, made some months earlier, he had said of Jackson, "Such an executive officer the sun never shown on. I have but to show him my design, and I know that if it can be done it will be done."[2]

The bond between Lee and Jackson was a curious one. They had scarcely known each another before the war, and they appear not to have crossed paths during hostilities until their June 23 conference before the Seven Days' campaign. Both men were pious, crediting their successes to Divine Providence; but Jackson was Old Testament, Lee the New. Lee depersonalized the enemy, while Jackson demonized him. To Lee they were simply "those people" who had no business in Virginia; the enemy had a human face. Jackson, in contrast, once exhorted his generals to "Kill them all! Kill them all!" According to Gen. Richard Anderson, Jackson once said that his only objection to General Lee was that "he did not hate Yankees enough."[3]

Lee somehow overlooked Jackson's failures on the peninsula, and the Lee-Jackson combination became one of the most famous partnerships in military history, despite striking differences in their command styles. Lee thought in terms of broad campaign objectives, giving his subordinates wide discretion in matters of tactics. Jackson was secretive by instinct, leaving his subordinates in the dark about his plans, asking only that they be executed precisely as he had ordered. Between battles Lee never forgot that his army depended on volunteers, and he spent much of his time looking after their needs. Jackson, in contrast, was unsparing of his men, expecting and often achieving miracles of endurance.

Lee was sensitive to the feelings of his officers, winning them over with praise, rarely making ad hominem attacks. Jackson, in contrast, was inflexible in his dealings with subordinates, leaving a succession of feuds as part of his legacy. One of Jackson's staff officers, Charles M. Blackford, first met Lee during the Second Manassas campaign. He was impressed, as many others had been, with Lee's dignity and "natural grace," adding that the commanding general in some way made people feel "of some consequence." This was not the case with Jackson, Blackford wrote. "He is ever monosyllabic and receives and delivers a message as if the bearer was a conduit pipe from one ear to another. . . . All admire his genius and great deeds; no one could love the man for himself."[4]

On the battlefield, however, Lee and Jackson were equally committed to seizing the initiative, dividing enemy forces, and destroying them. Did the Army of Northern Virginia have among its generals a worthy successor to Stonewall Jackson? There were many able division commanders, but it was unclear which of these could manage a three-division corps in camp, on the march, and in battle. In the weeks after Jackson's death Lee reorganized his army. Aware that some of his divisions were as large as Scott's army had been during the war with Mexico, Lee decided that a corps in his army—as many as 30,000 men—was too unwieldy for one man to command. He received permission from Davis to structure his army into three corps.

One of these would be commanded by James Longstreet. Although obstinate, hard of hearing, and overly eager for independent command, the Georgian was a proven professional, unshakable in battle. Lee had been unable to bring Longstreet's divisions from southern Virginia in time for Chancellorsville, but he counted on his "warhorse" for future campaigns.

To command Jackson's Second Corps, reduced by one division, Lee chose Gen. Richard S. Ewell—"Old Bald Head"—a 46-year-old West Pointer who had served under Jackson for most of the war. Ewell lisped and complained regularly of insomnia and a variety of digestive ailments. He was a modest man, commenting on one occasion that the U.S. Army had taught him how to command fifty dragoons, but that he had forgotten everything else.[5] Ewell had lost a leg in the Second Manassas campaign, but had returned to the army and had maintained a reputation for solid competence.

Lee's choice to command the new Third Corps was Powell Hill, whose Light Division had saved the day at Antietam. Lee had long regarded the 37-year-old Hill as his most capable division commander, notwithstanding his penchant for quarrels, first with Jackson and later with Longstreet. Hill, who was noted for wearing a flaming-red shirt into battle, had a swagger that appealed to the unassuming Lee. Although Hill was a tough fighter, he had never fully recovered from a youthful brush with venereal disease that disabled him at crucial times. Remembering Hill's performance at Antietam, however, Lee chose him over two generals with greater seniority to command a corps composed of Hill's old division, that of Richard Anderson, and a newly created division under Gen. Henry Heth.

Lee's promotion of Ewell was predictable, but that of Hill was less so. There were rumors that Jeb Stuart, who had commanded Jackson's corps at Chancellorsville after Jackson had been wounded, aspired to corps command. He would have been an interesting choice—the one man who might have matched Jackson in daring and initiative. But Lee wanted Stuart as his cavalry commander, and there would have been complaints if Lee had passed over able division commanders and placed a cavalry officer in command.

Lee's headquarters staff, meanwhile, remained stable, if inadequate. Notwithstanding the demands on Lee, he operated with a minimal staff. The War Department had assigned as its chief Col. Robert Chilton, who had not worked out. One of Lee's weaknesses was a tendency toward carelessness in the wording of orders, and Chilton added to the problem. During the Battle of Chancellorsville, he so garbled an order to Jubal Early that Early evacuated Marye's Heights before Lee had planned. Lee saw to it that Chilton was reassigned.

Although aides came and went, Lee's staff included for extended periods Armistead Long, military secretary; T. M. R. Talcott, the son of Lee's friend from his time at Fortress Monroe, military engineer; and three aides without significant military experience: Charles Marshall, Charles Venable, and Walter Taylor. None of these staff members had the training, rank, or clout to follow up on Lee's orders to senior commanders and ensure that they were carried out.

Lee realized that he was operating with minimal assistance, and in theory favored a staff on the French model. He wrote to the War Department in 1863:

> We . . . have need of a corps of officers to teach others their duty, see to the observances of orders, & to the regularity & precision of all movements. This is accomplished in the French Service by their staff corps, educated, instructed & practiced for the purpose. . . . Can you not shape & form the staff of our army to produce equally good results?[6]

Lee could have developed a more professional staff of his own, but he apparently was satisfied to have a staff of dedicated amateurs with whom he was personally comfortable.

Meanwhile, Lee was engaged in a continuing debate with Richmond about how best to deal with Confederate setbacks in the West. The victory at Chancellorsville only briefly eclipsed a stream of bad news from the Mississippi. There, the Federal army of Gen. Ulysses S. Grant had crossed the river below Vicksburg and posed an immediate threat to the most important Confederate stronghold on the Mississippi. Joe Johnston watched the Federal advance, convinced that he lacked the force necessary to slow it. In Tennessee, Rosecrans's Army of the Cumberland was quiescent, but posed a continuing threat to Bragg's small army. Jefferson Davis, having learned that the Army of Northern Virginia could look after itself, was preoccupied with his inability to check the enemy in the West.

On May 6, on his way back to northern Virginia from Suffolk

County, Longstreet stopped in Richmond. In a meeting with Secretary of War Seddon, he expounded on the need to reinforce Confederate forces in the West. Longstreet proposed that instead of rejoining Lee he take his two divisions to Tennessee and reinforce Bragg. With Johnston's assistance they could defeat Rosecrans, and a Federal setback in Tennessee might lead Grant to break off his campaign against Vicksburg. Seddon expressed interest, but thought that reinforcements from the East could best be used directly against Grant.

The Confederates had the advantage of interior lines, and could presumably shift forces from one theater to another more easily than the Federals, but the distances were great and the railway links connecting the two theaters were overtaxed. The fact that Davis and Seddon felt obliged to borrow from the Army of Northern Virginia to meet the crisis in the West was ominous. Lee addressed the issue in a letter to Seddon on May 10. Noting that any division sent to the Mississippi would not arrive before the end of the month, he speculated that the need for it would have vanished "as the climate in June will force the enemy to retire." Meanwhile, Lee estimated that the enemy force facing the Army of Northern Virginia numbered about 160,000. If his army did not receive reinforcements, Lee wrote, he would have to return to the defenses around Richmond.[7]

It would take more than hot weather and mosquitoes to intimidate Grant, however, and Lee's reasons for not sending Longstreet west are suspect. But Lee had little confidence that his troops would be put to good use in the West, and he was sure they would be used effectively in Virginia. At about this time Lee discussed plans with his military secretary, Armistead Long, tracing on a map a route by which the Army of Northern Virginia might invade Pennsylvania. When Long asked whether Hooker might instead be engaged near Manassas, Lee replied that he had considered and rejected such an option. The Federal army, if defeated, would simply fall back on the Washington defenses, and would soon be ready to campaign again. Lee wanted to take on the enemy at a site where a Federal army could be routed and destroyed.

In Lee's view, the most promising venue was Pennsylvania. If the enemy could be brought to battle, Gettysburg might be the best locale because it was relatively close to Confederate supply lines in Virginia. And what would be the fruits of a victory? At a minimum, the presence of a victorious Confederate army in Pennsylvania would discourage the enemy from strengthening its forces in the West. And a defeated Army of the Potomac would be forced to retreat across the Susquehanna, giving the Confederacy temporary control over much of Maryland and western Pennsylvania. Such a development, Lee speculated, might cause the evacuation of Washington.[8]

There were other possible benefits. An incursion that threatened Philadelphia as well as Washington might create a financial panic, increase the price of gold, and prompt business interests in the North to demand peace. Jubal Early, one of Lee's division commanders, thought that a victory north of the Potomac was far more likely to produce a financial crisis in the North than any number of Confederate victories in Virginia.[9]

Lee also thought in terms of lesser objectives. One of these, which he mentioned on several occasions, was his desire to feed his army outside of northern Virginia. Another was simply to keep the enemy off balance. Lee remarked to Gen. Henry Heth, "An invasion of the enemy's country breaks up all his preconceived plans, relieves our country of his presence, and we subsist while there on his resources."[10]

There was already a strong peace movement in the North, and it appeared to be growing stronger. A peace rally in early June in New York City was estimated to have drawn a crowd of 30,000. The movement drew strength both from actions of the Lincoln administration and from Federal setbacks on the battlefield. In September 1862 Lincoln had suspended the writ of habeas corpus, and subjected to martial law all persons who discouraged voluntary enlistments, resisted conscription, or engaged in "any disloyal practice." This measure, which led to the arrest of thousands of draft resisters, newspaper editors, and others, was anathema to civil libertarians. Although the Emancipation Proclamation, issued in December 1862, gained support for the Lincoln administration in Europe, it was controversial in the North— denounced by most Democrats and unpopular in the army.

These dissident voices might have been ignored if not for the succession of Union military failures in the East. For Northerners, as for Southerners, Virginia was the principal theater of the war. There were to be found the rebel capital and the South's most formidable army, and there the Federals had met nothing but disaster. Joseph Medill, the staunchly Unionist editor of the *Chicago Tribune*, had written early in the year that there was bound to be an armistice in 1863: "The rebs can't be conquered by the present machinery."[11]

Before proceeding with his projected offensive Lee would have to gain support for it in Richmond. Meeting with Davis and his cabinet from May 14 to 17, Lee found the president preoccupied with the threat to Vicksburg. Lee recommended that Johnston attack Grant, but resisted any detachment of troops from his own army. He outlined his own plan and its promise. By implication, the benefits of shifting assets from Virginia to the Mississippi were far less certain. Lee was not noted for his persuasiveness in council, but such was his prestige that he carried the cabinet with him. Only Postmaster General John H. Reagan, a Texan, continued to believe that Vicksburg should be given top priority.[12]

Lee was sure that Virginia would remain the war's main theater. The loss of Vicksburg would be unfortunate; but the fall of Richmond would probably mean an end to the war. Lee had no illusions about the Confederacy's long-term prospects, however. In June he wrote Davis a letter in which he emphasized that time was not on the side of the Confederacy. "We should not therefore conceal from ourselves that our resources in men are constantly diminishing, and the disproportion in this respect . . . is steadily augmenting." Already his army was receiving too few replacements to make up for its casualties:

> Under these circumstances we should neglect no honorable means of dividing and weakening our enemies that they may feel some of the difficulties experienced by ourselves. It seems to me that the most effectual mode of accomplishing this object, now within our reach, is to give all the encouragement we can to the rising peace party of the North.[13]

Politics aside, Lee was gaining support for his plan for a second invasion of the North. Longstreet's corps, back on the Rappahannock, found an army that was reasonably well fed and in excellent spirits after the victory at Chancellorsville. Longstreet had second thoughts about the relative priority of the Virginia and Tennessee theaters, writing to a confidant in Richmond, Sen. Louis Wigfall, "When I agreed with the Secy [Seddon] & yourself about sending troops west I was under the impression that we would be obliged to remain on the defensive here. But the prospect of an advance changes the aspect of the affair to us entirely."[14]

Lee appears to have convinced Longstreet of the merits of a move into Pennsylvania. The tactics to be adopted on any battlefield there, however, would become a subject of bitter dispute. Longstreet believed that Lee's army must assume the tactical defensive. He considered Second Manassas and Fredericksburg to have been Lee's greatest victories largely because the Army of Northern Virginia had been attacked in strong defensive positions. Lee and Longstreet doubtless discussed tactics for future battles, in Pennsylvania and elsewhere. Whatever Lee may have said to Longstreet with respect to the tactical defensive, Longstreet apparently believed that he had sold his case to the commanding general.

Having gained Davis's approval for a new offensive, Lee put his army in motion. He and his staff left Fredericksburg on June 6, arriving at Culpeper the following morning. He planned to cross the Blue Ridge Mountains and move north through the Shenandoah Valley, but in response to a longstanding invitation from Jeb Stuart he reviewed Stuart's cavalry corps at Brandy Station on June 8. Lee wrote to Mary that the cavalry had put on a splendid show, with Stuart "in all his glory." [15]

The pageantry was short-lived, as the real war quickly intruded. On the day after the grand review, 10,000 Federal troopers crossed the Rappahannock and caught Stuart's cavalry by surprise. The Battle of Brandy Station—the largest cavalry battle ever fought in North America—became a struggle for Fleetwood Hill, where Stuart had staged his recent extravaganza. The Confederates eventually prevailed, but the Yankee troopers not only had surprised but had outfought the Confederates on some parts of the field. One of the Confederate casualties was Lee's son Rooney, who encountered his father while being taken to the rear with a bullet in his thigh. Rooney was sent to his wife's home, Hickory Hill, and Lee found time for a letter to his daughter-in-law:

> I am grieved, my dear daughter, to send Fitzhugh to you wounded. . . . With his youth and strength to aid him, and your tender care to nurse him, I trust he will soon be well again. . . . I want all the husbands in the field, and their wives at home encouraging them, loving them, and praying for them. We have a great work to accomplish, which requires the cordial and united strength of all. [16]

Before entering Pennsylvania, Lee ensured that sufficient forces were left to protect Richmond in case Hooker attacked the Confederate capital while the Army of Northern Virginia was moving north. However, Lee had been unable to gain President Davis's agreement to the movement of some of Beauregard's troops from South Carolina to the Culpeper area to distract the enemy. At a minimum, Lee reasoned, the presence of a Confederate force around Culpeper would make the Federals hesitate before sending the entire Army of the Potomac into Pennsylvania. Three times Lee petitioned the president for such a force, but Davis rejected the request on grounds that transport was inadequate.[17]

Lee's army continued its march, much of the time in stifling heat. By June 17, Ewell's corps was in Winchester, Longstreet had reached Upperville, and Hill, bringing up the rear, had left Fredericksburg. Lee was pleased; on about June 18 he remarked to one of his generals that they had once again outmaneuvered the enemy, who did not know where the rebels were or what they were planning. "Our whole army will be in Pennsylvania day after tomorrow," he mused, "leaving the enemy far behind."[18] Lee was unaware that documents captured by the Federals at Brandy Station revealed that the Army of Northern Virginia was moving north.

Even if the Army of the Potomac was far behind, Lee needed to know where it was. Stuart's troopers had been screening Lee's right as it passed through the Shenandoah Valley; on June 22, Lee gave new orders to his cavalry leader. These directed Stuart to leave two brigades to watch the valley passes while taking the rest of his cavalry to scout ahead of the Confederate army. Lee's poorly worded order invited misinterpretation:

> If General Hooker's army remains inactive you can leave two brigades to watch him, and withdraw the three others, but should he not appear to be moving northward, I think you had better withdraw this side of the mountains tomorrow night, cross at Shepherdstown next day, and move over to [Frederick].[19]

Using the freedom that he had long enjoyed in implementing Lee's orders, Stuart planned to lead three of his brigades along a route between Hooker's army and Washington, thereby playing on Lincoln's concern for the capital. The Federals had plans of their own, however.

Hooker was also moving north—he got under way at the same time as Stuart—forcing the Confederate cavalry to take a circuitous route on June 25 to emerge east of the enemy columns. Stuart later claimed to have sent a message to Lee telling him that the enemy was on the move, but Lee never received it.

By June 25, when Lee himself crossed into Maryland, virtually all of his 75,000-man army was north of the Potomac. The foraging was good. Southern soldiers appropriated food, cattle, horses, medicines, and clothing, occasionally laying specific requisitions on an occupied town or hamlet. All goods were paid for in Confederate currency, but in Pennsylvania this was essentially confiscation.

On June 27, Lee issued General Order 73, a proclamation that was both a skillful piece of Confederate propaganda and a reflection of Lee's beliefs as to how wars should be fought:

> The commanding general has observed with marked satisfaction the conduct of the troops on the march, and confidently anticipates results commensurate with the high spirit they have manifested. . . .
>
> The commanding general considers that no greater disgrace could befall the army, and through it our whole people, than the perpetration of the barbarous outrages upon the unarmed and defenseless, and the wanton destruction of private property that have marked the course of the enemy in our own country. . . .
>
> It must be remembered that we make war only upon armed men.[20]

On this, the most critical campaign Lee had yet waged, he was curiously accessible to a variety of people, some of them Federal sympathizers. One day a woman identified only as a Mrs. McLellan came to request that the invaders, in their foraging, make some provision for the hungry of Chambersburg. Lee told her to tell his commissary officers how much flour was required to meet the emergency. Mrs. McLellan then asked Lee for his autograph:

> "Do you want the autograph of a rebel?" Lee asked.
>
> "General Lee," she replied, "I am a true Union woman, and yet I ask for bread and your autograph."

"It is to your interest to be for the Union, and I hope
you may be as firm in your principles as I am in mine."

Lee told her that his autograph might be a dangerous souvenir, but he
gave it to her and went on to speak of the war and its cruelties. His
only desire, Lee said, was to be allowed to go home and eat his bread
in peace.[21]

·→≡⊃ ⊂≡←·

THE FIRST PART OF LEE'S PREDICTION REGARDING THE
enemy was remarkably accurate; Hooker had crossed the Potomac on
June 26 and 27 and had two corps at Frederick. But the Federal commander was also out of a job. A running dispute between Hooker and
Halleck regarding whether to evacuate Harpers Ferry had proved to
be the last straw for Lincoln. On June 28, at a crucial moment in the
history of the Army of the Potomac, the president named Gen. George
G. Meade to be its commander.

The 47-year-old Meade had been born into a middle-class Philadelphia family; his parents had sent him to West Point for a free education, much as Lee had been sent. Like many West Pointers, Meade
had resigned his commission to pursue a career in civil engineering,
but he was strongly opposed to slavery and had returned to uniform in
1861. He had performed capably as a division and corps commander
without showing any promise of brilliance. Meade reminded one
Massachusetts soldier of "a good sort of family doctor." To *New York
Tribune* correspondent Whitelaw Reid he appeared "a thoughtful student more than a dashing soldier."[22] Meade sometimes demonstrated a
nervous irritability that made it difficult for others to work with him;
his nickname in the army was "Old Snapping Turtle." But he had a
reputation for competence on the battlefield and for integrity in his
personal dealings.

·→≡⊃ ⊂≡←·

IT WAS A CONFIDENT, ALMOST COCKY, CONFEDERATE ARMY
that marched into Pennsylvania that June. One of Longstreet's officers
gave his impressions of Lee's headquarters at Chambersburg:

The general has little of the pomp and circumstance of war about his person. A Confederate flag marks the whereabouts of his headquarters, which are here in a little enclosure of some couple of acres of timber. There are about half a dozen tents and as many baggage wagons and ambulances. The horses and mules for these, besides those of a small—very small—escort, are tied up to trees or grazing about the place.[23]

One of Ewell's officers would recall that Lee's army was never in better spirits than in the days leading up to Gettysburg, and "never seemed to me as invincible as on the 1st [of] July 1863."[24] Out of privation and hard-won victories Lee had molded an army of "ragamuffins"—Lee's term—that had a certain threadbare jauntiness. Shortages of shoes and clothing were endemic, but the men themselves were as tough as leather. And considerable bonding had taken place since Lee had assumed command a short year before. The army had come to worship its commander; it would go wherever he led, and fight as he directed. The respect in which the army held Robert E. Lee was fully reciprocated. In a letter the previous month Lee had said of his troops, "There never were such men in an army before. They will go anywhere and do anything if properly led."[25]

Lee did not know at this point that the Army of the Potomac was on the move, and he might have been surprised to learn that morale in that army was almost as high as in his own. Even in defeat many Yankee regiments had developed a pride of unit. As for leadership, the Army of the Potomac, if given the choice, would probably have favored the return of McClellan as army commander. Nevertheless, Meade's promotion found favor with officers and men alike. An Illinois officer wrote home that everyone felt that a Federal victory in Pennsylvania would be the beginning of the end of the rebellion. An Ohio officer wondered about the command change but concluded that "a feeling had taken hold of the army that it had suffered disasters enough, and that [its] time had now come whatever leader and at whatever cost."[26]

Lee, meanwhile, considered how best to bring the enemy to battle on favorable terms. He had sent Ewell's corps to threaten Harrisburg in an attempt to flush out the Army of the Potomac, but in the absence of reliable information about Meade's whereabouts he could not risk having Ewell beyond recall. The town of Gettysburg began to take on importance in Lee's thinking. Gen. Isaac Trimble, a brigade commander who had been wounded at Second Manassas, traveled with Lee for part of the march into Pennsylvania. On June 27, according to Trimble, Lee had pointed at a map and indicated that the area around Gettysburg might well be the site of the next battle:

> Our army is in good spirits, not overly fatigued, and can be concentrated on any point in twenty-four hours or less. I have not yet heard that the enemy have crossed the Potomac, and am waiting to hear from General Stuart. . . . They will come up, probably through Frederick, broken down with hunger and hard marching. . . . I shall throw an overwhelming force on their advance, crush it, follow up the success, [and] drive one corps back and another . . . create a panic and virtually destroy the army.[27]

ON THE EVENING OF JUNE 28, ONE OF LONGSTREET'S STAFF officers asked to see the commanding general. Admitted to Lee's tent, he said that a spy, known by Longstreet to be reliable, had told the general that two Federal corps were close by, on the eastern side of the Blue Ridge. The enemy knew the Confederates were in Chambersburg. The spy also informed Longstreet that Hooker had been succeeded by Meade.* This change did not please Lee, who had considerable respect for Meade, more so than for his predecessor. Lee passed an uneasy night, complaining to visitors about the absence of any word from Stuart.

Lee had no choice but to begin concentrating his forces. Fortunately, Ewell had been ordered that morning to return to either Cashtown or Gettysburg, as circumstances might dictate. On the morning of the 29th Lee told his staff that they would not be going to Harrisburg, "but will go over to Gettysburg and see what General Meade is after."[28] Lee's first move was to send Hill's corps east to Cashtown on a

---

* Little is known of the spy, Henry Harrison, whose information helped precipitate the Battle of Gettysburg. He is known to have served Longstreet before, and the information that he brought to the Confederates on June 28 was remarkably accurate.

reconnaissance in force. Lee remained with Longstreet at Chambersburg, still hoping for word from Stuart. (Lee erred in not sending for the two cavalry brigades that Stuart had left behind; long after Lee had crossed the Potomac, the cavalry brigades of Gen. Beverly Robertson and Gen. William E. "Grumble" Jones were still watching the empty passes of the Shenandoah Valley.) On June 30, Lee followed Hill in the direction of Cashtown, making camp just west of South Mountain.

That evening a courier from Hill reported that part of Pettigrew's brigade, going into Gettysburg for supplies, had encountered Federal cavalry. Lee was passing through Cashtown Pass on the morning of July 1 when he heard cannon fire and musketry to the east. Leaving Longstreet, Lee and his aides spurred ahead. Two great armies were about to collide.

CHAPTER THIRTEEN

"THIS IS ALL MY FAULT"

As LEE RODE WITH LONGSTREET FROM Cashtown to Gettysburg on July 1, his first wish had already been granted. He had brought his army to Pennsylvania to do battle, and a battle was his for the asking. The day before, Gen. James Pettigrew had led his South Carolina brigade to Gettysburg, a town of 2,400 and a hub for no fewer than ten roads, where the Confederates had skirmished briefly with enemy cavalry. The next morning Powell Hill—who was skeptical of Pettigrew's belief that he had encountered the Army of the Potomac—sent Henry Heth's division to Gettysburg on a reconnaissance in force.

When Heth approached Gettysburg on the morning of July 1, he encountered not the local militia that Hill had led him to expect but two brigades of battle-hardened Federal cavalry. The dismounted Yankee troopers under Gen. John Buford gave battle, and in midmorning they were reinforced by elements of the Federal First Corps. In violation of Lee's orders—Lee had told Hill that he wanted no "general engagement"—the volatile Hill sent in reinforcements. By the time Lee reached Gettysburg, about two o'clock, three Confederate divisions had been engaged with elements of two Federal corps for six hours. Some 24,000 Confederates faced 19,000 Federals along a three-mile crescent west and north of Gettysburg.

Lee was not happy with the way the battle was unfolding. He told his staff that he did not want a battle until Longstreet was present, and that would not be until evening. But even as Lee pored over his maps the situation changed. Elements of Ewell's corps began arriving from the direction of Harrisburg in accordance with Lee's earlier orders to pull back. The unplanned result of Ewell's arrival was the establishment of Confederate battle lines north and west of Gettysburg, with the Federals between.

Lee felt that Ewell's arrival offered an opportunity. He ordered an attack, and watched as Hill's and Ewell's men drove the enemy with the élan that had become the hallmark of the Army of Northern Virginia. Howard's Federal corps—the "Flying Dutchmen" of Chancellorsville—retreated precipitously through Gettysburg to Cemetery Hill, immediately south of the town. The streets were choked with blue-clad soldiers. Milling refugees, intent only on escape, crowded the road to Baltimore.

Another Chancellorsville appeared to be in the making. But Lee still had no idea of what forces he faced, and the enemy held Cemetery Hill south of the town. Lee dispatched aide Walter Taylor to tell Ewell to press ahead and to seize Cemetery Hill "if practicable"—a fatal qualifier. Generations of historians have pointed out that whereas Jackson would have acted immediately and vigorously, Ewell did not act at all. Uncertain about what lay behind Cemetery Hill, and influenced by cautionary advice from Jubal Early as well as by Lee's discretionary orders, Ewell busied himself processing Federal prisoners. Lee also was hesitant, and did not commit Hill to support Ewell.

Night fell, and Cemetery Hill was no longer vulnerable. One of Ewell's officers later recalled how the sound of axes "rang out clearly on the night air, and bespoke the preparations the enemy were making for the morrow."[1] After the war, Gen. Winfield S. Hancock, whose Federal corps arrived at Cemetery Hill late on the first day, maintained that if the Confederates had continued their pursuit of Howard's disorganized command they would have captured Cemetery Hill easily.[2]

Lee, meanwhile, had pitched his headquarters tents in a field near the Cashtown road, on the west side of Seminary Ridge. When Longstreet arrived in late afternoon Lee was at the summit of the ridge studying the terrain through his field glasses. Longstreet, too, surveyed the scene and did not like the prospect of a frontal attack. He remarked to Lee that they had the Federals exactly where they wanted them—the Confederates had only to move around the enemy left and find a good defensive position between the Federals and Washington. Lee did not like the idea; probably his face flushed and his head jerked, signals that his staff had come to recognize as irritation. "If the enemy is there, we must attack him," Lee replied. "If he is there," Longstreet claimed to have responded, "it will be because he is anxious that we should attack him—a good reason, in my judgment, for not doing so."[3] Longstreet, as a veteran corps commander, was within his rights to question Lee's plans at this stage. As yet, Lee had issued no orders.

A number of observers would later recall that Lee was not his usual, confident self during the three days of Gettysburg. A Prussian officer who accompanied the army at both Chancellorsville and Gettysburg wrote later that in contrast to Chancellorsville, where Lee had been a model of self-possession, at Gettysburg he was not at his ease, "but riding to and fro, frequently changing his position, making anxious inquiries here and there, and looking care-worn."[4]

Much of Lee's anxiety concerned Stuart. After eating supper on July 1, Lee took action that bordered on the incongruous—he initiated a search for his cavalry, ordering a Maryland officer, James D. Watters, to send riders in various directions with orders for Stuart. They were to find him at all hazards, and order him to join the army at Gettysburg immediately. It was well that Lee acted as he did because on the afternoon of July 1, Stuart, encumbered by a captured wagon train, was thirty miles north of Gettysburg at Carlisle, demanding the surrender of the town. His demand was refused, and Stuart was preparing to shell the Federal garrison when one of Lee's messengers arrived. Stuart turned his weary troopers south.

Meanwhile, Lee waited with growing impatience for the sound of Ewell's guns in front of Cemetery Hill. Finally, at dusk, he rode to Ewell's headquarters in the town. There was no longer any question of an attack—the light was failing and it was evident that the Federals were fortifying Cemetery Hill—but Lee needed to check on morale at Second Corps headquarters. Two of Ewell's division commanders, Jubal Early and Robert Rodes, were with him at his headquarters at the Blocher house. After the exchange of amenities that marked even the most urgent Confederate councils, Lee listened to Ewell's explanation as to why he had not attacked that afternoon, then asked if he was prepared to attack in the morning.

Some authors have contended that the once pugnacious Ewell was almost paralyzed with his new responsibilities, deferring repeatedly to Early, who was unenthusiastic about any frontal assault but who thought that the southern end of Cemetery Hill might be turned. When Lee asked bluntly whether the Second Corps could attack Cemetery Hill, Early shook his head: The ground was steep and rough, the streets of the town would impede the formation of a battle line, and the hill was now heavily defended.

Lee, who could sense Ewell's irresolution, found the conference disturbing. Nor was Lee himself especially confident. Remarking on the extended Confederate lines—his army manned a front more than five miles long—Lee asked whether the Second Corps should not move to the Confederate right. Early thought not. He did not wish to give up the ground won that day, much less the arms that had been captured.[5] Lee changed the subject, saying that he was thinking of sending Longstreet against the Federal left the next morning and suggesting that Ewell demonstrate in support. Perhaps the demonstration could even be turned into a general attack. Ewell and his division commanders agreed to this proposal—a demonstration that would be expanded into a general attack "if practical."[6]

In his report on Gettysburg, Lee explained the motives that prompted him to continue the battle that had developed so unexpectedly:

> I had not intended to deliver a general battle so far from
> our base unless attacked, but coming unexpectedly upon the
> whole Federal Army, to withdraw through the mountains
> with our extensive trains would have been difficult and dan-
> gerous. At the same time we were unable to await an attack,
> as the country was unfavorable for collecting supplies in the
> presence of the enemy.[7]

The signs were mixed. On one hand, the Confederates had won a clear-cut victory on July 1, clearing the Federals from the town and capturing more than 5,000 prisoners. On the other hand, Lee knew little of the enemy's dispositions and had no cavalry to discover them. Still more disquieting, he was working through two untried corps commanders, and a third who had no confidence in Lee's plans.

Late that night, when Lee lay down for a few hours of sleep, his last thoughts were of Stuart. Thinking out loud, he asked Armistead Long if it would be wise to attack without Stuart. Would the absence of cavalry deny the Confederates the fruits of a victory? Long responded that, considering the uncertainty as to Stuart's whereabouts, it would be better to go ahead without him.[8]

⋯⋙ ⋘⋯

LEE ROSE AND BREAKFASTED BEFORE DAYLIGHT ON JULY 2, then made his way to a cleared area on Seminary Ridge. The first rays of the sun showed the ridge sloping down to the Emmitsburg Road. About a mile and a half to the south he could discern two rocky protuberances, known locally as Big Round Top and Little Round Top. Here and there he could see scattered groups of soldiers in blue, but no signs of an enemy concentration.

The terrain around Gettysburg has long been described in terms of an inverted fishhook south of the town. Gettysburg itself lay directly in front of Lee, the curve of the fishhook immediately to his right. Cemetery Hill and Culp's Hill, southeast of the town, formed the barb of the hook. Its shaft ran north and south along Cemetery Ridge, between the Emmitsburg and Taneytown Roads. At the end of the shaft, in front of the Round Tops, was a rocky formation soon to be known as Devil's Den. The entire "fishhook," from barb to Devil's Den, extended about four miles.

Although the sun had risen, Lee had not yet issued orders for the day. He had some time, in part because Longstreet's corps was not yet in position. Hood's division had marched much of the night, reaching Gettysburg only at dawn. But Lee sought to retain the initiative. He sent one of his aides, Charles Venable, to see whether Ewell would commit himself to a full-scale attack rather than the demonstration agreed on the previous evening. Lee also ordered a reconnaissance. Capt. Samuel R. Johnston, one of Lee's engineers, led a small party through the Federal pickets to explore the ground between Seminary and Cemetery Ridges, working his way as far as Little Round Top. The Federals were even then in the process of moving a corps into line south of Cemetery Ridge, but from Little Round Top Johnston could see no concentrations of enemy troops.[9] His report, delivered to Lee about nine o'clock, suggested that Federal lines across from Longstreet were not strongly manned.

By this time Lee had decided on his plan of attack, one based on Johnston's outdated intelligence. Longstreet's corps—minus Pickett's Virginians, who were not yet available—was to drive in the enemy left. Hill was to threaten the Yankee center so as to prevent reinforcement of the enemy left. Ewell was to demonstrate against the enemy right, moving at the sound of Longstreet's artillery. In part because his and Longstreet's headquarters were close to each other, and in part, perhaps, because of concern about Longstreet's attitude, Lee involved himself in First Corps dispositions. Sitting on a log and holding a map, he showed Gen. Lafayette McLaws how he wished his division aligned relative to the Emmitsburg Road. Longstreet then joined the conversation, tracing a line on Lee's map parallel to the road and telling McLaws, "I wish your division placed so." "No, General," Lee responded, "I wish it placed perpendicular to that."[10] Lee then rode off to consult with Ewell, leaving Longstreet to get his two divisions into line.

The controversy, now in its second century, regarding Longstreet's performance at Gettysburg stems not from the placement of McLaws's division but from how Longstreet occupied himself for the next few hours. Lee's orders may have given him some discretion, but the army commander had made clear that he expected an attack on the Federal left that morning. In midmorning Lee listened for the sound of Confederate artillery, asking aides, "What can detain Longstreet? He ought to be in position by now."[11] Longstreet understood what Lee wanted and should have begun getting his corps into position immediately; instead he delayed, ostensibly for Law's brigade and Pickett's division to come up, but perhaps in the hope that Lee would reconsider.

Returning to Seminary Ridge about eleven o'clock, Lee gave Longstreet a direct order to attack. Preparations for the attack took an additional five hours. Longstreet first asked for time for his rear-most brigade to come up. Lee reluctantly assented and Longstreet began to bring his divisions into position. He wanted their movements to be out of sight of the enemy, and Hood's and McLaws's divisions marched and countermarched in the heat and the dust before finding a route that afforded concealment. Not until about three o'clock were Longstreet's troops in their assigned positions.

Meanwhile, the enemy front had changed in important respects. The commander of the Federal Third Corps, Gen. Daniel Sickles, had been unhappy with the poor cover available on the southern end of Cemetery Ridge and had moved his two divisions a half-mile forward toward the Emmitsburg Road. Although Sickles had made his move without orders and his corps was now vulnerable on both flanks, the move disrupted Confederate battle plans. Should the Sickles salient be attacked or outflanked? What attention should be given to the Round Tops, which scouts reported to be still unoccupied?

Lee had ordered Longstreet to attack at an angle from the Emmitsburg Road to the enemy flank on Cemetery Ridge. By the time Longstreet was ready, however, Cemetery Ridge was defended in strength, the enemy flank was farther south, and for Longstreet to attack at the angle Lee had specified would expose him to enfilading fire. One of his division commanders, McLaws, noted later that the Federal front was one "certainly not contemplated when the original battle order was given." He believed that if Lee had known of the changed conditions he would have called off the attack.[12]

But the attack was on. Confederate artillery opened up at four o'clock, bringing the soon-to-be-legendary Peach Orchard under fire. The infantry assault was delivered with all the fury for which Lee's veterans were famed. Hood's division, shrilling the rebel yell, crushed the left flank of Sickles's corps in the Peach Orchard and fought through Devil's Den to Little Round Top. Longstreet, for reasons that remain unclear, waited for more than an hour to send McLaws in behind Hood, and that delay took some of the impact out of the Confederate charge.

For three hours Cemetery Ridge was the scene of some of the fiercest fighting in the war. A regiment of Alabamians attempted to capture Little Round Top, still unoccupied at about five o'clock. Had the Confederates seized the hill and brought up artillery they might have made the Federal line untenable. But Meade's chief of engineers, Gen. Gouverneur K. Warren, recognized the danger in time to send a brigade that included Col. Joshua Chamberlain's Twentieth Maine to throw back the Confederate assault. Little Round Top was secure and the Federal line on Cemetery Ridge intact. Elsewhere, McLaws's division pushed the Federals out of the Peach Orchard and back to Cemetery Ridge, and elements from Hill's corps managed to break through the enemy center, but they could not hold the ground won.

A Federal outpost on Little Round Top at Gettysburg. LIBRARY OF CONGRESS.

Lee followed the afternoon's action from his command post on Seminary Ridge. He conferred with Hill, but asked relatively little of Hill's corps. To Lee's left, the movement of Federal defenders from the area of Cemetery Hill to meet Longstreet's assault gave Ewell the opportunity that Lee had hoped for, but Ewell seemed unable to act. Far from attacking at the sound of Longstreet's guns, as instructed, "Old Bald Head" had done nothing more than send out patrols and engage the enemy artillery. At about seven o'clock, Ewell sent Early's division against Cemetery Hill, but the attack was badly coordinated and Early was thrown back. Not only was Ewell unable to capture Cemetery Hill but the delay in launching his attack had allowed Meade to devote his full attention to Longstreet.

Altogether, the Army of Northern Virginia had turned in a poor performance. In a day of uncoordinated assaults, it had been unable to exploit such successes as it gained. The fault was at the top. Of Lee's three corps commanders, Longstreet was disgruntled, Ewell was inept, and Hill was unwell. Lee himself seemed much less disposed to assert control than at Antietam and Chancellorsville; even Freeman would write that on July 2 "the Army of Northern Virginia was without a commander."[13]

The one positive development for Lee was the arrival, after the second day's fighting, of Stuart and his three cavalry brigades. There are two versions of what took place between Lee and Stuart. The accepted version of their meeting at Lee's tent has the commanding general greeting his protégé with the cool remark, "Well, General Stuart, you are here at last."[14] Coming from Lee, this was a stern rebuke. Other accounts suggest that Stuart received a severe dressing down in the privacy of Lee's headquarters tent. In his official report Lee would allude to Stuart with but a single pejorative sentence: "The movements of the army preceding the Battle of Gettysburg had been much embarrassed by the absence of the cavalry."[15]

EARLY ON THE MORNING OF JULY 3, LEE SOUGHT OUT Longstreet. They had scarcely exchanged greetings when the Georgian resumed a familiar refrain: He had sent out scouts during the night, and the information they had brought him confirmed the feasibility of a move to the right of the Federal army that would force Meade to attack. The sun had scarcely risen, and already Lee's patience was being tried. "No," Lee told his corps commander, "I am going to take them where they are." He went on to say that he wanted Pickett's fresh division to spearhead the attack, but that Pickett would be supported by Heth's and Pender's divisions from the Third Corps. After the war Longstreet reconstructed his response:

> "That will give me fifteen thousand men," I replied. "I have been a soldier, I may say, from the ranks up to the position I now hold. I have been in pretty much all kinds of skirmishes . . . and I think I can safely say there never was a body of fifteen thousand men who could make that attack successfully."
> The general seemed a little impatient at my remarks, so I said nothing more.[16]

Lee spent most of the morning with Longstreet and Hill arranging the details of the attack. As on the day before, the target was Cemetery Ridge, but this time at a point closer to the Federal center. Lee designated a clump of trees near the crest of Cemetery Ridge as an aiming point for the attack which, if successful, would split the enemy line.

Once again Lee ordered Longstreet to attack, and once again Longstreet required hours to prepare. The delay was significant because Ewell had been ordered to attack that morning in conjunction with Longstreet. In the confusion, a key element of Lee's order—that Ewell's attack be coordinated with the main thrust against Cemetery Ridge—was somehow ignored. Gen. Edward "Allegheny" Johnson attacked Culp's Hill at dawn, but the assault by his division was spent well before Longstreet was prepared to move.

About noon, Lee mounted Traveller and rode along the western edge of Seminary Ridge to a hollow where Pickett's Virginians were already suffering from the heat. The men were under orders not to cheer, but as Lee passed by they silently raised their caps and Lee nodded in acknowledgment. An hour later he was back at his command post.

Shortly after one o'clock Longstreet's artillery commander, Porter Alexander, began the greatest artillery bombardment of the war. Alexander had more than 150 guns, but he knew that the enemy had at least as many and he was worried about his own ammunition supply. For nearly two hours an artillery duel involving some 300 guns shook the Pennsylvania countryside. Along the Federal front, men and horses were killed and some guns disabled. Unfortunately for the Confederates, however, their aim tended to be high, and the enemy infantry on Cemetery Ridge was largely protected by stone walls and impromptu breastworks.

Shortly after two o'clock, Alexander, running short of ammunition, sent a note to Pickett that he must move quickly. The message reached Pickett when he was in conversation with Longstreet. Pickett, eager for action, passed the note to Longstreet and asked whether he should advance. Later, Pickett would write that he had never seen his corps commander so troubled. Longstreet turned away and nodded. Pickett saluted and sprang to his horse.[17]

The story of Pickett's Charge has been told so frequently and in such detail that it need hardly be recapitulated here. Pickett's brigade moved out with parade-ground precision and was joined in a separate advance by six brigades from Hill's corps. The Confederates advanced across open ground in the face of a withering fire, yet for the briefest of moments they gained a toehold near the clump of trees designated by Lee. Valor was not enough, however, and the handful of Confederates who reached the Federal lines either became casualties or turned back.

Of the 14,000 Confederates who went forward, about half returned. Three brigadier generals and thirteen colonels were killed or wounded in Pickett's Charge.

Lee observed the action from Seminary Ridge. About the time the attack stalled he joined Longstreet and Alexander, watching the broken regiments as they streamed back to the Confederate lines. He had words of comfort for the distraught Pickett: "Come, General Pickett, this has been my fight and upon my shoulders rests the blame." He rode among the units, re-forming one, encouraging another. "This is all my fault," Lee told one brigadier. "It is I who have lost this fight and you must help me out of it the best way you can." [18]

In the space of an hour, Lee's hoped-for victory had turned into disaster, his first defeat since Malvern Hill. Lee's initial response was to prepare for an attack from Meade, but the Federal commander was not disposed to follow up his victory. The Army of Northern Virginia was free to retreat, something it had rarely done before.

⊷⟞⊙ ⊙⟝⊶

THE BATTLE OF WATERLOO AND THE BATTLE OF GETTYS-burg are the two most thoroughly analyzed engagements in military history. The former marked the end of the age of Napoleon in Europe; the latter is widely seen as the high-water mark of the Confederacy in the American Civil War. Played out over three days in Pennsylvania, the Battle of Gettysburg, like Waterloo, was the setting for more than the usual number of heroics, missed opportunities, and decisions made under the greatest pressure.

In terms of strategy, Lee's plan for a second invasion of the North is difficult to judge. Recent scholarship suggests that not even a Confederate victory at Gettysburg would have assured foreign intervention on behalf of the South; Britain recognized that Canada was highly vulnerable if Britain were to antagonize the Lincoln government. As for Northern morale, Lee could not remain in Pennsylvania indefinitely, and his withdrawal to Virginia even after a victory would have been interpreted in the North as a Federal triumph. These historical judgments were not available to Lee in 1863, however, and his hopes for the Pennsylvania campaign—that it would take some pressure off the Confederacy in the West and hold out the prospect of a decisive battle—were not unreasonable.

Stuart's absence got Lee off to a bad start. Some senior Confederates wanted to court-martial the dashing cavalryman for ignoring his intelligence responsibilities, but Lee, though chagrined by defeat, would have no part of this. Lee's orders had been so general that no reasonable person could accuse Stuart of disobedience; what had been lacking was the cavalryman's usually keen judgment. The conventional wisdom is that Stuart was still smarting from the surprise at Brandy Station and eager to pull off a daring raid to silence his critics. Whatever Stuart's thinking, his absence effectively blinded Lee, who was slow to bring up the two cavalry brigades that he had left behind in the Shenandoah Valley.

Lee had a right to expect better of Stuart, but he made errors of his own. His first was to expect Ewell to perform like Jackson. Lee knew Ewell well, regarding him as a brave and effective division commander. But Lee had indicated to intimates that he recognized a certain indecisiveness in Ewell, a serious handicap in corps command. Lee may not have wanted to go outside his own army for a successor to Jackson, and he may have felt that the Second Corps would be best led by one of Jackson's lieutenants. Given his options, Lee's error was not in promoting Ewell but in failing to supervise him closely. Ewell was a product of Jackson's style of command, in which orders were carried out exactly as given, not of Lee's style, in which corps commanders were encouraged to use judgment and initiative. If Lee considered it essential for Ewell to capture Cemetery Hill on the first day, he should have provided detailed, imperative orders, or even have commanded in person.

Lee was misled by the Confederate success on the first day. His rout of two Federal corps on July 1 encouraged overconfidence. Would the Army of Northern Virginia not deliver anything that was asked of it? The result of this mind-set was two days of poorly coordinated frontal attacks against the best defensive position the Army of Northern Virginia had faced since Malvern Hill. Even if the timing of Confederate attacks on the second and third days had been perfect, which it was not, there was no element of surprise as there had been at Second Manassas and Chancellorsville.

Lee can be excused for continuing the fight at Gettysburg, even in the absence of good intelligence, because the first day had gone so easily. But his failure to adjust his remote command style to the fact that two of his three corps commanders were new to their jobs is less defensible.

In Churchill's phrase, the terrible *Ifs* accumulate. If Stuart had not been embarrassed at Brandy Station, he would have paid more attention to his reconnaissance responsibilities. If Ewell had attacked and captured Cemetery Hill, the Federal line might have become untenable. If Johnston's July 2 reconnaissance had been undertaken an hour later, Lee would have gained an accurate appreciation of Meade's strength. And if Jackson had been present . . .

What about Longstreet's performance? There is little doubt that he behaved badly in delaying his attack on the second day, and then in committing his divisions piecemeal. However deplorable his attitude and dilatory movements, it is not clear that they determined the outcome of the fighting on the second day. Indeed, had he attacked in the morning or early afternoon, he would probably have encountered a more formidable enemy line than at four o'clock, because it was only about three o'clock that Sickles moved his corps into an exposed position in the Peach Orchard.

Any discussion of Longstreet at Gettysburg must acknowledge that he was correct in advising Lee against what became Pickett's Charge. Had Lee broken off the battle after the second day, he would have spared his army some 7,000 casualties and could have claimed a drawn battle. However, Longstreet's suggested alternative—a flanking move around the Federal left—was so unpromising that Lee's dismissal of it is understandable. For Lee to have uncoiled his five-mile line, and moved it south, would have been possible only if the Federals had been too timid to strike the Confederates while they were moving. And even if Lee had "stolen" a march on Meade, he could not simply have found a defensive position and awaited attack. The provisioning of his army, as well as the safety of Richmond, depended on movement. If Lee had simply hunkered down in Pennsylvania, in the hope of inviting attack, he would have handed the initiative to the enemy.

Gettysburg was Robert E. Lee's worst battle. It is so judged not only because of the faulty decisions made by Lee himself, but also because he failed to compensate for the loss of Stonewall Jackson. The circumstances of the Army of Northern Virginia had changed, but Lee's style of command had not.

Lee offered no apology for the defeat at Gettysburg; it was not his nature to do so. His earliest recorded comment on the battle was to one of the foreign observers with the Army of Northern Virginia, whom Lee told that he would never have attacked had he realized that

Meade's entire army was on the scene. But Lee's success on July 1 had led him to believe that he was facing only a portion of Meade's army.[19]

Lee's most detailed discussion of what went wrong may have been in a conversation after the war with Col. William Allan, a one-time Confederate officer who interviewed him in Lexington in 1868. Allan's notes of Lee's comments relative to Gettysburg read as follows:

> [Lee] did not know the Federal army was at Gettysburg, *could not believe it*, as Stuart had been specifically ordered to cover his (Lee's) movement & keep him informed of the position of the enemy, & he (Stuart) had sent no word. He found himself engaged with the Federal army therefore, unexpectedly, and had to fight. This being determined on, victory wd. have been won if he could have gotten one decided simultaneous attack on the whole line. This he tried his utmost to effect for three days and failed.[20]

By the time of this interview Lee could speak dispassionately of lost opportunities in Pennsylvania. At the time, however, defeat was hard to bear. On the evening of July 3, Lee rode over to one of his cavalry commanders, Gen. John D. Imboden, to discuss the forthcoming retreat. Imboden thought Lee "almost too tired to dismount." When he alighted "the moon shone upon his massive features and revealed an expression of sadness" that Imboden had never seen before. "General," Imboden ventured, "this has been a hard day on you." Lee nodded; indeed it had been a sad, sad day:

> Being unwilling again to intrude upon his reflections, I said no more. After perhaps a minute or two, he suddenly straightened up to his full height, and turning to me with more animation . . . than I had ever seen in him before . . . he said in a voice tremulous with emotion:
>
> "I never saw troops behave more magnificently than Pickett's division of Virginians did today in that grand charge upon the enemy. And if they had been supported as they were to have been—but, for some reason not yet fully explained to me, were not—we would have held the position and the day would have been ours." After a moment's pause he added in a loud voice, in a tone almost of agony, "Too bad! *Too bad! OH TOO BAD!*"[21]

CHAPTER FOURTEEN

A MILITARY
SACRAMENT

IN THE DAYS AFTER GETTYSBURG, THE ARMY OF Northern Virginia retreated through driving rain to the Potomac and across it to Virginia. The groans of the wounded in makeshift ambulances made it seem that the entire army was in pain. In its reports the army acknowledged 2,600 killed, 12,700 wounded, and 5,200 captured or missing, for a total of 20,500. Because of a rash of postbattle deaths and desertion, actual Confederate losses for the campaign were considerably higher, perhaps as high as 28,000.[1] Approximately one-third of Lee's army had become casualties in Pennsylvania.

Meade, in cautious pursuit, demonstrated no zeal for renewed battle. Although the Federals held a hard-won field at Gettysburg, the victors were only slightly better off than the vanquished. Federal losses—a total of 23,000, or one-quarter of Meade's strength—approached those of the Confederates. The Federal commander seemed astonished at his own victory. When a cavalry officer urged a vigorous pursuit of the rebels, Meade responded that the army had done well enough.

News of Lee's defeat sent a shock through Richmond, in part because it was unexpected. The first rumors were of a great Confederate victory. Secretary of War Seddon heard that Lee was driving the enemy toward

Baltimore, and passed the good news to President Davis. A Richmond paper sold a run of extras by claiming that Lee had routed the enemy at Gettysburg, taking 40,000 prisoners. Enthusiasm gradually gave way to doubt, and doubt evolved into shocked surprise. A letter from Lee to Davis on July 7 acknowledged "the unsuccessful issue of our final attack" at Gettysburg and left Confederate partisans to ponder the implications of twin disasters, for Vicksburg had surrendered to Grant on July 4.

The reaction in Lee's army to defeat was one of pain and bewilderment. One group of artillerymen assured the British observer, Colonel Arthur Freemantle, that all would be well: "'Uncle Robert' will get us into Washington yet; you bet he will!"[2] Others were less certain. A Maryland soldier wrote in his diary that he had gone to Gettysburg confident of victory "and that God would certainly declare himself on our side. *Now* I feel that unless He sees fit to bless our arms, our valor will not avail." One of Lee's brigadiers, Gen. Stephen D. Ramseur, was perplexed and shaken. "Our great campaign," he wrote home after the battle, "admirably planned & more admirably executed up to the fatal days at Gettysburg, has failed." Although insisting that the setback in Pennsylvania did not mean defeat, Ramseur anticipated a series of crises before the Confederacy could gain its independence.[3]

Morale among Lee's soldiers quickly rebounded, however, and the loss of Vicksburg probably damaged Southern confidence more than the defeat at Gettysburg. Lee himself treated Gettysburg as a setback but not a disaster. The mask that had slipped ever so briefly in his impassioned remarks to Imboden was quickly back in place; in official dispatches Lee spoke of objectives only partially achieved, of valor insufficiently rewarded. He wrote to Mary that she will have learned that Confederate success at Gettysburg was not so great as first reported. He remained confident that "our merciful God, our only help & refuge, will not desert us in this our hour of need, but will deliver us by His mighty hand."[4]

A formal report on the battle was mandatory, and Lee provided it on July 31. He wrote to Davis:

> No blame can be attached to the army for its failure to accomplish what was projected by me, nor should it be censured for the unreasonable expectations of the public. I am alone to blame, in perhaps expecting too much of its

prowess & valour. It, however, in my opinion achieved under the Most High a general success, though it did not win a victory.[5]

Here Lee himself appears to have been in denial. No other Confederate in a position of responsibility appears to have regarded Gettysburg as other than an unmitigated defeat.

Lee had no words of criticism for Stuart, Ewell, or Longstreet. The irrepressible Stuart passed through Martinsburg on the retreat with a large cavalcade of staff and couriers "and two bugles blowing furiously."[6] Lee and Longstreet consulted daily, and onlookers could discern no tension between them. When Pickett submitted an official report that was harshly critical of the failure of other units to support his July 3 charge, Lee ordered the report suppressed. But Lee himself could be testy about Gettysburg. During the winter of 1863–64, Henry Heth, who knew his commander well, mentioned to Lee some of the mistakes in that campaign. "After it is all over," Lee responded, "as stupid a fellow as I am can see the mistakes that were made. I notice, however, my mistakes are never told me until it is too late, and you, and all my officers, know that I am always ready and anxious to have their suggestions."[7]

If the Army of the Potomac was numbed by its victory, the North as a whole was exultant. The coincidence of two great victories near Independence Day inspired scores of editorials and sermons. A thoughtful New York City diarist, George Templeton Strong, called the victory at Gettysburg "priceless," in part because "the charm of Robert Lee's invincibility is broken."[8]

Lee's real enemy had long been the willingness of the North to wage war for a constitutional principle. Even after Gettysburg, however, there were signs of disaffection in the North that Lee found encouraging. Only a week after the battle, resentment against the draft exploded into violent riots in New York City. Conscription offices went up in flames, and blacks were attacked by Irishmen who perceived free blacks as an economic threat and a cause of the war. Confederates exulted at the news; John B. Jones, the perceptive Richmond clerk who kept a diary throughout the war, wrote of "*awful* good news from New York: an INSURRECTION . . . with a suspension of conscription."[9]

Order was restored, conscription resumed, and the war went on.

Secretary of State Seward, worried that Europeans might be unduly influenced by the recent unrest, promoted a trip by the diplomatic corps intended to impress them with the North's vast resources. Traveling across New York State, the diplomats could not help noting the signs of a booming economy, with factories and mills seemingly operating at capacity. In contrast to the beleaguered South, which some diplomats had visited, there were few signs of war in upstate New York.

In June, Napoleon III had hinted to Confederate emissaries that France was prepared to press Britain for joint action to recognize the Confederacy. Encouraged by this, the Confederates arranged for a friendly member of Parliament, John Roebuck, to introduce a motion that Britain should begin talks with the European powers aimed at recognition of Confederate independence. Roebuck's motion gained little support in the ensuing debate, in part because everyone wanted to see how Lee's invasion of Pennsylvania would turn out. Word of Gettysburg reached London on July 16, followed immediately by reports of Vicksburg's surrender. Confederate bonds tumbled and there was no more talk of diplomatic recognition.[10]

Meanwhile, in his camp near Culpeper, Lee dealt with family problems. A few days before Gettysburg, Federal raiders had reached Hickory Hill, the estate north of Richmond where Rooney Lee was recovering from the wound received at Brandy Station. The younger Lee was captured and moved to Fortress Monroe. Other such prisoners might expect a period of convalescence followed by exchange, but Rooney Lee was not an ordinary prisoner. In July, Confederate authorities, angered by alleged enemy atrocities in Kentucky, threatened to hang two Federal officers then in Libby Prison. The Federals responded that if these executions were carried out, Rooney Lee would be hanged in retaliation. Both sides backed down, but young Lee would spend eight months in prison before being exchanged in 1864.[11]

Although Rooney's welfare was Lee's most immediate domestic concern, his wife was never far from his mind. Mary was living in a rented house in Richmond with two of their daughters, Agnes and Mary. She suffered acutely from arthritis, but as the wife of General Lee she had many privileges, including the use of a private railroad car for travel to mountain spas where the waters provided a degree of relief. When, in March 1863, Mary complained to Lee of his irregular correspondence, he chided her gently, "You forget how much writing, talking & thinking

I have to do." Although he was often unable to write, "my thoughts are always with you." [12]

Mary Lee appears to have taken some of her husband's admonitions to heart. In December 1863 she moved into more comfortable accommodations on East Franklin Street. But instead of holding court there, as she might easily have done, Mary and her daughters set an example in making clothes for the army. Diarist Mary Chesnut, after a call at the Lee residence, was impressed with the work going on there. "What a rebuke to the taffy parties!" [13]

Meanwhile, Lee sought to restore his army to something approaching its prowess prior to Gettysburg. The army's numbers began a slow climb, as some of those wounded in Pennsylvania returned to their units and prisoners were exchanged. Conscripts who had previously evaded service were absorbed into the ranks, though many of these deserted at the first opportunity. With Lee's approval Davis issued a proclamation offering pardons to deserters who returned within a twenty-day period, but the offer had the unintended effect of encouraging new unauthorized absences by soldiers long separated from their families.

Lee addressed the problem of diet by turning some units to farming. He dealt with the desertion problem by instituting a system of furloughs. Having done so, he urged President Davis to take a hard line with respect to future instances of desertion. "Nothing will remedy this great evil . . . except the rigid enforcement of the death penalty in future cases of conviction." [14]

Lee was hard on deserters, but he was also hard on himself. He heard, from various sources, the carping in Richmond about the Gettysburg campaign. Although he did not seek the role of scapegoat, he wrote to Davis on August 8 offering his resignation:

> I have seen and heard of expression of discontent in the public journals at the result of the [Gettysburg] expedition. I do not know how far this feeling extends in the army. My brother officers have been too kind to report it, and so far the troops have been too generous to exhibit it. It is fair, however, to suppose that it does exist, and . . . I therefore, in all sincerity, request Your Excellency to take measures to supply my place.

Thus far, there is a pro forma quality to Lee's offer of resignation. Did he really expect Davis to remove the victor of the Seven Days, Second

Manassas, and Chancellorsville? But Lee went on to discuss his health in a way that suggests he genuinely felt a diminished capacity for field command, and there was nothing pro forma about his self-criticism:

> I sensibly feel the growing failure of my bodily strength. I have not yet recovered from the attack I experienced the past spring. I am becoming more and more incapable of exertion, and am thus prevented from making the personal examinations and giving the personal supervision to the operations in the field which I feel to be necessary.[15]

Lee may have concluded privately that a more vigorous commander at Gettysburg would have supervised Ewell more closely on the first day, and would have made a personal reconnaissance on the third day that might have brought victory.

Lee's letter prompted the warmest possible reply from Jefferson Davis. The president assured Lee that he, too, had been obliged to bear "the criticisms of the ignorant." Such critics apart, the people will demonstrate the fortitude "needful to secure ultimate success." He then articulated the obvious:

> But suppose, my dear friend, that I were to admit, with all their implications, the points which you present, where am I to find that new commander who is to possess the greater ability which you believe is required? . . . To ask me to sub-stitute you by someone in my judgment more fit to com-mand, or who would possess more of the confidence of the army, or of the reflecting men of the country, is to demand an impossibility.[16]

Lee had wanted to clear the air, and his exchange of letters with Davis did so. Even after Gettysburg, the president's confidence in Lee was unshakable. His position secure, Lee considered how to regain the initiative in the field. "As soon as I can get the vacancies in the army filled," he wrote back, "and the horses and men [restored] a little, if General Meade does not move, I wish to attack him."[17]

But Davis had other priorities. In late August he called Lee to Richmond, where he found the president's office heavy with gloom. Charleston was under siege by the Federal navy, and Beauregard was sending alarmist reports. The surrender of Vicksburg had effectively cut the Confederacy in two. An army under Gen. William S. Rose-crans was threatening Chattanooga, loss of which would allow the

Federals into Atlanta and the Confederate Southeast. Commanding the Western Department was Gen. Braxton Bragg, a favorite of President Davis but a man who enjoyed little respect from his generals.

What could be done to avert disaster in Tennessee? Davis could offer no solution to his problems in the West other than to transfer troops from Lee's army in numbers sufficient to allow Bragg to go on the offensive. Longstreet had favored such a move, and saw himself as a logical successor to Bragg. Davis hoped that Lee himself would accept the command in the West and take some of his army with him. Lee spent the last week of August "in the hot & badly ventilated rooms in the various departments"; he was prepared for a decision that would separate him from the Army of Northern Virginia, and he feared the worst.

As the days passed, Lee gradually began to score some points in conference. He knew nothing about the Army of the Tennessee, he insisted, and the Federals in Virginia were unlikely to allow the good autumn weather to pass without making some move. Lee suggested, by implication, that no good would result from his taking command in the West. Davis finally decided that Lee should stay in Virginia, but that Longstreet, with his First Corps, would go to Tennessee to reinforce Bragg. Grateful that he would not be leaving the Army of Northern Virginia, Lee wrote Davis, "I did not intend to decline the service [in Tennessee] if desired that I should undertake it, but merely to express the opinion that the duty could be better performed by the officers already in that department." [18] Implicit in Lee's position was his belief that although the West might cost the Confederacy the war over time, defeat in Virginia could end the war in an afternoon.

Lee returned to Orange Courthouse on September 7 to see Longstreet off for Tennessee. His movement would be on a roundabout route on ramshackle railroads, but it was a reminder that the South retained the advantage of interior lines. With Longstreet gone, Lee had no alternative but to assume the defensive along the Rapidan River. Nevertheless, on hearing that the Federals had weakened Meade's army by sending two corps west, Lee sought a means to take the initiative. On October 9 he sent Hill's and Ewell's corps around Meade's right flank to threaten Washington and force Meade to abandon his field fortifications. This maneuver was reminiscent of the Second Manassas campaign, and for a time it held considerable promise. Meade withdrew toward Washington, and Lee pursued him to Culpeper, to Warrenton, and then to Centreville. Meade had great respect for his opponent, and not until October 14, as Meade's rear guard withdrew from Bristoe Station, did a portion of the Federal army appear vulnerable. Lee told Hill to attack.

Hill saw Federal soldiers crossing a small stream and ordered Heth to strike. Hill acted without taking time for a reconnaissance, and not knowing that a Federal corps was concealed in a railway cut on the Confederate right. Suddenly, the attackers found themselves in an ambush. Heth's division suffered more than 1,300 casualties, and Lee's hopes for results like those of Second Manassas evaporated. The next morning Lee and Hill went over the battleground, where a chastened Hill took responsibility for the debacle. Lee heard him out in silence, then said, "Well, General, bury these poor men and let us say no more about it."[19]

The setback at Bristoe Station came only days after mixed news from Tennessee. On September 19, Bragg, with notable assistance from Longstreet's corps, defeated Rosecrans at Chickamauga. The Federals were allowed to retreat to Chattanooga, however, and Bragg's failure to pursue led his generals to revolt. On October 6 a careworn Jefferson Davis traveled by train from Richmond to Bragg's headquarters to try to make peace among his generals. It was a doomed mission. In Bragg's presence, his four corps commanders told Davis that Bragg must be replaced. The president had long resisted pressure to remove his old friend, and now he temporized. Bragg's logical successor was Joe Johnston, but Davis considered him partly responsible for the loss of Vicksburg. Bragg continued in command, his generals remained sullen, and Davis returned to Richmond.

In the last week of November, Federal troops under Ulysses S. Grant won a crushing victory over Bragg at Chattanooga. The Confederates retreated all the way to Dalton, Georgia, and once again Bragg asked to be relieved. This time Davis complied, although his respect for the acerbic Bragg was such that he soon brought him to Richmond in an advisory role.

The disaster at Chattanooga prompted a summons to Lee for another round of conferences on how best to stretch the Confederacy's waning resources. Lee disliked these conferences both because he disliked conferences and because they posed the threat of new transfers from the Army of Northern Virginia. Lee fully expected to be named to succeed Bragg, and he warned Stuart that he would be returning to

Culpeper only to gather his belongings. Whatever the future held, he wrote, "my heart and thoughts will always be with this army."[20]

Lee spent two weeks in Richmond and in the end was again able to prevent the president from sending him west. If Davis was not convinced that others could handle the assignment better than Lee, the president knew better than to tamper with the leadership of his most effective army. Lee at first suggested Beauregard as a successor to Bragg, but when he perceived that Davis was irrevocably opposed to Beauregard, Lee suggested Johnston, and the appointment went to him.

Did Davis and Lee discuss still more sensitive matters, including emancipation? Lee had spoken enough with Colonel Freemantle and other European observers to realize that the question of foreign recognition had been irrevocably bound to the slavery issue. Even more germane, the willingness of Yankee soldiers to fight in some instances grew out of their hostility toward slavery as the underlying cause of secession. Lee remarked after the war that he had told Davis often that emancipation was the only way "to remove a weakness at home and to get sympathy abroad . . . but Davis would not hear of it."[21]

THE WINTER OF 1963–64 WAS THE SECOND ONE IN SUCCESsion that the Army of Northern Virginia was so starved for supplies that Lee was obliged to send alarming entreaties to Richmond. At one point Davis authorized Lee to impress supplies from local residents, but Lee was unwilling to place an additional burden on people he was attempting to defend.

In late February a Federal cavalry raid caused a major furor in Richmond. Led by Col. Ulrich Dahlgren and launched with Lincoln's specific approval, the raid was designed to free Federal prisoners in two locations near the Confederate capital. Dahlgren's column reached the western outskirts of the city, but there it ran into unexpected resistance from local militia and turned north. Confederate pursuers caught up with the raiders, killing Dahlgren and dispersing his troopers.

The episode would have been quickly forgotten except for papers found on Dahlgren's body. His special orders included instructions that, once the prisoners were released, Richmond was to be destroyed and

Davis and members of his cabinet killed. When Davis released the documents to the Richmond press there were loud demands for reprisals. Lee wrote to Meade asking whether he endorsed assassination as a means of warfare, and Meade repudiated the documents. In Richmond there was talk of executing captured troopers from Dahlgren's force, but Lee would not countenance reprisals. He wrote Secretary of War Seddon that Dahlgren's troopers were probably unaware of his orders, and the matter was closed.

Lee devoted much of the winter of 1863–64 to attempting to feed and equip his army. It was an unrewarding task, in part because the commissary general, Col. Lucius Northrop, was a favorite of President Davis and largely immune from criticism. On January 22 Lee wrote Secretary Seddon that short rations were weakening his army physically and were contributing to the high desertion rate. "Unless there is a change," he wrote, "I fear the army cannot be kept together."[22] But Lee's concerns did not always find an attentive audience in Richmond. Within the government and elsewhere, Southerners were accustomed to good news from the Army of Northern Virginia. With no appreciation of the vastly superior resources available to the Federals, confidence in Lee remained boundless.

In early April, Longstreet was ordered to return east and rejoin the Army of Northern Virginia. His soldiers had not enjoyed their sojourn in Tennessee. After the barren victory at Chickamauga, the malaise that seemed to affect all Confederates in the West struck Longstreet's corps as well. Longstreet had quarreled with his division commanders, and a campaign to liberate Knoxville had failed in the winter mud. "What a slow old humbug is Longstreet," wrote Southern diarist Mary Chesnut. "Detached from General Lee, what a horrible failure."[23]

Having the First Corps back in Virginia pleased Robert E. Lee. Longstreet set up camp near Gordonsville, and Lee arranged to ride over to greet him on April 29. The result was one of those moments of sheer theater that helped create the Lee legend. Lee and his staff rode up a small knoll and halted near an oak grove. Longstreet's two divisions were drawn up in an open field in front of them. Lee doffed his hat, and the artillery thundered a salute. Past hardships forgotten, the soldiers cheered themselves hoarse. Porter Alexander wrote how "each man seemed to feel the bond which held us all to Lee. . . . The effect was that of a military sacrament."[24] A soldier recalled,

The men hung around [Lee] and seemed satisfied to lay hands on his gray horse or to touch the bridle or the stirrup, or the old general's leg—anything that Lee had was sacred to us fellows who had just come back. And the General—he could not help from breaking down . . . tears traced down his cheeks.[25]

A chaplain asked Lee's aide, Charles Venable, if it did not make Lee proud to see how his men loved him. "Not proud," Venable replied. "It awes him."[26]

CHAPTER FIFTEEN

"WE HAVE GOT TO WHIP THEM"

IN THE SPRING OF 1864 THE CIVIL WAR ENTERED a new phase. Union victories in the West had divided the Confederacy and sharply eroded its resources. Federal forces continued to increase in strength, while the Confederates neared the limit of their manpower. So critical was the recruiting situation in the South that the congress in Richmond required soldiers whose three-year enlistments were about to expire to continue to serve. All white men between the ages of 17 and 50 were made subject to the draft.

To many Northerners, the success of Union arms seemed assured. Apart from the Federal successes in the West, Lincoln had discovered in Ulysses S. Grant a general who campaigned with solid competence and dogged persistence. Congress revived the rank of lieutenant general—one last held by George Washington—and in March 1864 Lincoln promoted Grant to this rank with the title of general-in-chief. Halleck was moved to a staff post and Gen. William T. Sherman placed in command of Federal armies in the West. For Grant, the objective was to be Lee's army. Although Meade remained in nominal command of the Army of the Potomac, Grant planned to campaign with him. The Army of the Potomac would go down in history as "Grant's army."

For three years, Northern generals—believing somehow that they were emulating Napoleon—had marched against strategic points in the Confederacy: Memphis, Fredericksburg, and Richmond. Content to occupy key locations, they had allowed Confederate armies to escape to fight again. In Grant, however, Lincoln had a general who recognized the importance of pressing the Confederates everywhere and destroying their armies. Grant's plans called for Sherman, with 100,000 men, to move against Atlanta so as to oblige Johnston to fight. A force under Gen. Franz Sigel was to occupy the Shenandoah Valley. A 35,000-man army under Gen. Benjamin Butler was to advance up the James River toward Petersburg and threaten Richmond from the southeast. Elsewhere, the Army of the Gulf was to march on Mobile and prevent Confederate forces in Alabama from reinforcing Johnston. But the Federals' primary concern would be the Army of Northern Virginia. "Lee's army will be your objective point," Grant told Meade. "Wherever Lee goes, there you will go also."[1]

As Lincoln and Grant viewed the situation from Washington, there were grounds for optimism. Not only was the Mississippi River under Federal control, but also Tennessee, West Virginia, and portions of Louisiana and Virginia were occupied by Federal forces. Many of the coastal forts along the Atlantic and Gulf Coasts were in government hands. The naval blockade, although not totally effective, curtailed the Confederacy's foreign trade.

Grant's offensive, when it came, would be undertaken by the greatest army ever assembled in the Western Hemisphere. He would field some 120,000 men, many of them combat veterans. Federal artillery was as potent as ever, and Grant's rapidly improving cavalry, now under Gen. Phil Sheridan, numbered more than 12,000 troopers. The "new" Army of the Potomac reflected McClellan's intense training, the individual survival skills gained from two years of tough campaigning, and, finally, competent leadership. The army's most serious problem was a lack of self-confidence. When Grant sent aides to confer with Meade's staff officers, seeking to instill a degree of his own optimism, the most common response was polite skepticism. Grant, they were told, hasn't met "Bobby" Lee yet.[2]

To confront Grant's host Lee had about 45,000 infantry, 8,000 cavalry, and 200 guns. Shortly, with the return of Pickett's division and other detachments, the Army of Northern Virginia would number more than 60,000 for the last time. Notwithstanding the enemy's numerical advantage, most Southerners were optimistic about the coming campaign. The Confederate heartland, after all, was largely untouched by war. The Shenandoah Valley continued to serve as the breadbasket of the Confederacy, and factories in Richmond, Atlanta, and elsewhere in the South continued to produce ordnance. Two combat-wise armies—Lee's in Virginia and Joe Johnston's in northern Georgia—would contest any new invasion.

However, all was not well with the Army of Northern Virginia, camped near Orange Courthouse. Whereas a process of trial and error had brought capable leadership to the Army of the Potomac, Lee's army was hard hit by the casualties suffered during two years of heavy fighting. This was evident especially at the top. Of Lee's three corps commanders—Longstreet, Hill, and Ewell—only Longstreet was a proven quantity. Powell Hill was volatile in battle but prone to lapses in judgment and to sickness. As for Ewell, Lee doubted whether the one-legged officer was equal to the strains of the forthcoming campaign. He suggested as much to Ewell, but "Old Bald Head" failed to take the hint and Lee could not bring himself to sack so brave an officer.

At the division and brigade levels Lee's army was vastly changed from the previous year. Of the twenty-eight brigades that Lee had commanded on the eve of Chancellorsville, only eleven had the same commanders a year later. Five brigade commanders were dead, three had been promoted to divisional command, and nine had departed for a variety of reasons.[3] But the Army of Northern Virginia had competent division commanders—men such as William Mahone, John B. Gordon, and Robert E. Rodes—and morale was high throughout the ranks. Many of Lee's veterans had reenlisted even before the Confederate congress had extended their terms of enlistment. They were devoted to their cause, to their general, and to their fellow soldiers. A sergeant in one Virginia regiment wrote of his comrades, "All express a determination to do their utmost when [fighting begins] and have confidence in the protection of Providence, their Leader, and themselves."[4]

In any case, the Army of Northern Virginia was truly "Lee's army." At a time when Grant was a stranger to the Army of the Potomac, Lee knew not only his generals but also many subordinate officers, in most cases well enough to judge their strengths and weaknesses. He himself seemed genuinely optimistic about his chances of turning back any new Yankee offensive, writing to President Davis on April 15:

> If Richmond could be held secure against the attack from
> the east, I would propose that I draw Longstreet to me
> & move right against the enemy on the Rappahannock.
> Should God give us a crowning victory there, all their plans
> would be dissipated, & their troops now collecting on the
> waters of the Chesapeake will be recalled to the defence of
> Washington.[5]

In one part of his mind Lee probably recognized that the war was
turning into the war of attrition that he had long feared. He probably
recognized also that there could be no new invasions of the North,
no slashing offensives such as Second Manassas. At the same time,
his confidence in his troops was such that he could scarcely imagine defeat. Some of Lee's confidence grew out of poor intelligence;
whereas McClellan had been guilty of constantly overestimating Confederate strength, Lee initially underestimated Grant's numbers, crediting him with no more than 75,000 men. Whatever the numbers, Lee
was ready to fight. "Colonel," he remarked to Walter Taylor, "we have
got to whip them; we must whip them; and it has made me feel better
to think of it."[6]

Lee had long argued for more effective use of the scattered forces
under Beauregard that were defending the South Carolina coast. He
had been unable to borrow any of these troops at the time of Gettysburg, but in mid-April 1864 Davis assigned Beauregard to command
the Department of North Carolina and southern Virginia, with responsibility for the defense of Richmond. Lee would be free, at least for a
time, to concentrate his attention on Grant.

◆➤══◑ ◐══◆◆

THE DOGWOOD BLOSSOMS OF EARLY MAY MARKED THE
beginning of the campaign season, and it was clear that Grant was
about to move. On May 3, Lee rode with his corps commanders to
the top of Clark's Mountain, a rise on the south bank of the Rapidan
that afforded a good view of the enemy's tent city outside Culpeper.
Through his glass Lee could see dust and wagons, evidence of an army
about to move. But in which direction? The enemy had a number of
options. He might move southeast, making Fredericksburg his immediate goal. Or he might advance directly south by way of the Ely

and Germanna fords, much as Hooker had done two years before. Or he might swing west and attempt to attack Richmond from the rear. The stakes were high. "If victorious, we have everything to live for," he wrote to Custis. "If defeated, there will be nothing left for us to live for."[7] This letter may represent Lee's first acknowledgment that defeat was a possibility.

Lee was soon made aware of the enemy's intentions. In the early morning of May 4, Grant moved three corps across the Rapidan by two fords, moving toward Lee's right. The next day Butler's army landed on the south side of the James at Bermuda Hundred, with orders to move on Richmond. Beauregard was not yet on the scene, and Richmond and Petersburg together were defended for a time by only 5,000 men. Had Butler moved quickly he might have seized the Confederate capital, but his cautious advance allowed Beauregard time to improvise a defense. The Federals had lost a golden opportunity, but Butler's mere presence south of Richmond would further stretch Confederate resources.

Lee was pleasantly surprised that Grant had chosen almost the same route that Hooker had used in the Chancellorsville campaign. He decided not to contest the crossing of the Rapidan, but to challenge the enemy amid the "ghosts" of the Wilderness, where the advantage of artillery and superior numbers would be mitigated and where the Confederates might be able to strike an enemy on the march. Lee's intention was to intercept Grant's column by using the Orange Turnpike and the Orange Plank Road, the same east-west links that had figured so prominently in the Chancellorsville campaign. Lee ordered Hill and Ewell to march east and strike the enemy column on May 5; Longstreet, who was forty miles away on the Confederate left and rear, was to come up as fast as possible.

The initiative, however, passed to the Federals. When Grant discovered Confederates attacking from the west, he ordered his column, strung out along the Brock Road, to attack without changing formation. Ewell was hard-pressed for a time, but the Confederates stabilized their front and, in the early afternoon, beat back attacks by Warren's and Sedgwick's corps, inflicting heavy losses.

While Ewell was engaged, Hill was moving east along the Plank Road two miles to the south. Lee was traveling with Hill, and knew from the sound of heavy firing that Ewell was in a fight. Lee was in the process of shifting one of Hill's divisions to the left, to establish contact with Ewell, when the Federals attacked in front with more than

30,000 men. Hill led a skillful defense, but at the end of the day he and his men were exhausted and their lines in disarray. Lee sent Walter Taylor to hurry Longstreet along, but his corps was not expected until midnight at the earliest.

The next morning Longstreet was still not up when the enemy attacked again. Hill's weary regiments were quickly overrun, and the Federals advanced a mile to near the Tapp Farm, where Lee had established his headquarters. Lee, alarmed, mounted Traveller and attempted to rally Hill's fleeing men. Then he spied the vanguard of Longstreet's tardy corps, led by Gen. David Gregg.

"Who are you, my boys?" Lee called.

"Texas boys!" came the response.

Lee shouted a welcome, then attempted to make himself heard above the sounds of battle. "When you go in there," he cried, "I wish you to give those men the cold steel—they will stand and fight all day and never move unless you charge them!" Lee paused to study the approaching enemy line, then exploited to the full the affection in which he was held by his men. "The Texas Brigade has always driven the enemy, and I want them to do it now. And tell them, General, that they will fight today under my eye—I will watch their conduct!"[8]

Lee's fighting blood was up, and it appeared that he himself intended to lead the Texans into battle. Normally not given to theatrical gestures, Lee may have moved to lead the charge as a means of motivating his soldiers. Then, as Hood's men realized that Lee planned to join them, shouts rose over the din of battle, "Go back!"—"Lee to the rear!" One of Hood's soldiers wrote in his diary,

> The Texas brigade is moving to the charge, Genl. Lee following them slowly, soon the balls are whizzing by us and our rifles in fierce defiance are belching forth storms of leaden hail on the hated foe, now someone seizes Genl. Lee's bridle & says he must go no farther, he stops & to our great relief turns back.[9]

The Texans stemmed the Federal advance, and Lee looked for an opportunity to regain the initiative. One of Longstreet's officers knew of an unfinished railroad bed that ran past the enemy left and suggested that it could be a concealed route to the Federal flank. Longstreet sent three brigades on the flanking expedition and about noon they assailed Grant's left. At this crucial juncture the terrain was neutral. A North Carolina officer recalled, "Imagine a great, dismal forest . . . so thick with small pines and scrub oak, cedar, dogwood and other growth . . . [that] one could see scarcely ten paces."[10] The fighting became so close, and the smoke so dense, that soldiers on both sides thrust their bayonets through the underbrush in the hope of killing or wounding one of the enemy.

As Longstreet's three brigades attacked on the Confederate right, the remainder of the First Corps began to advance up the Orange Plank Road. There, the misfortune that had repeatedly decimated Lee's senior ranks struck again. Confederate soldiers mistook a group of riders for enemy cavalry and fired, seriously wounding Longstreet only a few miles from where Stonewall Jackson had met a similar fate the year before. Several hours passed while Lee attempted to organize a final attack that would crush the enemy left. Occasional crescendos of firing gave him a clue as to the fighting in the smoking undergrowth, but the Federals threw up breastworks along the Brock Road and the Confederate attack lost its momentum.

In the late afternoon Lee rode over to Ewell's headquarters on his left. There he found one of Ewell's brigadiers, John B. Gordon, attempting to convince his corps commander that the enemy right was exposed and should be attacked while there was still light. Lee authorized Gordon to attack, and his assault drove the enemy right for about a mile. But darkness fell and the Confederates pulled back. Lee could not have known it, but the fighting on May 6 represented his last opportunity to overwhelm Grant, and the Confederate effort had fallen short.

Nevertheless, in two days of fighting the Army of the Potomac had been roughly handled. Grant had suffered more than 17,000 casualties, Lee no more than half that number. But if Lee hoped for a victory that would drive the enemy back across the Rapidan he was disappointed. Many Federal soldiers probably expected that the setback they had met in the Wilderness would prompt a withdrawal behind the Rapidan. In this they were mistaken, for while the two armies skirmished on May 7, Grant prepared to move south toward Spotsylvania. That evening the blue divisions pulled out of line in succession, but instead of turning north they headed south, prompting some men in the ranks to raise a cheer. "For the first time in a Virginia campaign," writes historian James McPherson, "the Army of the Potomac stayed on the offensive after its initial battle."[11]

Lee had no special insight into Grant's thinking, but he knew on May 7 that there would be no enemy retreat, for Grant no longer had pontoons across the Rapidan. Lee could not be certain whether the next enemy move would be south toward Spotsylvania or east toward Fredericksburg, but recognizing that occupation of Spotsylvania would place Grant between his own army and Richmond, Lee ordered a night march south by Longstreet's corps, now commanded by Anderson. May 8 saw a close race for Spotsylvania, a race won by the Confederates in part because of hard fighting by their cavalry in harassing the Federals along the Brock Road.

At Spotsylvania came a forecast of the type of warfare that would mark the final year of the war in Virginia. There, Lee put his men to work on field entrenchments. North and west of Spotsylvania gray-clad soldiers constructed a hasty network of trenches, traverses, and abatis—felled trees placed at angles designed to entangle attackers. No longer did such work bring sarcastic references to the "King of Spades"; both armies had come to realize that entrenchments were often the key to survival.

Grant probed the Confederate lines on May 9 and the next day he launched a series of assaults. He attacked Anderson's corps on the Confederate left in late afternoon and was repulsed. He next attacked the Confederate center, a bulge in the line manned by Ewell's corps that soldiers had labeled the Mule Shoe. At about six o'clock, the Federals achieved a breakthrough, and the Confederate line was for a short time broken.

When Lee heard of the penetration he mounted Traveller and started for the front. Aides Charles Venable and Walter Taylor, however, urged him to remain at his command post. "Then *you* must see that the ground is recovered," Lee directed Taylor, who had long sought an opportunity to prove himself in combat. The erstwhile Norfolk banker galloped off to the Mule Shoe, where he found a flag and personally led a counterattack. The initial Federal assault was not-supported as it should have been, and when darkness fell the Confederates had restored their line.

Lee was seeing an aggressiveness in his foe that he had rarely experienced before. Indeed, Grant had not finished testing the Confederate defenses. Lee had included the Mule Shoe in his defensive line to deny

A sketch by artist Alfred Waud of Federal troops during the battle for the salient at Spotsylvania. LIBRARY OF CONGRESS.

to the Federals some high ground for artillery, but it was a vulnerable salient bordered on three sides by the enemy. Lee had planned to build a second line of defense across the base of the salient, but on the night of May 11–12, work had scarcely begun.

Anticipating another flanking movement by Grant, Lee told Ewell to be ready to move on short notice. With Lee's instruction in mind, Ewell began withdrawing his artillery—about twenty guns—that night, only to be told of unusual noises from the Federal lines. After some delay Ewell ordered that the guns be returned. A wet fog hung over the woods, and for much of the night the uneasy Confederates could hear the sound of Yankee bands playing and soldiers marching.

The Federals struck at dawn. Two divisions of Hancock's Second Corps surged over the Confederate defenses against minimal opposition. Never had a portion of Lee's army been taken so completely by surprise. The Federals captured more than 2,000 prisoners, including a division commander, Gen. Edward "Allegheny" Johnson. For the second time in a week the Army of Northern Virginia was in danger of being cut in two.

Lee was finishing a predawn breakfast when he heard firing. Riding toward the sounds of battle, he reached the base of the Mule Shoe where he found the detritus of defeat: a stream of retreating soldiers confronted by a handful of officers attempting to form a line. Gen. John B. Gordon, commanding the Confederate reserves, watched as Lee rode to the front of Gordon's line, "with uncovered head and, mounted on old Traveller, [looking like] a very god of war." [12] Once again, Lee was preparing to lead a counterattack.

The scene that followed would be an enduring part of the Lee legend. A Georgia soldier recalled how

> Gen. Lee was trying to rally his men. His emotions had got the better of him. He was crying like a child. He started rite toward ther line of battle when Gen. Gordon . . . dashed right in and caught that old war horse and led him out. [13]

Gordon cried out that he would lead the charge. Addressing the army commander in a bellow that his men could hear, he told Lee that his Georgians, Virginians, and Carolinians would never let him down. "Will you, boys?" he roared. A group of soldiers led Traveller toward the rear as Gordon's men moved to check Hancock's advance. [14]

   The Federals had nearly erased the tip of the salient, but at the same time they had crowded so many men into a confined space that all order was lost. Gordon, with three brigades, halted the enemy advance and began to inflict heavy casualties. It began to rain. Some of the most grisly fighting of the war took place at the "Bloody Angle" of the salient, where blood and water turned the ground into a slimy ooze. A Confederate officer recalled,

> The trenches on the inner side were almost filled with water. Dead men lay on the surface of the ground and in the pools of water. . . . The water was crimsoned with blood. Abandoned knapsacks, guns, and accoutrements were scattered all around. . . . The rain poured heavily, and an incessant fire was kept upon us.[15]

Soldiers of both sides fired over the parapet, then threw their bayoneted guns like spears at enemy soldiers just a few feet away.

   At dawn Lee was able to bring reinforcements to the base of the Mule Shoe, and the enemy fell back. Burnside's corps, which was to have supported Hancock, never made its presence felt, and after a morning of hand-to-hand fighting the men in gray had reclaimed much of the salient. By nightfall Lee's men were constructing new defenses at its base, where the Confederate line should have been all along. Soldiers on both sides knew that they had been through hell but were not sure what to make of it. Federal soldier George Whitman, brother of the poet, wrote his mother that Grant "has got Lee in a pretty tight spot." But one of Lee's young officers wrote home that "the men are so confident of a decisive victory that they exhibit a delight in fighting."[16] A Georgia soldier wrote bluntly, "We [gave] old Grant a whipping."[17]

   Grant had indeed been whipped. In the week since he had crossed the Rapidan, the Army of the Potomac had suffered some 32,000 casualties, a greater total, notes historian James McPherson, than for all Federal armies combined in any previous week of the war.[18] The Federals' grand strategy was not going according to plan. Although Sherman was on the move in Georgia, Butler had been completely neutralized at Bermuda Hundred. Nor were things going well in the Shenandoah Valley. There, on May 15, a Confederate force of about 5,000, including cadets from the Virginia Military Institute, defeated Gen. Franz Sigel's army at New Market.

Although Lee had been guilty of tactical lapses in dealing with Grant, he had given the advancing Federals a bloody nose and the promise of more. At the same time, the senior ranks of the Army of Northern Virginia had been hard hit. In the campaign to date Lee had lost five generals killed or fatally wounded, and ten others had been wounded so badly they had to turn over their commands. In all, the army had suffered some 18,000 casualties, and because of the threat posed by Butler, Lee had not been able to persuade Davis to return Pickett's division to the Army of Northern Virginia.

The wounding of Longstreet underscored Lee's need for competent corps commanders. Anderson might prove an adequate replacement for Longstreet, but Hill had become ill on May 8 and Lee had been obliged to replace him with Jubal Early. Within a matter of days Lee had lost two of his three corps commanders.

The greatest blow, however, was the death, on May 12, of Jeb Stuart. Grant had sent Sheridan, with 12,000 troopers, on a raid toward Richmond designed to initiate a fight with the outnumbered Confederate cavalry. Stuart took only 4,000 riders with him to head off the Yankees, and clashed with the Federals a few miles north of Richmond at Yellow Tavern. There, the 31-year-old Stuart was fatally wounded by a dismounted Federal trooper.

Like Stonewall Jackson, Stuart was irreplaceable. When first informed of Stuart's wound Lee received the news stoically, remarking in tribute, "He never brought me a piece of false information." Word that Stuart had died came after the terrible fighting for the Mule Shoe. Lee had seen all the horrors of war, but when Stuart's death was confirmed that evening, he retired to his tent. Moments later he remarked to an aide that he could scarcely think of Stuart without weeping. A Federal cavalry officer, Gen. James H. Wilson, would write of Stuart's death, "From it may be dated the permanent superiority of the national cavalry over that of the rebels."[19]

CHAPTER SIXTEEN

NEVER CALL RETREAT

DESPITE THE CARNAGE AT THE MULE SHOE, Grant gave the Confederates no rest. Although continuing rain made offensive movements difficult, he repeatedly tested Lee's flanks. These probes were not threatening, and Davis was not alarmed. Lee was a prisoner of his success, for as long as he appeared to be holding his own, the authorities in Richmond were reluctant to send reinforcements, even though Beauregard now required comparatively few troops to contain Butler's enclave southeast of Richmond.

After the war, George C. Eggleston, a sergeant in one of Lee's artillery units, clearly defined Lee's problem in the Wilderness-Spotsylvania campaign:

> We had been accustomed to a programme which began with a Federal advance, culminated in one great battle, and ended in the retirement of the Union army, [and] the substitution of a new Federal commander for the one beaten. . . . But here was a new Federal general, fresh from the West, and so ill-informed as to the military customs in our part of the country that when the battle of the Wilderness was over, instead of retiring to the north bank of the

river . . . he had the temerity . . . to try conclusions with us again.[1]

Meanwhile, Grant had problems not of his own making. His plans to press Lee in the Shenandoah Valley and at Petersburg were integral parts of his strategy, but these secondary theaters were being badly handled. The first commander to fail was Ben Butler, whose influence as a War Democrat had secured for him command of a 30,000-man expedition aimed at Richmond and Petersburg. On May 5, Butler's force had steamed up the James River and landed at Bermuda Hundred, a point between the two cities. The area was defended by only 5,000 Confederates, and the road to glory lay open. But Butler, blind to his opportunity, moved slowly. By the time the Federals were able to threaten the railroad between Richmond and Petersburg, Beauregard had arrived with reinforcements from North Carolina and the opportunity was gone. On May 16 the Confederates drove the Federals back across the neck between the James and the Appomattox Rivers. They then proceeded to construct entrenchments that effectively sealed Butler in a cul-de-sac where he could do no damage.

Two telegrams from Lee to Davis on May 18 included an uncharacteristic note of pleading:

> If the changed circumstances around Richmond will permit I recommend that such troops as can be spared be sent to me at once. . . . The forts around Washington and the Northern cities are being stripped of troops. The question is whether we shall fight the battle here or around Richmond.[2]

Lee at last gained the president's full attention, and Pickett, who had been stationed on the James, rejoined the Army of Northern Virginia.

Lee's army remained Grant's objective. The Army of the Potomac to this point had moved almost directly south, first to the Wilderness, then to Spotsylvania. After failing to overrun Lee at Spotsylvania, Grant took a slightly different tack, marching southeast before turning west in another attempt to get between Lee and Richmond. But Lee held the inside track, and he was able to take up a position at Hanover Junction, south of the North Anna River, before the bluecoats arrived. Once again the question became: What route would Grant choose next?

Considering the Army of Northern Virginia's proximity to Richmond—Hanover Junction was only twenty-five miles away—the army's supply situation might have been expected to improve. Because of the inefficient commissary, however, Lee's situation was worse than it had been on the Rapidan. One Southern soldier would write about conditions later at Cold Harbor,

> We had absolute faith in Lee's ability to meet and repel any assault that might be made, and to devise some means of destroying Grant. . . . But there was an appalling and well-founded fear of starvation, which indeed some of us were already suffering. . . . In my own battery, three hard biscuits and one very meager slice of fat pork were . . . the first food that any of us had seen since our halt at the North Anna River two days before.[3]

On May 23, Lee met with his senior generals and set his army to digging a new set of entrenchments. The new line was in the shape of an inverted V, with the apex touching the river at a bend called Ox Ford. It was a trap, because any part of Grant's army that crossed close to Ox Ford was in the jaw of a vise formed by one arm of Lee's army and the river. For a few hours the Federal Second Corps was in one part of the vise and isolated by the river from the rest of Grant's army. Lee, even with his depleted force, should have been able to assault one segment of a divided enemy. But A. P. Hill failed to seize the moment, and Lee gave him no orders, in part because he himself was sick.

On May 24, Lee's illness confined him to his cot. When a malady that included severe diarrhea was added to the strain of command, Lee's self-control was an early casualty. To Hill he snapped, "Why did you not do as Jackson would have done—thrown your whole force upon those people and driven them back?"[4] Lee attempted to carry on business as usual, but was so irascible that his aides, though accustomed to flashes of temper from the Tycoon, had difficulty dealing with him. The faithful Venable left Lee's tent after a furious exchange over some matter lost to posterity. To an officer nearby he exclaimed, "I have just told the old man that he is not fit to command this army, and that he had better send for Beauregard."[5]

Beauregard was part of the problem, in that Lee was attempting to hold off Grant without the benefit of Beauregard's 14,000 men arrayed against Butler; Lee commanded only the Army of Northern Virginia.

On May 25 he wrote Davis to ask whether it might be possible to unite his army with that of Beauregard. Lee was the senior of the two generals, and when he spoke of "uniting" with Beauregard he was suggesting that he absorb Beauregard's troops in a unified command. Lee's logic was impeccable, but Davis's approval would have risked another public controversy with the volatile Beauregard. For the moment, Davis did nothing.

Beauregard, for his part, believed that Lee should remain on the defensive against Grant, and that he, Beauregard, should be reinforced so that he could destroy Butler's army. Through such a strategy, he believed, the Federals south of the James could be prevented from reinforcing Grant, and Lee's task made easier. Lee rebutted this argument in a letter to Davis on May 23:

> As far as I can understand, General Butler is in a position from which he can only be driven by assault. . . . Whether it would be proper or advantageous to attack it General Beauregard can determine, but if not, no more troops are necessary there than to retain the enemy in his entrenchments. [Meanwhile], General Grant's army will be in the field, strengthened by all available troops from the north, and it seems to me our best policy [is] to unite upon it and endeavor to crush it.[6]

On May 26, Grant withdrew from his position on the North Anna and again attempted to maneuver between Lee and Richmond. The Federals crossed the Pamunkey River only to find Lee's army entrenched behind Totopotomoy Creek, just ten miles from Richmond. After two days of skirmishing Grant again marched south, this time headed for a crossroads at Cold Harbor, close to the old battlefield at Gaines's Mill. Two years after the Seven Days' campaign, the Federals were again at the gates of Richmond.

Lee repeated his appeal for reinforcements, his argument strengthened by the fact that Grant had transferred an entire corps from Butler to his own army. Beauregard, however, persuaded Davis that the enemy he faced was proportionately as large as that facing Lee. On the evening of May 29 Davis visited Lee for what appears to have been inconclusive discussions. That evening Beauregard himself arrived and told Lee that he could provide no help.

Early on May 30, Lee learned that Grant was again moving against the Confederate right. That evening he sent Davis the most pessimistic telegram he had dispatched in three years of war. After quoting Beauregard as saying that troop movements were the prerogative of the War Department, Lee asked Davis to send him Robert Hoke's division immediately. Any delay, he warned, "will be disaster."[7]

Lee had never before used the term *disaster*. The sound of firing from his front could at this point be heard in Richmond, and this time Davis followed Lee's advice. The transfer of Hoke's division occurred on May 31. Beauregard may have been facing as many enemy proportionately as Lee, but Butler had no capacity to maneuver, and Beauregard had made his lines almost invulnerable.

Lee, still unwell, traveled south in a carriage and slept in a farmhouse while his troops entrenched along Totopotomoy Creek. When Dick Ewell reported himself sick, Lee gave command of the Second Corps to Jubal Early in a "temporary" arrangement that soon became permanent. For two days the armies skirmished along a north-south line before Grant concluded that Confederate defenses were too strong to warrant an attack. His patience wearing thin, Grant continued his march toward the dusty crossroads of Cold Harbor.

It is a commentary on Lee's aggressiveness that, though badly outmanned, he still sought an opportunity to strike at Grant's column. In a note to Hill, probably written on June 1, Lee said that the time had arrived "when something more is necessary than adhering to lines and defensive positions." The Confederates must prevent the Federals from freely selecting positions from which to assault his lines. He reiterated a familiar theme: "If [the enemy] is allowed to continue that course we shall at last be obliged to take refuge behind the works of Richmond and stand a siege, which would be but a work of time."[8] These comments echo those of 1862, when, preparing for the Seven Days' campaign, Lee indicated that Richmond could not withstand a siege.

Lee did not yet recognize that reduced numbers and a subsistence diet had robbed his army of the capability for vigorous offensive action. On the morning of June 1, Lee, still sick, ordered an attack by Anderson's corps plus Hoke's division to secure a strategic crossroads near Cold Harbor. In Lee's absence the attack was badly handled— Hoke's division failed to participate—and Anderson's corps was turned back by Federal cavalry armed with repeating carbines.

Unable to dislodge the enemy, the Confederates went to work

strengthening their entrenchments. When no Federal attack materialized on June 2, Lee's men used the respite to lay out one of the strongest defensive lines since Fredericksburg—"intricate, zig-zagged lines within lines, lines protecting flanks of lines, lines built to enfilade opposing lines."[9] Lee himself was well enough to mount Traveller for the first time in a week and to inspect the defenses. As a result of his entreaties, the Army of Northern Virginia now numbered about 50,000 men—almost exactly half the number available to Grant.

Grant had brought Lee's army to the brink of defeat with his flanking movements, but he now felt that new tactics were necessary, for another move south would entangle the Army of the Potomac in the same Chickahominy swamps where it had come to grief under McClellan. Perhaps influenced by the ragged appearance of recently captured Confederate prisoners, Grant concluded that Lee's army was all but whipped, and that a spirited attack might break his lines.

Once again, the enemy was about to come to Lee's rescue. Grant would have done well to have talked with some Army of the Potomac veterans. These men had no illusions about Lee's ragamuffins, especially behind entrenchments. One of Meade's staff officers regretted that Grant had postponed his attack from June 2 to the following day, remarking,

> It is a rule that, when the rebels halt, the first day gives them a good rifle-pit; the second, a regular infantry parapet with artillery in position; and the third a parapet with an abatis in front and entrenched batteries behind. Sometimes they put this three days' work into the first twenty-four hours.[10]

When they learned of the frontal attack planned for the next day, hundreds of Federal soldiers once again fastened name tags to their uniforms so that their bodies could be identified.

At dawn on June 3 came the first of a series of attacks by three Federal corps on Lee's north-south line at Cold Harbor. Each was easily repulsed. Succeeding waves only piled up the dead and wounded in front of Lee's trenches, but not until about nine o'clock did Grant halt the slaughter in which Federal dead and wounded totaled approximately 7,000. At the end of the day, Lee, who had been largely uninvolved in the fighting, reported to the War Department that Confederate losses had been light "and our success, under the blessing of

God, all that we could expect."[11] A South Carolina officer wrote home, "I have often heard about the yankees being piled up five deep around Richmond but I did not believe it until last week when I saw them with my own eyes."[12] In his memoirs, Grant would later express regret that the assault at Cold Harbor had been attempted.

During the three-day battle Lee received visitors from Richmond, including Postmaster General John Reagan. Two years earlier Lee might have sent them away from his front; now he was more hospitable. "General," Reagan asked, "if he breaks your line, what reserve have you?" "Not a regiment," Lee replied, "and that has been my condition since the fighting commenced on the Rappahannock. If I shorten my lines to provide a reserve, he will turn me; if I weaken my lines to provide a reserve, he will break them."[13] Lee may have been exaggerating slightly but he could not overlook a chance to make his needs known to a member of the president's inner circle.

THE CAMPAIGN FROM THE WILDERNESS TO COLD HARBOR was unlike any that Lee had fought before. For seventy miles and most of four weeks the Army of Northern Virginia had been in constant contact with the enemy. For Lee, the month had been one of successive crises—repeatedly he had sought to stem enemy breakthroughs in person—but his army had inflicted such appalling losses on the Federals that virtually the entire North was in mourning. The 60,000 casualties that Grant had suffered since May 6 were roughly equal to Lee's total numbers at the beginning of the campaign. "I think Grant has had his eyes opened," Meade wrote to his wife, "and is willing to admit now that Virginia and Lee's army is not Tennessee and Bragg's army."[14]

Lee had fought the war on the assumption that time was not on the side of the Confederacy—that he needed to inflict early defeats on the enemy to bring him to the negotiating table. That campaign had failed—Gettysburg had been its finale—and since then, Northern resolve had, if anything, stiffened. But Lee's army, forced to fight on the defensive, was inflicting such heavy casualties on the Army of the Potomac that its morale was shaken as it had not been shaken since Fredericksburg. Veteran Union soldiers spoke bleakly of the "butchering in the slaughter pens." A correspondent for the *New York Tribune* wrote privately that he was becoming discouraged about Grant, adding, "Lee is a great general and today [May 18] Grant has stood seemingly baffled and undecided what to do." [15] For several weeks after Cold Harbor, Federal officers were reluctant to order any attack lest their orders be defied and result in a mutiny.

Northern disillusionment about the war had an obvious political dimension. There was opposition to Lincoln's renomination within his own party, and even if Lincoln was renominated a Republican victory in November was far from certain. The election of 1864 and the war itself might well be decided along the banks of the James.

For a week the opposing armies hunkered down, miserable in the intermittent rain. Lee had little opportunity to savor his easy victory at Cold Harbor. On June 5 there was bad news from the Shenandoah Valley, where a Confederate force under Gen. W. E. Jones had been routed near Staunton by Sigel's replacement, Gen. David Hunter. Lee, sensitive to developments there, sent Breckinridge's division, which had rejoined Lee after the victory at New Market, back to the valley. When Lee heard that Hunter had penetrated as far as Lexington, he sent Early, with 8,000 men, to attempt to drive him out of the valley.

Meanwhile, Lee had his hands full in front of Richmond. Grant had not been idle in the days since Cold Harbor; rather, he had decided to move his army across the James and attack Petersburg, the "back door" to the Confederate capital. He advised Halleck on June 5,

> My idea from the start has been to beat Lee's army if possible north of Richmond; then after destroying his lines of communication on the north side of the James River to transfer the army to the south side and besiege Lee in Richmond, or follow him south if he should retreat.
>
> Without a greater sacrifice of human life than I am willing to make all cannot be accomplished that I had designed outside of the city. . . . I will move the army to the south side of the James River. [16]

It was a risky undertaking. The challenge to the Federals was to move an army of 100,000, one that was in daily contact with Lee's pickets, on a thirty-mile flank march undetected. But Grant's staff was equal to the task. On the night of June 12–13 the Army of the Potomac quietly withdrew from its lines at Cold Harbor. Screened by cavalry that Sheridan had left behind, Grant moved four corps across the

James via a pontoon bridge that was one of the longest constructed up to that time.

Lee knew that Grant was gone, and suspected that he was crossing the James, but, as he wrote to Davis, there was a chance that a good portion of the enemy would remain north of the river. On the afternoon of June 14, Lee sent Hoke's division to Drewry's Bluff, from where it could march to Petersburg if necessary. Even as he ordered Hoke's movement Lee speculated to Richmond that Grant "will cross" the James, not realizing that his opponent, moving with alacrity, already had portions of two corps across the river.

Located some twenty-five miles south of Richmond on the Appomattox River, Petersburg was an important rail hub. On June 15, two Federal corps totaling some 16,000 men reached the outskirts of the town, which was held by Beauregard with fewer than 3,000 men. The Federals could easily have overrun its defenses, but the Confederate breastworks were impressive and memories of Cold Harbor lingered. Only late in the day did the Federals launch an attack that carried portions of the Confederate works. While the enemy buildup continued, Beauregard stripped his lines at Bermuda Hundred to meet the new threat. Lee, however, remained uncertain about where the main threat lay, writing to Davis on the evening of June 16 that Beauregard had not yet informed him of the strength of the enemy in front of him. Nevertheless, Lee sent Pickett's division to recover the trenches at Bermuda Hundred that had been captured by the Federals, but which were still lightly manned.

Rarely was Lee so unaware of enemy movements as in the week of June 14. His response to the threat to Petersburg was inhibited by several factors: Beauregard's reputation, recognized over a period of weeks, for exaggerating the threat to his lines; a bureaucratic command structure, in which Lee and Beauregard commanded separate departments and normally communicated through Richmond; and Lee's shortage of cavalry, which made him slow to recognize that the bulk of Grant's army was already south of the James.

On June 17, Rooney Lee's troopers provided information that convinced Lee that the primary threat was to Petersburg. While Beauregard fended off a new Federal assault, Lee ordered Hill's and Anderson's corps to Petersburg. That evening Beauregard evacuated his main line, and when the Federals advanced the next morning the works that had stymied them for three days were empty. A mile closer to the town were new entrenchments. For all the problems that he had caused Lee, Beauregard had conducted a skillful defense.

In Bruce Catton's admirable summary, Grant's plan worked perfectly up to the point where it was about to win the war, and then did not work at all.[17] By June 15 the Federals had more than 50,000 men in Lee's rear, opposed initially by no more than 9,000 Confederates, but could not achieve a coordinated assault. Part of the problem was inept commanders, and part of it was the "Cold Harbor syndrome"—the unwillingness of units that had fought bravely throughout the campaign to assault Confederate entrenchments. The Federals had no way of knowing that the rebel works were virtually unmanned.

By June 18 Lee himself was on the scene, with most of his 45,000 men. The immediate threat to Petersburg was past, but the one development that Lee had feared for two years was at hand: The Army of Northern Virginia was under siege.

CHAPTER SEVENTEEN
SIEGE

As Lee built up his defenses east of Petersburg, there was no denying that his army and his capital were besieged—the fate he had fought for two years to avert. Lee remained stoic. On June 21 he wrote to President Davis,

> I hope your Excellency will put no reliance in what I can do individually, for I feel that will be very little. The enemy has a strong position, & is able to deal us more injury than from any other point he has ever taken. Still we must try & defeat them.[1]

The sounds of firing could be heard daily in both Richmond and Petersburg, but residents of both cities were so confident of Lee's ability to defend them that many went about business as usual. The London *Times* correspondent wrote from Richmond that "if a man were landed here from a balloon after six months' absence—if he were taken along Grace or Franklin Streets in this city on a summer evening, and told that two enormous armies are lying a few miles off and disputing its possession—he would deem his informant a lunatic."[2]

While Lee's men sought to resist the pinch of hunger as well as Grant's numbers, the immediate threat to the Confederacy appeared to be to the south. In Georgia, Joseph E. Johnston, with about 50,000 men, was attempting to hold back Sherman's army of nearly twice that number. In May, in a move timed to coincide with Grant's campaign against Lee, Sherman engaged Johnston with the goal of capturing Atlanta. In contrast to the siege warfare in Virginia, Sherman and Johnston waged a campaign of maneuver. Jefferson Davis had been unable to get Johnston to make an offensive move against Grant in the Vicksburg campaign, but Johnston now took full advantage of the mountainous terrain of northern Georgia to delay Sherman's advance. On June 27, in the one full-scale battle of the campaign, Johnston inflicted heavy casualties on Sherman at Kennesaw Mountain.

By retreating slowly, avoiding battle where possible, and fighting behind field entrenchments that neutralized the enemy's superior numbers, Johnston frustrated his opponent and bought time for the South. But his relations with President Davis were as strained as ever, and there was doubt in Richmond as to whether Johnston was prepared to fight for Atlanta. When Davis sent Braxton Bragg south to determine Johnston's intentions, the army commander refused to commit himself.

John B. Hood, one of Johnston's corps commanders, was as critical of Johnston as Davis was. Hood had lost an arm at Gettysburg and a leg at Chickamauga, but he had lost none of the aggressiveness that he had demonstrated in the Devil's Den at Gettysburg. He was a favorite of President Davis, and on July 12 the president asked Lee whether he should replace Johnston with Hood. Lee was always uneasy when asked for recommendations on matters outside his jurisdiction, and his reply to Davis reflected this unease. Lee hoped that Johnston "was strong enough to deliver battle." It would be desirable for cavalry to be used against Sherman's communications. As for Hood, he was "a good fighter, very industrious on the battlefield, careless off." Carefully refusing to endorse Hood for army command, Lee noted in closing that Gen. William J. Hardee had more experience than Hood in handling an army.[3]

Davis nevertheless appointed Hood to command the Army of Tennessee, and Hood fought three battles outside Atlanta in which the Confederates suffered more than twice the casualties they inflicted.

Southerners interpreted Hood's battles as victories, but Sherman was at the gates of Atlanta.

⊶⊷ ⊷⊶

ALTHOUGH HISTORY HAS REMEMBERED ROBERT E. LEE primarily for his daring, his most enduring contributions to the science of war may have been in the use of entrenchments. Field entrenchments were used periodically during the Civil War, and Lee had used them skillfully at Chancellorsville and Spotsylvania. In resisting Grant's army in the last nine months of the war, however, Lee created entrenchments of such depth and intricacy that they neutralized Grant's superior numbers and ensured that the Confederacy and its capital would survive until at least November 1864. At that time, Abraham Lincoln would either have been returned to office or been replaced by General McClellan, who was believed to favor a negotiated peace.

Confederate defenses of Petersburg ran on a north-south line just east of the city, but because the Federals occupied the north bank of the James, Lee had to defend a line nearly thirty miles long, from Chaffin's Bluff north of Richmond to the Appomattox River south of Petersburg. The same entrenchments that allowed Lee to hold off an enemy twice his numbers denied him any opportunity to maneuver.

Lee manned his line with the remnants of Hill's and Anderson's corps, supported by a number of other units, including Pickett's division. Anticipating a practice that would become routine in World War I, he devised a system of rotation in which a unit would serve in the forward trenches and then be posted to the rear for a few days' rest. Even so, life in the verminous trenches was hard. One Confederate officer recalled, "It was endurance without relief; sleeplessness without exhilaration; inactivity without rest; constant apprehension requiring ceaseless watching."[4] A measure of the Army of Northern Virginia's fading fortunes was the status of its cavalry, part of which was now without mounts. With no animal depot to provide replacement horses, perhaps one-third of Lee's cavalrymen now fought as infantry.

Grant's first offensive moves were against the extended Confederate flanks. On June 22 he sent the Second Corps south in an attempt to break the Weldon Railroad and to force Lee to stretch his line. Lee anticipated the move, however, and Hill repulsed the Federal attack with heavy losses. Other assaults followed, some of them little more than demonstrations, but all of them forced Lee to make countermoves.

The Army of Northern Virginia was in dire straits, but living conditions for the Yankees were almost as onerous. The summer was proving to be exceptionally dry, and the dust lay inches deep. Both sides used sharpshooters—men loathed by blue and gray alike because the briefest lapse in attention could bring a bullet in the head. Surgeons remarked on the unusually high proportion of head wounds during the siege of Petersburg.

Lee established his headquarters on the north bank of the Appomattox near Petersburg, on a farm belonging to a Mrs. Shippen. He had not developed a great deal of respect for his opponent—he wrote to Custis that Grant's strategy "consists in accumulating overwhelming numbers"—but he had considerable respect for those numbers. In a rare attempt at humor Lee wrote Mary on July 10, "Grant seems so pleased with his present position that I fear he will never move again."[5]

Lee attended church in either Petersburg or Richmond when he could, and sometimes made other arrangements. In mid-July he asked the rector of St. Paul's Episcopal Church, Petersburg, to hold an open-air service at his headquarters. A sergeant of artillery recorded his impressions of Lee, "humbly kneeling on the ground among the sunburnt soldiers of his army, & joining in the impressive ceremony of the day."[6] Although Lee maintained an outward show of confidence, he must have begun to wonder whether Providence was on the side of the Confederacy.

Notwithstanding his dwindling personnel, Lee was convinced that he must defend the farms of the Shenandoah Valley if the Confederacy was to survive. He had earlier sent Jubal Early's corps to the valley, where a Federal army under Gen. David Hunter had attempted to take up where Sigel had left off. In mid-June, Early, assisted by Breckinridge, had turned back Hunter's attempt to capture Lynchburg, and then had pursued the Federal army into present-day West Virginia.

Without Early's corps Lee had only about 40,000 men to man the lines against Grant. Nevertheless, near the end of June, Lee asked Early whether he could cross the Potomac and threaten Washington. Even from his Petersburg lines, Lee sought a way to keep his enemy off balance; he wrote to President Davis in regard to Early's planned advance, "I still think it is our policy to draw the attention of the enemy to his own territory."[7]

On July 6 Early crossed the Potomac with 12,000 men, and three days later brushed aside a scratch Federal defense force at Monocacy, Maryland. For a few days the situation in the east appeared to have undergone a stunning reversal; Northern hopes for the capture of Richmond gave way to fears for the safety of their own capital. By July 11, Early's vanguard had reached the lightly manned Federal defenses on the northern outskirts of Washington.

Early's soldiers were exhausted, however, and Grant had belatedly reacted to the threat to his rear. Elements of the Federal Sixth Corps manned the capital's defenses, and Early wisely decided not to test them. He turned back to the Shenandoah Valley, but not before burning the home of Lincoln's postmaster general in Silver Spring and the town of Chambersburg, Pennsylvania, which had refused to provide the $500,000 ransom demanded by the Confederates. Anger at Hunter's depredations in the valley found many outlets during Early's raid.

Lee had given the enemy a scare and had briefly removed a Federal corps from his own front, but nothing had really changed. Richmond and Petersburg were still under siege, and when Early returned to the valley his adversary was not the bumbling Hunter but Grant's aggressive cavalryman, Phil Sheridan.

PARADOXICALLY, GRANT WAS NO MORE EAGER FOR A SIEGE than Lee. He wanted to end the war quickly, before the November elections, and when an officer in Burnside's Ninth Corps came up with a proposal to explode a mine under part of Lee's line he found a receptive audience. Meade was dubious about the project, but—probably influenced by Grant—he allowed it to go forward. Digging began in late June, and in four weeks a Federal regiment drawn from the coal-mining regions of Pennsylvania had completed a 500-foot shaft running under a section of Lee's line east of the Jerusalem Plank Road. To distract his opponent, Grant sent a strong force north of the James, the weakest point in the Confederate line, on July 28. Lee moved elements of Hill's corps to meet the threat, which was eventually repulsed.

At dawn on July 30, after a number of mishaps, the Federals exploded 8,000 pounds of gunpowder in what may have been the greatest man-made explosion up to that time. A Federal officer recalled it as "a magnificent spectacle . . . as the mass of earth went up into the air, carrying with it men, guns, carriages, and timbers."[8] The blast created a pit 170 feet long and 30 feet deep, killing more than 300 Confederate defenders in the process. Five hundred feet of entrenchments were destroyed.

The way to Petersburg was open, but Federal hopes were dashed by the ineptitude of Burnside and his division commanders. Nothing had been done to remove the abatises along the Federal lines, which delayed the advance to the crater. Then Burnside rushed so many men into the pit—many of them black soldiers—that it became a death trap. The explosion had taken place in a sector manned by the Virginia troops of Gen. William Mahone, and the Confederates quickly recovered from their initial surprise. They poured a deadly fire into the crater, where the Federals were so densely packed that many could not use their weapons.

The Battle of the Crater represented the first time that Lee's army had encountered black soldiers in appreciable numbers, and the reaction of the men in ranks was one of fury. Shortly after noon Mahone's men charged the crater, some with cries of "Take the white man—Kill the nigger!" One Confederate soldier wrote that captured blacks were being executed "when Gen. Mahone with drawn sabre and awful threats caused them to desist from their barbarous work."[9] The Battle of the Crater was another disaster for the Union, with Grant suffering some 3,800 casualties to less than half that total for the Confederates.[10]

Lee hurried from Petersburg to the scene of the fighting and observed the action from the Jerusalem Plank Road. With the enemy self-destructing, his presence was hardly required. Lee appears to have had no comment on the racial hatred that flared so markedly in the fighting, informing Richmond of the outcome in the briefest of telegrams and writing to Mary only that the enemy had "suffered severely."[11]

⊷⟾ ⟾⊷

TWO MONTHS INTO THE SIEGE THE CONFEDERATE LINE SUF-fered a permanent breach. A Federal attack on the southern end of Lee's line on August 21 gave the enemy control over a stretch of the

Weldon Railroad, the source of supplies to Lee's army from the Carolinas. Lee inspected the breach and concluded that the cost of restoring the line would entail a greater effort than was justified. Accepting the break in the railroad line as irreparable, Lee arranged for a wagon link around the break to ensure a supply line of sorts.

Along with his constant worry about supplies Lee faced the chronic problem of getting enough soldiers to man his lines. The Confederate conscription system had almost broken down. On August 23 Lee wrote Secretary of War Seddon about the large number of men detailed to the Conscript Bureau and the few recruits being delivered to the army. If Conscript Bureau staffers could not deliver recruits, they themselves should serve in the lines:

> Our numbers are daily decreasing, and the time has arrived in my opinion when no man should be excused from service, except for the purpose of doing work absolutely essential for the support of the army. If we had here a few thousand men more to hold the stronger parts of our lines . . . it would enable us to employ with good effect our veteran troops.[12]

Seddon assured Lee that he would give the matter his attention, but he rejected Lee's proposal to put the staff of the Conscript Bureau in the lines. Not satisfied with this response, Lee wrote directly to Davis on September 2. In one of his longest letters, Lee urged the revocation of virtually all draft exemptions and reiterated his recommendation that men of the Conscript Bureau be called to arms. "If the officers and men detailed in the Conscript Bureau have performed their duties faithfully, they must have already brought out the chief part of those liable to duty. . . . If not, they have been derelict, and should be sent back to the ranks." As for black soldiers, "It seems to me that we must choose between employing negroes ourselves, and having them employed against us."[13]

Lee was not alone in believing that the South must derive some advantage from its black work force. In January 1864, Gen. Patrick Cleburne of the Army of Tennessee had proposed creating regiments of black slaves, who would be emancipated after the war. Davis had pigeonholed Cleburne's radical proposal, probably anticipating the furor it would create in congress. In November of the same year, however, Davis endorsed a bill that would have allowed the government to purchase 40,000 slaves for service in the army in support functions, slaves who would be freed after service "faithfully rendered." Remarkably, even this modest measure failed to pass. One Richmond paper pointed out that the promise of freedom would constitute a repudiation of the view that blacks were better off in slavery.

⊷⟹ ⟸⊶

HIMSELF BESIEGED, LEE WAS UNABLE TO CONTROL EVENTS beyond his immediate front. As mentioned previously, Grant had named Sheridan to command the 35,000-man Army of the Shenandoah, with instructions to follow Early "to the death." Sheridan sparred for several weeks, but on September 19 he defeated Early's foot-weary little army at Winchester. Early retreated up the valley to Fisher's Hill, where Sheridan attacked on September 22. The Confederate infantry fought well, but Early's cavalry was overpowered and eventually his entire army was overwhelmed. The Confederates suffered more than 5,000 casualties in the two battles, and Early could no longer contest the valley. Sheridan put his men to a systematic destruction of the region, and the Shenandoah Valley, so long the breadbasket of the Confederacy, fell under enemy control.

Nevertheless, Lee declined to withdraw Early from the valley. Two years earlier he had concluded that Stonewall Jackson was more useful there than defending Richmond. Now he chose to keep a pale shadow of Jackson's army within striking distance of Washington as a distraction to Grant. When Early described his force as "very much shattered," Lee could offer little comfort. "I have given you all I can," he wrote. "You must use the resources you have to gain success."[14]

Nevertheless, when the governor of Virginia, William "Extra Billy" Smith, assailed Early in a letter, Lee sprang to his defense. A judgment based on the outcome of a single battle, Lee wrote, does not consider "all the circumstances surrounding the officer, his resources as compared with those of the enemy, his information as to the movements and designs of the latter, the nature of his command, and the object he has in view."[15] Lee's defense of Early was especially appropriate, for Lee had badly underestimated the force arrayed against the Army of the Valley. Indeed, notwithstanding his careful perusal of the Northern press, for most of 1864 Lee had underestimated enemy strength in Virginia. "My regret is equal to your own at the reverses that occurred at Winchester and Fisher's Hill," Lee wrote to Early on October 12. He advised Early to "keep your troops well together, restore their confidence, improve their condition in every way you can, enforce strict discipline in officers and men, keep yourself well advised of the enemy's movements and strength, and endeavor to separate and strike them in detail." [16]

Lee's letter is an excellent summary of his own military philosophy, but his recommendations were not easily implemented. And while Lee continued to give Early moral support, he suggested also that if Early could not make good use of his troops, some would have to be returned. Stung into action, Early returned to the offensive. On October 18, near Cedar Creek, he detected a weak flank in Sheridan's line. Early attacked at dawn the next day, routing two Federal divisions and capturing eighteen guns. By ten o'clock Early believed he had won a victory, and he did little to keep his hungry soldiers from sacking the Yankee camps.

But the battle was not over. The Federals regrouped a few miles north, and it was there that Sheridan—who had been in Winchester—found them when he galloped toward the sound of fighting. While Early ignored the urgings of his generals to complete the victory, Sheridan launched an afternoon counterattack that was all the more devastating because it was unexpected. Driving the Confederates across Cedar Creek, Sheridan not only recaptured the guns lost in the morning but also captured more than twenty of Early's. Sheridan had turned imminent disaster into one of the most decisive victories of the war.

Lee refused to yield to the new clamor for Early's removal, but he reluctantly concluded that little could be expected from the Army of the Valley. Before the year ended he transferred all except a fraction of Early's army to the Richmond-Petersburg defenses, a move that marked the end of his efforts to maintain a viable second front. Interestingly, even this shadow force led Sheridan to station two infantry corps and two cavalry divisions in the valley—units that Grant would have liked to have had in his lines at Petersburg.

⚬══◦ ◦══⚬

BY LATE SUMMER THE PRESIDENTIAL ELECTION IN THE North was a topic of overwhelming interest on both sides of the lines.

The Confederate diarist, John B. Jones, wrote in late August that "everything depends upon the result of the Presidential election in the United States."[17] A few weeks later a Federal cavalry officer reported a curious incident in which two Union pickets were surprised and captured by the Confederates. Upon being asked whom they would vote for, and replying that they were McClellan men, the two were promptly released, and allowed to return to their lines.[18] No one was more apprehensive about the election outcome than Abraham Lincoln. "You think I don't know I am going to be beaten," he told a friend, "but I do, and unless some great change takes place *badly beaten.*"[19]

The South had been losing the war ever since Gettysburg and Vicksburg, but in the latter half of 1864 even the illusion of stalemate finally began to crumble. In August, David Farragut's victory in Mobile Bay closed one more Confederate port. In September, Sherman occupied Atlanta. The collapse of Confederate operations in the valley was only the last of a series of Federal victories that ensured Lincoln's reelection. The only bright spot for the Confederates was Lee's tenacious containment of Grant.

✦══ ══✦

MARY LEE ONCE REMARKED THAT PERHAPS HER HUSBAND'S most conspicuous characteristic was his attention to detail. Whatever the fortunes of the Confederacy and however desperate the situation of his army, this characteristic at times took odd forms. Lee had encouraged his wife to knit socks and gloves for the army, and biographer Emory Thomas has noted that out of fourteen surviving letters from Lee to his wife in the first four months of 1864, only one does not contain some reference to sock production. In one instance Lee complained that the number of socks enclosed "scarcely ever agrees with your statement," noting that the latest shipment had contained 67 rather than 64 pairs.[20]

With his lines so close to Richmond, Lee could now visit his wife and daughters Agnes and Mildred in their house on Franklin Street. There, to Lee's distress, the ladies had tamed a squirrel. Lee viewed the squirrel as one more trial, for he was sure it would turn vicious. From his headquarters outside Petersburg, Lee ordered his family to get rid of the pet. "Immerse his head under water for five minutes," he wrote Mildred, assuring her that this would relieve her of "infinite trouble."

The Lee ladies paid no attention, even after the squirrel bit a doctor who was visiting. The general again took pen in hand, urging that the squirrel be turned into soup for wounded soldiers. Lee wrote, presumably in humor, "It would be most grateful to his feelings to be converted into nutritious aliment for them and devote his life to the good of the country."[21]*

Lee's antisquirrel campaign reflected his occasional preoccupation with trivia, but was otherwise out of character. A quality that Lee shared with his opponent, Grant, was an abhorrence of cruelty to animals. Grant, it was said, once knocked down a teamster who refused to stop beating a recalcitrant mule. Lee, for his part, often rebuked officers who failed to show consideration for their horses. During the siege of Petersburg the sight of an overworked mule team carrying lumber for a stable prompted Lee to write a letter to General Anderson that reflected both his solicitude for animals and his respect for the Sabbath:

> The mules were dreadfully poor, weary & worn & one in particular, the off leader, could scarcely be gotten along. . . . There are many things of necessity that we are obliged to do on Sunday, but I think this stable might have waited. Existing orders require that all work on Sunday to cease, except those of necessity, in order that man and beast have one day to rest.[22]

⋆⇒ ⇐⋆

THE SIEGE OF PETERSBURG, ALONG WITH LINCOLN'S RE-election, made Confederate defeat all but certain. The last remaining hope was for Lee to unite with Johnston and attempt to destroy Sherman, even at the price of yielding Richmond. Lee, with his usual diffidence, doubtless indicated as much in his many conferences with Davis, but the president would not consider such a course. Lee's aide, Walter Taylor, wrote in his postwar memoir that although the govern-

---

* The squirrel escaped the pot, at least temporarily, when the women turned him loose.

ment had supported Lee well in most of his campaigns, an exception was "the persistent effort to hold Richmond and Petersburg, after it became evident that it . . . would probably involve the complete exhaustion of the principal army of the Confederacy."[23]

But Lee had maintained good relations with Davis for more than three years by avoiding confrontation. He accepted his lot in the threadbare winter of 1864–65, even while pleading for reinforcements. On September 30, Federal troops successfully stormed Fort Harrison, a strong point in the Confederate line north of the James. After establishing a thin line west of the fort, Lee warned Secretary of War Seddon that Richmond was likely to fall soon unless the Confederacy mobilized the entire arms-bearing population of Virginia and North Carolina—in which case he might be able to keep the enemy in check until the beginning of winter.[24]

Lee managed to hold his lines well into the winter, however, and to keep his manpower at nearly 50,000 despite a rise in desertions. In February he wrote to the sponsor of a bill in the Confederate congress that provided for the arming of slaves. The measure was important to the survival of the Confederacy, Lee wrote, and if slaves were expected to fight they must receive something in return:

> The negroes, under proper circumstances, will make efficient soldiers. . . . Those who are employed should be freed. It would be neither just nor wise . . . to require them to serve as slaves.[25]

It was one thing for a relatively obscure officer such as Cleburne to propose the arming of slaves; for Lee to do so, and to endorse emancipation for those who fought, was nothing short of revolutionary.* In Bruce Catton's words, Lee was proposing not only to arm slaves, but also to accept those who served as free men. Although there was little that the Richmond government would deny Robert E. Lee, nothing could move the mossbacks of the Confederacy on so sensitive an issue as arming slaves. Howell Cobb, one of the founding fathers of the Confederacy, put the issue bluntly: "If slaves will make good soldiers," he wrote, "our whole theory of slavery is wrong."[26] The influential

---

* Given the foregoing, one of Alan Nolan's more remarkable conclusions is that Lee "embraced the preservation of slavery as a Confederate war aim." *Lee Considered,* 16.

Richmond Examiner, commenting on Lee's proposal, expressed doubt as to whether the general was a "good Southerner."

The Confederate house passed a watered-down bill that permitted the use of black soldiers but did not mandate their being freed. Even this measure was narrowly defeated in the senate. The Virginia legislature then passed a similar bill providing for the enlistment of black soldiers, but making no provision for freeing those who served. James McPherson notes that the two companies of black soldiers hastily organized in the final weeks of the war never saw action. "Nor did most of these men obtain freedom until the Yankees—headed by a black cavalry regiment—marched into the Confederate capital."[27]

CHAPTER EIGHTEEN

A SURRENDER OF QUALITY

As October turned into November, the stalemate along Lee's lines continued. To the south, Sherman was marching inexorably through Georgia, with Savannah his goal; the city would be Sherman's "Christmas present" to President Lincoln. For Lee, the Confederacy's collapse outside Virginia meant that it was only a matter of time before Sherman turned north to unite with Grant. There was bad news from Tennessee as well. On November 30, the impetuous Hood hurled his army in a series of assaults against well-entrenched Federals at Franklin, Tennessee. The Confederates were turned back with heavy losses, and two weeks later Hood was again defeated at Nashville.

These reverses had an insidious effect on morale in Lee's army. Many of his soldiers concluded that they were needed more at home than in trenches that were eventually going to be overrun. An Alabama soldier deserted after receiving a letter from his wife that read, "We haven't got nothing in the house to eat but a little bit o' meal. . . . I don't want you to stop fighting them Yankees . . . but try and get off and come home and fix us all up some and then you can go back."[1] Lee sought to combat desertion with strict discipline, but from Davis on down there was a marked reluctance to execute deserters.

The atmosphere in Richmond, where the realities of war had been so long ignored, was now marked by fear and recriminations. Davis had made many enemies with his rigidity; now he was a lightning rod for criticism. In the Confederate congress he was widely viewed as responsible for the setbacks in the West. Some of his critics, in their desperation, saw Lee as a miracle worker. Diarist John B. Jones noted in December, "There is supposed to be a conspiracy on foot to transfer some of the powers of the Executive to Gen. Lee."[2]

With Lincoln reelected and Atlanta and Savannah gone, there were whispers of surrender everywhere except in the presence of Davis, who was so determined to continue the war that no one dared raise the subject. Having been disappointed by virtually all his other generals, the president leaned increasingly on Lee, consulting him on all important military matters.

Davis was zealous in guarding his presidential prerogatives. Nevertheless, when the Confederate congress passed a resolution urging the appointment of Lee as general-in-chief and the restoration of Joe Johnston to his former command, the president was amenable, at least with respect to Lee. On February 1 the president named him general-in-chief. Lee was unclear about the new duties of his position, and, in acknowledging his appointment to Davis, he devoted most of his letter to recommending a final pardon for deserters who returned to their units within thirty days.[3] Lee could hardly have failed to note the irony of his latest honor. At the time of the Gettysburg campaign he could not persuade the president to allow him a few of Beauregard's troops. Now, with the war all but lost, Lee could have all the responsibility he desired.

ON FEBRUARY 3, THREE CONFEDERATE COMMISSIONERS MET with President Lincoln and Secretary of State Seward at Hampton Roads in a conference seen as perhaps the first step toward peace. The Confederate emissaries drew cheers from both armies as they passed through the lines. As Davis had anticipated, however, Lincoln gave no ground in reiterating that peace must come through reunion and the abolition of slavery. The Confederates had no bargaining position and Lincoln was giving nothing away; the main result of the conference was to appease pacifist elements in both the North and the South.

One of the Confederate commissioners was Robert M. T. Hunter, who had once represented Virginia in the U.S. Senate. Hunter was convinced that, notwithstanding Lincoln's hard line, the Confederates had more to gain if they surrendered while their armies were still in the field. When Hunter spoke to Davis along these lines, he was rebuffed.

Lee also wanted peace, and in the days after the Hampton Roads conference he sought out Hunter, whom he had known before the war. The two talked through much of a February night. If Hunter knew of any prospect for peace short of surrender, Lee said, it was his duty to propose it. Hunter then told Lee of his confrontation with Davis, and said he would have no more dealings with the president. Lee countered that he, as a soldier, could not propose negotiations against Davis's wishes. Hunter asked whether Lee could not go to Davis and tell him that it was "over." To this, according to Hunter, Lee made no reply. In Hunter's recollection,

> [Lee] never said to me he thought the chances were over; but the tone and tenor of his remarks made that impression on my mind. He spoke of a recent affair in which the Confederates had repelled very gallantly an attempt by the Federals to break his line. The next day, as he rode along . . . one of his soldiers would thrust forth his bare feet and say, "General, I have no shoes." Another would declare, as he passed, "I am hungry; I haven't enough to eat." These and other circumstances betraying the utmost destitution he repeated with a melancholy air and tone which I shall never forget.[4]

At this juncture, Lee's religion was not the comfort that it might have been. If God controlled events and if Confederate victories derived from the blessings of Providence, what was one to make of recent defeats? If God was on the side of the right, could it be that the Confederacy was in the wrong? And if the Confederacy did not enjoy God's blessing, was it right to prolong the war and its suffering?

The possibility of surrender negotiations would arise again soon. In the last week of February, Longstreet—who had recovered from his wound and was commanding Lee's troops north of the James—received a note from his counterpart, Gen. E. O. C. Ord, requesting a meeting on prisoner-of-war matters. In fact, Ord had other things on his mind. Because the politicians had failed to end the war, Ord told Longstreet, it was time for soldiers to try. He suggested a suspension of hostilities, to be followed by talks between Grant and Lee. Longstreet said that he had no authority to respond to Ord's proposal but would report it to Lee.

That evening, Davis, Lee, Longstreet, and a new secretary of war, John Breckinridge, met at the Confederate white house. They agreed to pursue Ord's approach, and Longstreet so informed Ord. Lee did not expect anything to come of the proposed meeting, but on March 2 he wrote to Grant suggesting that he and Grant meet to discuss a "military convention" to end the war.[5] Lee's pessimism proved amply justified, for Grant replied that he had no authority to participate in any such meeting.

⊷⊐⊏⊷

EXCEPT IN HIGH-LEVEL CONFERENCES SUCH AS THOSE WITH Davis, Lee attempted, in difficult times, to project an impression of confidence. A staff officer, John Esten Cooke, wrote of Lee, "His countenance seldom, if ever, exhibited the least traces of anxiety, but was firm, hopeful, and encouraged those around him in the belief that he was still confident of success."[6] Lee's stock with officers and men alike had never been higher. A young brigadier, John Bratton, who had several dealings with Lee in the fall of 1864, wrote to his wife, "The nearer [Lee] comes, the higher he looms up. It is plain, simple, unaffected greatness. It is just as natural and easy for him to be great as for me to be ordinary."[7]

A Texas soldier wrote to the *Richmond Examiner* to criticize a proposal that soldiers who had been present for duty from April to October should be awarded a $100 Confederate bond. The soldier insisted that two-thirds of Lee's soldiers would prefer "a certificate setting forth their good conduct and soldierly qualities, signed by General R. E. Lee."[8]

The greater the affection accorded him, the more Lee was haunted by the ethics of surrender. Totally respectful of civil authority, he recognized and admired Davis's willingness to fight on. But he also felt an obligation to the men in the trenches who had followed him for so long. Lee had pointed out to Davis the likelihood that Richmond would have to be evacuated, but he had not gone the next step and raised the critical issue of surrender. As long as his government chose to continue the fight, Lee could only do his duty. A February visitor to Lee's headquarters was Adm. Raphael Semmes, erstwhile commander of the cruiser *Alabama*, who had returned to Richmond via Texas after losing his ship off the French coast. When Semmes told Lee of the war weariness he had observed in his travel across the South, the general exhibited no surprise. Semmes thought that Lee, more by his manner than by words, recognized the inevitability of defeat.[9]

There were few men with whom Lee could speak freely, particularly on so sensitive a subject, but John B. Gordon, the 32-year-old Georgian who had risen to command one of Lee's corps, was such a man. Gordon was not only a fighter—he had been wounded three times—but he had impressed Lee as a thoughtful soldier. On a cold night in early March, Gordon received a message directing him to come to Lee's headquarters outside Petersburg.

Gordon arrived at 2:00 A.M. on March 3 and found Lee alone. To Gordon, his commander looked like "one suffering from physical illness." A long table in the room was littered with reports from every part of the army. After the briefest of amenities Lee motioned Gordon to a seat and told him to read the reports, which showed the actual strength of various units as opposed to their nominal order of battle. What Gordon saw startled him. He recalled in his memoir, "Each report was bad enough. . . . [but] I was not prepared for the picture presented by these reports of extreme destitution—of the lack of shoes, of hats, of overcoats, and of blankets, as well as of food."[10]

When Gordon had finished reading, Lee summarized the numbers. He had no more than 35,000 men fit for duty against Grant, who had an army of about 150,000 and who could expect reinforcements from Sherman and from Sheridan. Lee asked Gordon what he would recommend under these circumstances. The thought crossed Gordon's mind that no commander could ever have had a heavier burden than Robert E. Lee, but he went on to lay out three possibilities in order of their practicality: Make terms with the enemy, abandon Richmond and unite with Johnston, or fight "without delay."

In the silence that followed, Gordon asked Lee what he thought. Lee said somberly that he agreed completely. Gordon then asked whether Lee had made his views known to Davis and to the Confederate congress. In Gordon's recollection,

> [Lee] replied that he had not; that he scarcely felt authorized to suggest to the civil authorities the advisability of making terms. . . . He said that he was a soldier, that it was his province to obey the orders of the Government, and to advise or counsel with the civil authorities only upon questions directly affecting his army and its defense of the capital and the country.[11]

The two men talked on. They agreed that the army was in such dire condition that the two alternatives to surrender were scarcely alternatives at all. It was nearly sunrise when Gordon left, but Lee told him that he would be seeing Davis shortly and would inform him of the result of their meeting.

If Lee was prepared to be more blunt with Davis than in the past, circumstances were against him, for it was probably on March 3 that Lee received Grant's note stating that he had no authority to negotiate a military convention. Lee, in reporting to Gordon after meeting with Davis, again had kind words for the president's courage and persistence, but added that "nothing could be done" at Richmond.[12]

In fact, most of the discussion with Davis appears to have centered on Gordon's second alternative, the abandonment of Richmond in favor of a link-up with Johnston. When Lee said that the evacuation of Richmond and Petersburg was merely a matter of time, Davis claimed later to have said that if this was the case, it might be better to move sooner rather than later. Lee replied that this was impossible because of the weakened condition of the horses, but that he was arranging for the horses to receive extra rations.

It may have been on this visit that Lee met with Virginia's delegation to the Confederate congress. To them he repeated a familiar litany: thinning lines, weakened soldiers, starving animals. The legislators said that they were confident that the people of Virginia would respond to the challenge, but Lee had heard it all before. From the capitol he went to Franklin Street, where he spent the night with his family—Mary, Agnes, Mildred, and Custis. Lee was grave throughout the evening, and after supper he felt a need to get something off his chest. He turned to his son,

Well, Mr. Custis, I have been up to see the Congress and they do not seem to be able to do anything except to eat peanuts and chew tobacco, while my army is starving. I told them the condition the men were in, and that something must be done at once, but I can't get them to do anything.

Lee's visits with his family had usually been tranquil reunions, but this time the general was angry and bitter. He went on:

Mr. Custis, when this war began I was opposed to it, bitterly opposed to it, and I told these people that unless every man should do his whole duty, they would repent it; and now, they will repent.[13]

Lee would continue to do *his* duty, but where did that duty lie? His initial commitment to the Confederacy had sprung from a sense that he owed a stronger loyalty to Virginia than to the Union. Now, facing defeat in the field, he was torn between his loyalty to the Confederacy and his obligation to the soldiers who had followed him so long and fought so bravely. Perhaps the Federals would resolve his dilemma.

⋆⇒○⇐⋆

LEE'S THINKING TURNED INCREASINGLY TO HOW HE MIGHT evacuate his lines and make for open country. In the hope of forcing Grant to contract his left flank and perhaps provide an opening for a Confederate march south, Lee planned a surprise attack on a portion of Grant's line.

Fort Stedman was a link in the Federal entrenchments that invited attack because it was only about 150 yards from the Confederates' own lines. Lee turned the operation over to John Gordon, who developed an elaborate plan whereby a picked group of "deserters" would pretend to surrender and then overwhelm enemy pickets in the predawn darkness and pave the way for an infantry assault. Once Fort Stedman was captured, the attackers were to spread north and south, and assail several adjacent forts.

Gordon achieved total surprise and seized a half-mile of entrenchments. But the attack bogged down as the Confederates, after their initial success, milled about beyond Fort Stedman. A Yankee counterattack regained all the lost ground and captured several thousand dispirited Confederates, many of whom made no effort to return to their own lines. Lee not only had failed in his modest tactical objective, but also had lost 5,000 men, perhaps one-seventh of his entire force. Fort Stedman was not one of Lee's better engagements, for he had underestimated the difficulty of disengaging from the enemy lines after he had captured the fort. As Lee wrote to Davis, it was in retiring that Gordon's troops suffered the greatest casualties.[14]

Grant all but ignored the Confederate strike. He massed 50,000 men on his left and continued to stretch Lee's line south and west. The Confederates now had only two rail lines out of Petersburg, the Southside Railroad and a single link to Richmond. The Southside was the more important of the two because it was the route through which Lee could attempt to join Johnston. Lee instructed Pickett to protect the railroad by defending his position at Five Forks at all costs.

On April 1, however, Sheridan's cavalry attacked Five Forks and easily defeated Pickett's men, taking 5,000 prisoners—a figure indicative of the crumbling morale in the Army of Northern Virginia. In an equally ominous development, Lee had been compelled to move three brigades from his center to meet the threat at Five Forks. Grant, sensing his enemy's weakness, ordered an attack, and in the early hours of April 2 the Federal Sixth Corps broke Lee's center just above Petersburg. All Lee could do was inform Davis that the government must evacuate Richmond at once.

Atlanta and Columbia had been torched by Sherman; Richmond's fate came at the hands of the city's defenders. In accordance with an agreed procedure, the local garrison, commanded by Dick Ewell, was to set fire to the munitions and rations that could not be taken by the retreating troops. But with the enemy at the gates, discipline—the quality that Lee cherished above all others—dissolved. Ewell attempted to destroy a warehouse full of whiskey, but his guards could not prevent a mob from becoming drunk and ugly. By the time the last Confederate soldiers had left the city, Richmond was in flames.

Lee's attempt to escape was doomed from the start. Because he had lost the Southside Railroad he was obliged to march northwest on a circuitous route that gave the enemy ample time to block his movement. His goal was Amelia Courthouse, where he expected to find rations for his hungry soldiers. But there were no rations at Amelia Courthouse, and the Army of Northern Virginia entered a final stage of disintegration. Lee had intended to follow the rail line south to Danville, but

Sheridan captured Danville on April 5, forcing Lee to turn west. The next day, at Saylor's Creek, three Federal corps discovered a gap in Lee's line and attacked. When the day was over the Confederates had lost some 8,000 men—one-third of the army—mostly as prisoners. From the crest of a hill, Lee viewed the disorganized remainder of Richard Anderson's corps. "My God," Lee exclaimed, "has the army been dissolved?"[15]

Somehow the remnants of the Army of Northern Virginia kept moving. The detritus of defeat was everywhere—broken-down caissons, abandoned knapsacks, rifles. Starving horses collapsed and died in harness. Some soldiers had cast away their arms and sat along the roadside, waiting for the enemy to pick them up as prisoners. But others marched on, out of loyalty, habit, or both. There were rumors of food at Appomattox Station, where the army's line of march would once again cross the Southside Railroad. Meanwhile, many of the marchers carried a few grains of corn in their pockets, corn that probably had been intended for the horses. An army that had once numbered more than 80,000 had perhaps 11,000 men ready for duty—some 8,000 infantry and 3,000 cavalry. A hungry North Carolina soldier at the rear of Lee's column poked around some bushes hoping to flush a squirrel or chicken. Suddenly he found himself surrounded by soldiers in blue, and heard a shout, "Surrender! We've got you!" The Carolinian dropped his musket and raised his hands. "Yes," he said, "you've got me. And a hell of a git you got!"[16]

Even as his army crumbled Lee expected his officers to do their duty, and on April 8 he relieved three senior officers. When Lee learned that George Pickett had been socializing at a shad bake while his division was routed at Five Forks, he took action that he may have been contemplating for some time. The specifics that led to Gen. Richard Anderson's ouster are unclear, but that unlucky officer had lost control of his corps. The third officer relieved was Gen. Bushrod Johnson, who appears to have deserted his command in the fighting at Saylor's Creek.[17]

The inevitable could not be long postponed. On April 7 Grant sent a note through the lines calling on Lee to surrender. Lee handed it to Longstreet without comment, and Longstreet passed it back with the remark, "Not yet." Lee called for writing materials and penned a reply. Although not conceding the hopelessness of further resistance, he asked what terms Grant was prepared to offer. The next day passed quietly—neither army was willing to incur eleventh-hour casualties—and Lee received a second note from Grant summarizing the terms he was offering. The main point was that the Confederates who surrendered could not take up arms against the United States unless properly exchanged.

Lee now replied in a puzzling note that hints at the conflicting pressures he felt. He had not intended to propose the surrender of his army, he wrote, but to learn what terms would be offered in such an event. As the restoration of peace "should be the sole object of all," he sought broader discussions—very like those that Grant had declined on March 2. Lee closed by proposing that he and Grant meet at ten o'clock the next day along the old stage road to Richmond.

Grant knew a trap when he saw one. He replied that he had no authority to negotiate terms, but insisted that he was as eager for peace as Lee. "By the South laying down their arms, they would hasten that most desirable event, save thousands of human lives, and hundreds of millions of property not yet destroyed." Lee received this letter at his forward picket line, where a temporary cease-fire had been declared. His apparent delaying tactic having failed, Lee replied that he now asked for an interview in accordance with Grant's earlier letter. He carefully avoided the word *surrender*.[18]

That evening, after the cease-fire had expired, Lee called a council of war among his few remaining commanders. Lee stood by a fire, Longstreet sat on a log, and cavalry commander Fitz Lee shared a blanket with John Gordon. Lee summarized his exchanges with Grant and asked for comment. Remarkably, the consensus was not for surrender but for attack. Federal cavalry blocked their line of march but there was no sign of infantry as yet. It was agreed that Gordon would test the enemy at first light.

The last attack by the Army of Northern Virginia was briefly successful. But as Gordon advanced, he discovered a heavy force of infantry that threatened to cut him off from the remainder of the army. Word soon came from Gordon that he had fought his corps "to a frazzle" and could do no more. Lee conferred briefly with Longstreet and with William Mahone. Would further sacrifice on the part of the Army of Northern Virginia achieve any purpose? The consensus appeared to be that it would not.

Then Porter Alexander, the artillery commander, joined the group. He suggested that the men take to the woods, make their escape, and report to their state governors. This would spare Lee's army the humiliation of surrender, and might even improve prospects for a negotiated peace. But Lee appears to have considered this alternative and rejected it. The few thousand men who might escape could not change the outcome of the war, he told Alexander, and the by-products of guerrilla warfare would be disastrous. Lee went on:

> Already [the country] is demoralized by the four years of war. If I took your advice, the men would be without rations and under no control of officers. They would be compelled to rob and steal in order to live. . . . We would bring on a state of affairs it would take the country years to recover from. . . . You young fellows might go to bushwhacking, but the only dignified course for me would be to go to General Grant and surrender myself and take the consequences of my acts.[19]

Lee turned to his staff and said, "There is nothing left me but to go and see General Grant, and I would rather die a thousand deaths."[20]

Lee took with him his military secretary, Charles Marshall, and an orderly bearing a flag of truce. Early that Sunday afternoon Federal general Joshua Chamberlain, who had so bravely defended Little Round Top at Gettysburg, heard some commotion behind him:

> I turned about, and there behind me, riding in between my two lines, appeared a commanding form, superbly mounted, richly accoutered, of imposing bearing, noble countenance, with expression of deep sadness overmastered by deeper strength. It is none other than Robert E. Lee! . . . I sat immovable, with a certain awe and admiration.[21]

✧⇒◯ ◯⇐✧

AS NOTED IN THE FIRST CHAPTER, LEE'S RECENT CRITICS have attacked his performance in several areas. Of these criticisms, the most curious is that Lee did not surrender soon enough. Nolan devotes several pages to insinuating that Lee continued the war largely to vindicate his personal honor at the expense of several thousand Confederate casualties.[22]

With the advantage of hindsight, it is clear that Lincoln's reelection had sealed the fate of the Confederacy. With Richmond and Petersburg under siege and Sherman advancing through Georgia, Confederate prospects were indeed bleak; the growing defeatism was reflected in the increased number of desertions. Nevertheless, Lee's soldiers did not regard themselves as defeated. (Indeed, in any clash between forces of comparable size, the Army of Northern Virginia held its own to the end, as in the brief success at Fort Stedman.) Lee's soldiers were aware, too, of an erosion of morale among the Yankees, as the enemy's reliance on conscripts increased during 1864.

What was Lee to do? No American soldier has ever been more respectful of civilian control than Robert E. Lee, and Jefferson Davis proved unwilling to evacuate Richmond, much less consider surrender. Had Lee proposed surrender in the early months of 1865, when Grant was still at bay, he would have been opposed by Davis, by most of his generals, and by many of those serving in the ranks.

The situation changed after the fall of Richmond, and Lee was not bound by Davis's dictates. But not even the army's disorderly flight dictated immediate surrender. Lee by then had the modest objective of uniting with Johnston in North Carolina, where the existence of a Confederate army of significant size might have improved the South's bargaining position. As late as April 8, Lee's generals were opposed to surrender. But when it was clear that his army was surrounded, Lee took it upon himself to accept the inevitable.

THE SURRENDER OF HIS ARMY COMPLETED, LEE STRODE OUT of the McLean house at Appomattox, a dwelling that soon would be picked clean by Federal officers eager for souvenirs. Lee called for Traveller, and mounted with what some observers would recall as an audible sigh. He now had to tell his veterans, camped only a mile away, that their war was over. Just as Lee mounted, Grant, who had given Lee the most generous terms possible, came to the porch of the house and doffed his cap. Other Federal officers followed his example. Lee raised his hat and, followed by Marshall, set out for the Confederate camp.

The McLean house at Appomattox not long after Lee's surrender. LIBRARY OF CONGRESS.

The two riders crossed a small ridge, passed gray-clad pickets, and entered the Confederate lines. Rumors of surrender had swept through the camp, and many soldiers broke ranks when they saw their commander. A few cheered; others asked whether it was true that they were surrendered. "Men," Lee said, in a voice that he could not keep free of emotion, "we have fought the war together, and I have done the best I could for you. You will all be paroled and go to your homes until exchanged."[23]

He then rode slowly among the soldiers, some of whom were weeping, to his headquarters tent in a nearby apple orchard.

CHAPTER NINETEEN

A DRY AND THIRSTY LAND

LEE LINGERED AT APPOMATTOX FOR ABOUT three days after the surrender of his army. There were housekeeping details to attend to, and even friendships to mend with Federal officers such as George Meade and Henry J. Hunt. Lee issued a farewell order to his army, the drafting of which he delegated to Charles Marshall:

> After four years of arduous service, marked by unsurpassed courage and fortitude, the Army of Northern Virginia has been compelled to yield to overwhelming numbers and resources.
>
> I need not tell the brave survivors of so many hard fought battles, who have remained steadfast to the last, that I have consented to the result from no distrust of them.
>
> But feeling that valor and devotion could accomplish nothing that would compensate for the loss that must have attended the continuance of the contest, I determined to avoid the useless sacrifice of those whose past services have endeared them to their countrymen.
>
> By the terms of the agreement officers and men can return to their homes and remain until exchanged. You will

take with you the satisfaction that proceeds from the consciousness of duty faithfully performed, and I earnestly pray
that a Merciful God will extend to you His blessings and
protection.

With an increasing admiration of your constancy and
devotion to your country, and a grateful remembrance of
your kind and generous considerations for myself, I bid
you all an affectionate farewell.[1]

On about April 13, Lee reached the house in Richmond that had
been home to his wife and daughters for most of the war. Whatever
relief the family may have felt at the end of the fighting was muted by
the physical evidence of defeat and concern for missing members of the
family. Although Rooney Lee had accompanied his father to Richmond, Custis had been captured in the final days of the war and young
Rob was not accounted for. Both would show up in a few days.

Lee had no idea what the future held. He had no job and no income.
Other than the rented premises in Richmond he had no home; Arlington had been confiscated by the Federal government, ostensibly for
nonpayment of taxes, and Rooney's estate on the James had been burned
by Federal soldiers. Lee's holdings of some $20,000 in Confederate
bonds were worthless. However, he was not bankrupt. He owned shares
in the Erie Railroad and a Northern canal company, and in this respect
he was better off than most former Confederates.

Public security in Richmond was tenuous; demobilized soldiers and
newly freed blacks roamed the streets. Not a few found time to gawk
at the house on Franklin Street, hoping for a glimpse of the South's
foremost soldier. The Federals, thoughtful of their late opponent,
posted a sentry at the door, and Mary Lee, Yankee-hater though she
was, arranged for breakfast to be provided the sentry each morning.[2]

Rooney Lee and Walter Taylor tried to protect the general from
unwanted visitors, but not all callers could be deterred. There were
farewell handshakes, some tearful, with soldiers whom Lee did not
know by name but who were returning to homes from which they
could not expect to see their old commander again. Other veterans
wrote letters. An army doctor, en route to Alabama, wrote to Lee,

To belong to General Lee's defeated Army is now the proud-
est boast of a Confederate soldier. Though overwhelmed by

superior numbers and forced to surrender, we yet preserved intact our honor as men & soldiers. May the calamity which has befallen us be sanctified to the good of us all; and may the richest blessings of Heaven be vouchsafed to our noble Commander in Chief.[3]

One evening Lee, with daughter Mildred, called unannounced at the house of Lee's one-time aide, Robert Chilton. There he found not only Chilton but also his nephew, Channing Smith, who was serving with Mosby's rangers in northern Virginia. Smith, who had slipped into the city on Mosby's behest to determine whether the rangers should fight on, found himself face to face with Robert E. Lee. When he asked Lee what Mosby should do, the answer was dictated by Lee's legal status. "Give my regards to Colonel Mosby," Lee said, "and tell him that I am under parole, and cannot, for that reason, give him any advice." Smith took this in and wondered, wistfully, what he himself should do. Lee had no trouble this time. He had known young Smith before the war and now he told him, "Go home, all you boys who fought with me, and help build up the shattered fortunes of our old state."[4]

Lee was still in Richmond in June when word came that a Federal grand jury in Norfolk had indicted him for treason. The reaction in the South was one of indignation, for Lee had been scrupulous in observing the terms of his parole. In addition to the threat posed by the grand jury action, Lee, as a senior Confederate officer, fell into a category of persons for whom pardons would be considered on a case-by-case basis only.

Lee obviously did not want to be tried for treason, and he hoped that he might be granted a pardon as a conciliatory gesture by President Andrew Johnson's administration. On June 13 he wrote to Grant, and enclosed an application for pardon:

> I am ready to meet any charges that may be preferred against me, and do not wish to avoid trial; but, if I am correct as to the protection granted by my parole, and am not to be prosecuted, I desire to comply with the provision of the President's proclamation, and, therefore, inclose the required application.[5]

On receiving Lee's letter, Grant wrote to President Johnson urging that Lee be pardoned and that the grand jury indictment be quashed.

A still-proud Lee posed for this famous photograph by Mathew Brady in Richmond shortly after the surrender at Appomattox. LIBRARY OF CONGRESS.

The result was a partial victory. Federal prosecutors halted legal proceedings, but no pardon was forthcoming. The latter would have required a positive action by the president, and Johnson was reluctant to take an action that would be unpopular in much of the North.

By the autumn of 1865 Lee was forced to make plans. He and Mary had been welcomed at the homes of friends and relatives, but Lee was ready to put down some roots for the first time since his boyhood in Alexandria. He wrote to Rooney that he planned to buy a farm with which he could support himself and Mary. He hoped also to write a history of the Army of Northern Virginia, but circumstances were against him. Although Lee wrote to a number of his wartime colleagues requesting data on their campaigns, the records that he sought had invariably been abandoned in the last days of the war. Lee would never write the story of his "ragamuffins," and history is poorer for it.

Nor would he try his hand at farming, for in the Shenandoah Valley the trustees of a small college had other plans for the general. Washington College was an undistinguished school in Lexington, Virginia, that had been seriously damaged during the war. Federal troops had occupied it in 1864, scattering the library and damaging other facilities. Most of the students had joined the Confederate army at one time or another, leaving an underage student body that numbered about forty at the end of the war. The college's main asset, apart from bricks and mortar, was some canal stock donated by George Washington—a gift that had led the college to be named for the first president.

College trustees, meeting in August 1865, considered many needs, among them finding money to reopen the school and hiring a new president. Lee's name arose in the discussion of possible heads for the school. His daughter Mary had recently visited Lexington, and had remarked that her father's plans were uncertain. Might General Lee be willing to take on a struggling provincial college? Without even sounding him out, the trustees unanimously elected Lee president. The next step was to inform the general of his good fortune. Nervous trustees took up a collection on behalf of one John Brockenbough, who they believed was the best man to approach Lee but who had no money for travel expenses.[6]

Some warriors are restless in times of peace. Lee was not one of these, however, and he found the offer from Washington College appealing. The annual salary of $1,500 was modest, but it would be ample for the frugal Lees. Lexington was off the beaten track, but that is exactly where Lee wished to be. He had been urging others to work to rebuild the South; now he would be able to contribute personally in the field of education—a field in which, as a former superintendent of West Point, he had some expertise. In writing to the trustees, Lee made it clear that he would be looking to the future, not the past:

> I think it the duty of every citizen, in the present condition of the Country, to do all in his power to aid in the restoration of peace and harmony. . . . It is particularly incumbent upon those charged with the instruction of the young to set them an example of submission to authority.[7]

The college reopened in October 1865 with about fifty students. As superintendent of West Point, Lee had been responsible for managing a viable institution, one with a clear mission and a chain of command leading to the secretary of war. At Washington College he was handed a blank sheet of paper. The trustees did not expect Lee to be a full-time administrator; their hope was to use his name for fund-raising purposes. Instead, they found themselves with a hands-on president. Lee assessed each of his five professors, had a long talk with every incoming student, and began updating the course of study.

Like many institutions North and South, Washington College had a curriculum that was heavily weighted toward the classics. Prodded by Lee, the trustees established five new chairs, three of them in scientific courses. At the same time, Lee set about soliciting funds. Begging did not come easily to the general, but in January 1866 he received a commitment of $15,000 from Cyrus McCormick, the Virginia-born inventor of the reaper. Other donations followed.

Lee set up his office in the basement of the college chapel. The furnishings were spartan: a combination desk and bookcase along one wall, a sideboard along another, and a small round table in the middle of the room. They evoked the observation by Walter Taylor during the war that Lee was "never so uncomfortable as when comfortable."[8]

For most of his five years at Washington College, Lee had no secretary. He normally arrived at his office at eight o'clock in the morning after prayers. He worked until about two o'clock, much of the time on correspondence, and then went home for the midday meal. If there was no faculty meeting or other special business that afternoon, he would nap and then go for a long ride on Traveller, usually unaccompanied. These rides were his primary recreation.

Lee may have been deep in thought one day when he passed another rider who stopped and identified himself as one of Lee's veterans. He was so proud to meet the general, he said, that he was tempted to let out a cheer. That would not be necessary, Lee suggested; there were just the two of them in the forest. That did not matter, the old soldier replied, and he rode off shouting, "Hurrah for General Lee! Hurrah for General Lee!"[9]

Lee was a strong believer in moral education, one with a Christian bias. But he knew that there were good and bad ways to achieve this goal, and one of his first actions as president was to abolish compulsory chapel. "As a general principle," he told a professor, "you should not force young men to do their duty, but let them do it voluntarily, and thereby develop their characters. The great mistake of my life was

One of a handful of photographs of Lee on Traveller, taken by Michael Miley in Lexington in 1866. LIBRARY OF CONGRESS.

taking a military education."[10] This last sentence has been quoted out of context as the embittered reflection of a defeated general. But what Lee meant is that moral values can best be inculcated in a situation where rank plays no role.

At Lexington, Lee intervened repeatedly in incidents of racial friction between Washington College students and local blacks. Had his race-baiting students been cadets, Lee could have invoked traditional military punishments. At Lexington, he attempted to show his "boys" the error of their ways.

Lee never alluded to the fact that, although a college president, he was still under indictment for treason. He wrote in a philosophical vein to his wartime aide, Charles Marshall:

> The truth is this: The march of Providence is so slow and our desires so impatient; the work of progress is so immense and our means of aiding it so feeble; the life of humanity is so long, [and] that of the individual so brief, that we often see only the ebb of the advancing wave and are thus discouraged. It is history that teaches us to hope.[11]

Lee's legal status improved on Christmas Day, 1868, when President Johnson extended a general amnesty to former Confederates. The proclamation restored Lee's civil rights, except that he could not hold public office without congressional approval.

Happiness did not come easily to Robert E. Lee, but his years at Washington College provided him with a degree of fulfillment. He enjoyed working with young people. He was doing his *duty*, but it no longer involved killing people. One wonders how history might have been different if, in the dull years before the Civil War, Lee had been offered a professorship in engineering or moral philosophy at a school like Washington College.

At Lexington, Lee's relations with Mary were as warm as at any time in their marriage. She felt keenly the loss of Arlington and its Washington family memorabilia, but her childhood home did not exert its earlier pull. Her parents were gone, and so was the property. Like her husband, Mary had been a reluctant secessionist in 1861, but the war had changed her. Friends and sons of friends had been killed. She herself had had three sons in uniform. As the war went on she had become vitriolic in her denunciations of the Yankees and appreciative of the husband who had found time to look after her amid his many cares.

By the end of the war Mary's arthritis had become crippling, and she was largely confined to a wheelchair. In deference to her condition, the college built a new president's house with a wheelchair-accessible porch on three sides. Mary wrote to a cousin in 1867,

> We are expecting to move into a new house by the spring that they are building for the President of the College & hope then to have more room to entertain our friends & that some of you may get to see me. Life is waning away, and with the exception of my own immediate family I am cut off from all I have known & loved in my youth.[12]

The one indulgence the Lee family allowed itself consisted of trips to various spas, most of them in West Virginia, where the warm-water springs were widely believed to provide relief to such arthritis sufferers. In 1867 and again the next year, the Lees made a tour of these fashionable resorts, one of which provided the occasion for one of Lee's rare political pronouncements.

The general distrusted politicians and was uncomfortable discussing political topics. He epitomized the nonpolitical tradition in the U.S. military, and his lifelong attempt to remain aloof from the political turmoil about him would be emulated by twentieth-century soldiers as different as George C. Marshall and George Patton. At White Sulphur Springs, however, in the election-year summer of 1868, Lee was approached by a prominent Federal officer, Gen. William S. Rosecrans, on a sensitive matter. Rosecrans, a Democrat, was hoping that Lee would provide a statement—one to be endorsed by other prominent Southerners—to assure Northern voters that the South accepted the results of the war and was prepared to treat former slaves as free men. Lee mulled over Rosecrans's proposal and agreed to cooperate. The result was Lee's most comprehensive statement on the race problem of his day:

> Whatever opinions may have prevailed in the past with regard to African slavery or the right of a State to secede from the Union, we believe we express the almost unani-

mous judgment of the Southern people when we declare
that they consider these questions were decided by the war,
and that it is their intention in good faith to abide by that
decision. . . . The idea that the Southern people are hostile
to the negroes and would oppress them, if it were in their
power to do so, is entirely unfounded. . . . They still constitute an important part of our laboring population.

It was one thing for Lee to accept the end of slavery; the political
enfranchisement of the newly freed slaves was a different matter:

It is true that the people of the South . . . are, for obvious
reasons, inflexibly opposed to any system of laws that would
place the political power of the country in the hands of the
negro race. But this opposition springs from no feeling of
enmity, but from a deep-seated conviction that, at present,
the negroes have neither the intelligence nor the other
qualifications which are necessary to make them safe depos-
itories of political power. They would inevitably become
the victims of demagogues, who, for selfish purposes, would
mislead them to the serious injury of the public.[13]

Lee's thinking, unfashionable today, was typical of that of educated
Southerners, and not far from that of Northerners such as Lincoln and
Seward. Lee was wise enough to hedge his reservations about black
voting by saying that *at present* it was a bad idea.

It was one thing to accept the political realities that followed Appomattox; it was another to ally one's self with the government in Washington. In June 1868, James Longstreet published a letter in which
he espoused cooperation with the Radical Republicans. When the
Republicans gave his letter wide circulation and he was denounced
as an apostate by former Confederates, Longstreet wrote to Lee in
search of support. It was not forthcoming. Lee wrote back,

While I think we should act under the law and according
to the law imposed upon us, I cannot think the course pursued by the dominant political party the best for the interests of the country, and therefore cannot say so, or give
them my approval. . . . I am of the opinion that all who can
should vote for the most intelligent, honest and conscien-

tious men eligible for office, irrespective of former party opinions.[14]

Longstreet, heedless of the perils in associating himself with the erstwhile enemy, soon accepted an appointment from President Grant. In doing so, Longstreet ensured that his controversial behavior at Gettysburg would never be forgotten.

⟶⟳ ⟲⟵

ALTHOUGH LEE RARELY SPOKE OF THE WAR IT WAS NEVER far from his thoughts. One day he called in a student, Milton Humphreys, to caution him regarding an unusual vice: working too hard on his studies. Humphreys started to explain. He had served in the war, and now was "so impatient to make up for the time I lost in the army. . . ." He got no further. Lee, flushing, interrupted:

> Mr. Humphreys, however long you live and whatever you accomplish, you will find that the time you spent in the Confederate army was the most profitably spent portion of your life. Never again speak of having lost time in the army![15]

If Lee was very careful in what he said about the war, he and Traveller doubtless refought many a battle on their rides in the countryside. And, among friends, the general was prepared to reminisce. To Col. William Allan, a Confederate veteran and historian, he spoke of the Maryland and Pennsylvania campaigns. His invasions of the North, Lee said, were essentially defensive in their motivation, initiated in part to feed his army. But Lee emphasized different aspects of his campaigns in different conversations. To Edward Gordon, a Presbyterian minister who had served in the Confederate army, he attributed the result at Antietam to the lost order, saying, "I went into Maryland to give battle, and could I have kept General McClellan in ignorance of my position a day or two longer, I would have fought and crushed him."[16]

Lee had not known that the Army of the Potomac was at Gettysburg, and could not believe that it was there in force because he was confident that Stuart would have warned him. Lee dismissed as absurd a remark attributed to Longstreet—that Lee had promised his generals not to fight a general battle in Pennsylvania—and questioned whether Longstreet had in fact made such a statement.[17] Lee believed that Gettysburg would have been a victory if Jackson rather than Ewell had commanded the Second Corps, for Jackson would have carried Cemetery Hill on the first day and forced the Federals to evacuate their position along Cemetery Ridge.[18]

Asked who was the ablest of the Federal generals who had opposed him, Lee had a controversial reply. "McClellan, by all odds," he said.[19]

Lee rarely spoke of his crucial decision to throw in his lot with Virginia in 1861. Perhaps his most reasoned statement was in a letter to Beauregard in 1865:

> True patriotism sometimes requires of men to act contrary, at one period, to that which it does at another, and the motive which impels them—the desire to do right—is precisely the same. . . . Washington himself is an example. At one time he fought against the French under Braddock, in the service of the King of Great Britain; at another, he fought with the French at Yorktown, under the orders of the Continental Congress of America, against him. He has not been branded by the world with reproach for this; but his course has been applauded.[20]

⊷══ ══⊷

IN EARLY 1870, LEE'S HEALTH BECAME SO FRAGILE THAT HE thought of resigning the college presidency. He remarked to an associate that the short uphill walk from the chapel to his house so exhausted him that he had to stop and rest along the way. Lee did not resign, but he agreed to the change of scene that his doctors had long recommended. It was arranged that his daughter Agnes would accompany him on a trip as far south as Savannah.

In March 1870, Lee embarked on what became a farewell tour. Word of his travel prompted a surge of remembrance not only among war veterans but also among Southerners in general. Crowds gathered at every railroad depot. Agnes wrote home that wherever they went they were offered meals and other hospitality; "Even [United States] soldiers on the train sent in fruit."[21] The trip lasted more than two months and was not the rest cure that the general's doctors had in mind. But Lee must have felt a degree of satisfaction in seeing the affection in which he was held in so many parts of the South. A woman later remembered how Lee had been a guest at her parents' home:

> I can only remember the great dignity and kindness of General Lee's bearing, how lovely he was to all of us girls, that he gave us his photographs and wrote his name on them. . . . We regarded him with the greatest veneration. We had heard of God, but here was General Lee![22]

Back in Lexington, Lee prepared for another college year. He seemed to have regained a measure of strength, and he resumed his afternoon rides. In addition to his responsibilities at the college, Lee was senior warden at Grace Episcopal Church, and a meeting of the vestry was scheduled for the afternoon of September 27. The day was unseasonably chilly, but Lee donned an old military cape and made his way to the church.

The meeting lasted for three hours, with much of the time devoted to how to raise the rector's salary. As afternoon turned into evening the church grew colder and Lee appeared more weary. When it was discovered that the pledges fell $55 short of their goal, Lee said quietly, "I will give that sum."[23]

The meeting adjourned, and Lee bade his associates good night. He stepped into the rain and trod the familiar homeward path for the last time, at peace with the only entity that mattered, his God.

CHAPTER TWENTY

MEET GENERAL LEE

$\mathbf{D}$URING THE GETTYSBURG CAMPAIGN, IT IS said, Lee was watching one of his columns march under the hot sun when a soldier broke ranks and approached him. Perspiring heavily, the soldier apologized; he couldn't see because of the sweat in his eyes, and was looking for something to dry his face. Lee promptly took out his own handkerchief and handed it to the soldier. "Take it with you," Lee said, "and back quick to ranks." [1]

During the siege of Petersburg, Lee was in the front lines when the Federals opened up with artillery. After sending his companions to a less exposed position, Lee stepped into the open to pick up a sparrow that had fallen from its nest and returned it to the tree from which it had fallen. [2]

Both of these vignettes, of questionable provenance, are included in Douglas S. Freeman's four-volume *R. E. Lee*. Both incidents may have taken place, but in the absence of overwhelming evidence they present a target for critics of that biographer and his subject. There is a hint of irritation in Thomas L. Connelly's paraphrase of the Lee legend:

> He was the son who never disobeyed his mother, the per-
> fect student, and the man of flawless character. He was the

noble Lee of 1861, who supposedly loved the Union more
than others who espoused the Confederate cause. . . . He
was the tactical genius who was seldom—if ever—defeated
by mistakes of his own making.[3]

Edmund Wilson, the literary critic, once volunteered that the cruel-
est thing that had happened to Abraham Lincoln since his assassination was to fall into the hands of poet-biographer Carl Sandburg.[4]
Similarly, any "controversy" with respect to Lee is largely a result of the
extravagant praise accorded him by Southern admirers who in some
instances sought to denigrate others—most notably Longstreet—in
extolling Lee. The general was ensnared by his own myth. This fact has
enabled a modern generation of writers to focus on the background
noise of the Lee legend—the sometimes unseemly infighting among his
admirers on issues such as where a statue should be located—as somehow reflecting on Lee himself.

As noted earlier, many factors contributed to the growth of a Lee legend. But there would have been no legend if Lee himself had not been
almost universally admired by those who knew him best. His piety, in
addition to his bravery and modesty, had a special appeal in the Bible
Belt. The grim reality of defeat served as another impetus to the Lee
legend. The states of the former Confederacy not only had lost a generation of young men to war, but also had become the only part of
North America to experience military occupation. For many Southerners, Lee's character served to validate the Confederate cause and to
check any impulse to link the Union victory to God's will. There is no
doubt that the modest Lee would have been appalled at his canoniza-
tion in the decades after the war.

⋯⇒ ⇐⋯

IF WE DISPENSE WITH LOST CAUSE NOSTALGIA, WHAT CAN
be said with some degree of objectivity of Lee the soldier? A first step
will be to avoid the murky semantics that have grown up around
Confederate strategy. (Were both the grand strategy *and* the regional
strategy defensive, or only the grand strategy? Was the Lee of 1862
and 1863 waging an offensive war, or was his strategy one of offensive
defense?) The core questions with respect to any military commander
are: Did he undertake reasonable objectives and did he make the best
use of the resources available to achieve them?

The basis for most of the criticism of Lee as a soldier is that the South could have won the war if its commanders had been wiser and used their resources more skillfully. His critics are fond of citing battles from earlier eras in which a smaller force defeated a greater one; McWhiney and Jamieson note the victories of Epaminondas at Leuctra (371 B.C.) and Hannibal at Cannae (216 B.C.) as evidence that God is not always on the side of the heavier battalions.[5] For those who believe that the South could have won, it is easy to argue that it lost because Confederate commanders were reckless in their expenditure of life— as some of them were—and that Lee was one of the principal culprits. They ignore the fact that the South faced a determined foe with a vastly superior industrial base, a foe capable of putting about 2.8 million men into uniform, as opposed to about 600,000 in the Confederacy.

Although a step-by-step refutation of this thesis is beyond the scope of this volume, a few thoughts are in order. The Confederacy had a single objective in its short life: to compel the North to quit, to abandon its objective of reuniting the Union by force. Although this was a defensive objective, it was not one that could be achieved by static defense, given the North's superiority in number and resources. As Gary W. Gallagher points out,

> Strategically defensive campaigns often drained manpower at a rate almost equal to that lost by the side on the offensive. The problem lay in the fact that defenders usually reached a point where they had to attack in order to avoid a siege.[6]

The North could be brought to the bargaining table only if the Confederates could demonstrate that victory over the South would be prohibitively costly, and this is what Lee set out to do. Taking command of the Army of Northern Virginia in June 1862, he first saved Richmond from capture and, quite possibly, the Confederate cause from collapse. In the Second Manassas campaign that followed, he nearly drove the enemy out of Virginia. Although his brief incursion into Maryland was unproductive, Lee's easy repulse of Burnside at Fredericksburg brought Northern morale to perhaps the lowest point in the war. The next spring he brought off one of the classic victories in military history at Chancellorsville before embarking on the ill-fated Gettysburg campaign. In most of these campaigns Lee was outnumbered by two to one or more, and faced artillery far superior to his own.

It was Lee's recognition of the South's inferiority in resources that produced a sense of urgency in his thinking. His target was the North's willingness to fight, and Northern morale was most vulnerable in the period before the enemy could marshal its full resources. Although Lee was the opposite of a textbook general—he may have been one of the few generals of his era who never quoted Napoleon—he was very much like the emperor in seeking a climactic battle.

Lee's service as commander of the Army of Northern Virginia divides readily into two parts: from June 1862 until the end of 1863, when Lee was free to maneuver and sought to retain the initiative in the field; and from January 1864 until Appomattox, when he was constantly on the defensive against Grant. Few fault Lee's handling of his dwindling resources during this second period. Outnumbered at times as much as three to one, Lee proved able to defend Richmond far longer than the Confederacy had any right to expect, and his use of topography and field defenses showed him to be a master of defensive warfare.

The controversial period of Lee's career is the year that began with the Seven Days' campaign and culminated at Gettysburg. One must deal with two main indictments: first, that Lee accepted exorbitant casualties in the course of winning his victories, and in so doing "bled the Confederacy white"; and second, that he was preoccupied with developments in Virginia and failed to grasp the threat posed by Federal victories in the West.

Battlefield attrition certainly played a role in the defeat of the Confederacy, and the charge as it applies to Lee must be addressed. McWhiney and Jamieson conclude that Confederate armies on various fronts were the attackers in eight of the first twelve major battles of the war, and that in those battles suffered 20,000 more casualties than the Federals.[7] Using a statistical approach, the authors conclude that Lee incurred casualties of approximately 20 percent in twelve battles as army commander, as opposed to 10.5 percent for Joseph E. Johnston and 19 percent for the notoriously aggressive John B. Hood.[8]

Clearly, this trend in casualties is one that the Confederacy could not long sustain. Casualties, however, are the human toll of any war; they are not the principal standard by which campaigns should be judged. Lee accepted far heavier casualties than McClellan during the Seven Days' campaign, but in driving McClellan from Richmond he achieved a success for which the Confederacy would have paid almost any price. In battles such as Chancellorsville and Second Manassas, he sought not merely to defeat but also to destroy the enemy in front of him. Although the results fell short of Lee's hopes, the promise of decisive victory justified aggressive, potentially costly, tactics. At Malvern Hill and Gettysburg, Lee launched attacks that were ill advised. But war entails risk, and in each case Lee had reason to believe that the likelihood of success justified the risk.

Tactically, Lee sought to defeat the enemy "in detail"—without engaging his full force—and he was repeatedly successful. In the Seven Days he made use of the swollen Chickahominy River to isolate much of McClellan's army; at Second Manassas he executed a forced march on interior lines to defeat Pope, just hours before he would have been prohibitively outnumbered. At Chancellorsville, Lee defeated three wings of Hooker's army on three successive days, again making good use of interior lines.

Lee quickly gained a reputation for daring that was itself an asset. Except for the Seven Days' campaign, his campaigns were fought at places and times of Lee's choosing. Strategically, his insistence on maintaining a force in the Shenandoah Valley tied down Federal divisions that could have been used against Lee directly or in the West. Because of the threat from the valley, the Federals had to take measures to protect Washington throughout most of the war.

Should Lee have attempted to assume the defensive at Gettysburg, or even at Chancellorsville? If Lee could have persuaded the enemy to attack him in a strong defensive position in either engagement, the Army of Northern Virginia would probably have emerged a winner. The enemy knew this also, especially after Fredericksburg, and in the latter half of the war sought to avoid frontal assaults. To assume, as Longstreet did, that a general as astute as Meade could have been lured into attacking a strong defensive position is unwarranted.

But was a defensive battle ideal for the Army of Northern Virginia? Such an engagement would have allowed the Federals to take full advantage of their superiority in artillery, while allowing little scope for Lee's fine cavalry. Equally important, a static defense would have denied Lee the maneuverability with which he compensated for inferior numbers. Finally, such a course would have surrendered the initiative to the enemy. Lee's soldiers were aggressive in their approach to war, and any attempt to curb their élan, as opposed to using it on the offensive where possible, would have denied Lee one of his army's greatest assets. The rebel yell, delivered from behind a tree, lost much of its impact.

Antietam may have been a watershed for Lee. Although the battle itself was indecisive, his soldiers demonstrated such tenacity there that they can be said to have won the battle of wills. The resulting surge in Southern morale contributed to victory at Chancellorsville and, later, to defeat at Gettysburg. Had Lee not seen what his troops could accomplish at Antietam and Chancellorsville there would have been no Pickett's Charge. But when Lee ordered a frontal attack against Cemetery Ridge at Gettysburg, he could be excused for believing that his army was invincible.

By 1864, Lee was very selective in taking the offensive. At Spotsylvania and at least twice in the Petersburg campaign he rejected the urging of subordinates to attack Grant's lines. In Lee's words, "The lives of our soldiers are too precious to be sacrificed in the attainment of successes that inflict no losses on the enemy beyond the actual loss in battle."[9] If many of Lee's battles ended with frontal assaults, there was a practical reason. The time required to get troops into position for a flank attack was so great, and concealment so difficult, that successful flank assaults were rare. Jackson's famous attack at Chancellorsville was very much the exception.

Was Stonewall Jackson the essential element in Lee's greatest victories? Although another corps commander might have executed the flank march at Chancellorsville, it is doubtful that anyone could have matched Jackson's performance in the Second Manassas campaign. Still, Lee was entitled to at least one gifted subordinate. Certainly his other corps commanders, except for Longstreet on the defensive, were erratic in performance. Ewell and Anderson were promoted beyond their level of competence, although it is not clear that Lee could have made better choices from the talent available to him.

Lee himself was not without failings as a battlefield commander. His orders were at times imprecise, and contributed to tactical errors by A. P. Hill in the Seven Days' campaign, to a mistimed withdrawal by Early at Chancellorsville, and to Stuart's critical disappearance in the days before Gettysburg. And Lee's preference for giving his subordinates broad discretion worked for only as long as Jackson lived. It took the Battle of Gettysburg to impress on Lee that his corps commanders required closer supervision.

No amount of historical research has revealed what made Lee a great commander, but he demonstrated a number of identifiable skills. He made good use of every type of information on enemy intentions. He studied the Northern press and interrogated spies and informants. He could translate the sight of rations being cooked, or the availability of river-crossing equipment, into the intentions of his opposing commander. In some indefinable way, his engineering background helped him discover the weak points in an enemy line. Lee was extremely difficult to deceive on the battlefield. In the Seven Days' campaign, he appeared to anticipate McClellan's every move. At Chancellorsville, he required only minutes' study through his glasses to conclude that Sedgwick's corps did not pose a serious threat—the main attack would come from Hooker.

Beyond demonstrating his professional skill as a soldier, Lee put his personal stamp on any battlefield. He so preyed on the mind of the enemy that in early 1865, when Lee's army was a shadow of its former self, the Federals still feared some daring move. Outnumbered by two or three to one, Lee still had the ability to alarm and mystify his foe.

In dealing with his senior subordinates, Lee learned the strengths of each and used them to good advantage. Yet, in Freeman's term, he sometimes submitted to "mental bullying."[10] He twice allowed Longstreet to overrule his preference for an early attack on Pope at Second Manassas, and did little to speed him along on the crucial second day at Gettysburg. He put up with Ewell as a corps commander far longer than he should have. Still, even Lee's patience had its limits, as he demonstrated just days before Appomattox, when he sacked not one but three generals.

For the most part, the men in the ranks worshiped Lee. A North Carolina soldier wrote in 1863, "I felt proud that the Southern Confederacy could boast of such a man."[11] When, in April 1865, Lee speculated to Gen. Henry A. Wise about how the country might regard the Army of Northern Virginia's surrender, Wise responded, "Country be damned. . . . *You* are the country to these men."[12] One of Lee's later critics, Gen. John F. C. Fuller, would concede that "few generals have been able to animate an army as [Lee's] self-sacrificing idealism animated the Army of Northern Virginia. . . . What this bootless, ragged, half-starved army accomplished is one of the miracles of history."[13]

Not all military factors lend themselves to statistical analysis. If

Napoleon's presence on the battlefield was worth several divisions, how many was Lee's presence worth?

⊷≕⊃ ⊂≕⊷

THE SECOND MAJOR CRITICISM OF LEE—THAT HE WAS parochial in his focus on Virginia as opposed to other theaters of war— is more easily countered. Jefferson Davis, although relying increasingly on Lee for advice as the war went on, had carefully divided the Confederacy into military districts. Until June 1864, when Lee was nearly overwhelmed because he could not order reinforcements from Beauregard in southern Virginia, Lee commanded only in *northern* Virginia.

Lee's critics point out how reluctant he was to send any portion of the Army of Northern Virginia to reinforce Confederate armies in the West. He had good reason for misgivings. In May 1863, he opposed the transfer of Pickett's division to the West, citing both the time required in sending it and the "uncertainty of its application" under Gen. John C. Pemberton.[14] Lee's reluctance appears prescient, for three weeks later, Pemberton surrendered Vicksburg to Grant. In September, Lee reluctantly agreed to the transfer of two of Longstreet's divisions to assist Bragg, and rejoiced in Bragg's subsequent victory at Chickamauga. But Bragg failed to follow up on the victory or otherwise make the best use of Longstreet. Lee knew the men who led Confederate armies in the West, and he was properly, if privately, skeptical that they would put reinforcements from his own army to good use.

Should Lee have actively sought command of Confederate armies in the West? By the time Davis was considering such a move, Lee had a huge professional and emotional commitment to the Army of Northern Virginia. He knew the capabilities of his own officers in a way that he could never have known those in the West. But he had no need to fall back on personal considerations; Richmond remained the prize of war, and rarely in 1863 and 1864 was the Federal Army of the Potomac, 100,000 strong, more than fifty miles from the Confederate capital. In the words of historian Charles Roland, the "west was not intrinsically more valuable to the Confederacy than was the east; once the east was taken, the west would surely fall."[15] Lee *had* to do what he wanted to do: defend the capital of the Confederacy in the war's most important theater.

✦⟹ ⟸✦

ROBERT E. LEE WAS THE ABLEST COMMANDER OF THE CIVIL War and perhaps the greatest to come out of North America. But what can we say of Lee the man? Few men as prominent as Lee have been as successful as he in maintaining a degree of intellectual privacy. In the early months of the war, diarist Mary Chesnut reflected on the Lee brothers, Robert and Smith. "I know Smith Lee well," she wrote. "Can anybody say they know his brother? I doubt it. He looks so cold and quiet and grand." [16]

Quiet and grand Lee was, but not cold. He was in fact very emotional. He wept when tears were called for, as when he learned of daughter Anne's death in 1862, but on other occasions as well, including at least one of the "Lee to the rear" episodes when Lee saw manifest the affection in which he was held by his soldiers. Walter Taylor wrote that his chief was by no means one of those "invariably amiable men whose temper is never ruffled." The secret was his self-control: "General Lee was naturally of a positive temperament, and of strong passions; and it is a mistake to suppose him otherwise; but he held these in complete subjection to his will and conscience." [17]

The same language could have been applied to the man Lee most admired, George Washington.

In defining Lee we need to recall what he was not. He was in no sense a Renaissance man. His letters reflect no interest in art or music, and he once enjoined his wife not to allow young Rooney to read novels. And while it would be unfair to say that Lee lacked a sense of humor, his tended to be limited to the gentle teasing of family and close associates. He did not find relief in humor as Abraham Lincoln did. Lee's limited intellectual interests may have had something to do with his piety: If the Bible was the repository of all truth, why look elsewhere?

Spiritual himself, and married to a woman equally so, Lee from an early age sought personal self-improvement. He found time during the war to write down some of the thoughts he sought to live by:

> The manner in which an individual enjoys certain advantages over others is the test of a *true gentleman*. The power which the strong have over the weak, the magistrate over

the citizen, the employer over the employed, the educated over the unlettered, the experienced over the confiding, even the clever over the silly; the forebearing & inoffensive use of all this power or authority . . . will show the gentleman in a plain light. The gentleman does not needlessly and unnecessarily remind an offender of a wrong he may have committed against him. He can not only forgive, he can forget.[18]

Although Lee's religion appears to have provided him some comfort, it mainly served as a spur. His family letters, often filled with self-criticism and melancholy, have led some critics to portray Lee as troubled and insecure. Such a view, however, fails to distinguish between Lee's religious beliefs, in which piety and guilt went hand in hand, and feelings of personal inadequacy. In December 1863, Lee issued a proclamation calling on the Army of Northern Virginia to "humble itself in deep repentance for past sins" and to "bow submissively to His holy will."[19] The similar inferences of guilt in Lee's family letters have a pro forma quality; certainly, anyone who confronted Lee on a battlefield realized very quickly that he had no lack of self-confidence. But Lee's faith may have contributed to his preference for a remote command style: Once he had assembled his host, their fate lay with the God of Battles.

Some of the general's critics nevertheless contend that he was obsessed with a sense of personal failure, which made him unreasonably aggressive on the battlefield in some Wagnerian search for atonement. Before the war, Lee doubtless wondered whether his decades of peacetime service—a period devoid of tangible benefits and entailing long separations from his family—was time well spent. Such reservations were hardly unique to Lee, however; what is remarkable is that he accepted the mind-numbing routine of the peacetime army rather than pursue a career in civil engineering or teaching.

Less easily explained is how the outgoing, sociable young Lee evolved into so private a person. His only recreation was riding, the most solitary of diversions. He had few close male friends, and appeared capable of complete relaxation only with members of his family. Pleasure worried him. While his insistence on sharing the privations of his soldiers was a part of the Lee mystique, his spartan existence in Lexington is less readily explained. When an infant was brought to him for a blessing in 1870, Lee might have wished the child a life of happiness and service. Instead, Lee told the mother, "Teach him he must deny himself."[20]

It is not by accident that Lee's personality found a basis in his religion. He was not merely a pious soldier; he was a devout Christian whose profession happened to have been that of arms. In a different time he might have been a theologian. His belief that a divine Providence ruled human affairs made him a conservative in temporal affairs—slavery was an evil, but it would persist until Providence ruled otherwise. This perspective hardly put Lee in the vanguard of the anti-slavery movement, but we should not forget that Lee—born into a slaveholding society, and numbering many slaveholders among his friends—concluded that slavery was a moral wrong.

As a man and a soldier, Lee's most striking quality was his ability to wage war without demonizing the foe. Throughout the war the blue-clad enemy were simply "those people." After the war he became the South's most conspicuous advocate of reconciliation. He once declined an invitation to a dedication of monuments on the Gettysburg battlefield, writing that he preferred not to engage in activities that kept open the sores of war.[21]

An essential part of Lee's personality was his respect for constituted authority. When Virginia seceded he went along, despite grave doubts about the wisdom of its action. When Davis persisted in defending Richmond in the face of its imminent fall, Lee refused to invoke his authority and prestige to sway the president. After the war he not only set an example in his acceptance of the restored Union, but also, on his one postwar visit to Washington, paid a courtesy call on President Grant.

At the core of Lee's personality, as many writers have noted, was his sense of duty. When, in his farewell order to his soldiers, Lee said that they carried with them "the consciousness of duty faithfully performed," he was according them the highest praise of which he was capable. In part because he enjoyed so few earthly pleasures, "duty" was not a burden to Lee but an opportunity. Whether a sense of duty by itself constitutes a valid personal philosophy may be argued, but Lee made it one. To him, war was a heroic calling, but one to be waged in accordance with Christian values. Modest, thoughtful, and selfless as an unknown colonel in the U.S. Army, Lee did not change when he commanded an army of 80,000 and his name was revered throughout the South.

It is possible to refute some of the misunderstandings about Lee without fully comprehending this paradoxical figure. He abhorred personal confrontation but excelled in the profession of arms. A total realist in the logistics of war, he was enough of a romantic to reflect on the "glory" of death in battle. He was conservative in his philosophy and politics, yet audacious to the point of recklessness on the battlefield. He prayed for his enemies even as he waged aggressive war. For all of Lee's professions of unworthiness, he certainly demonstrated self-assurance in temporal affairs.

Not all rhetoric of the Lost Cause is without substance, and it was a Georgia politician, Benjamin H. Hill, who may have summed up Lee best. In Hill's words, Lee was "Caesar without his ambition, Frederick without his tyranny, Napoleon without his selfishness, and Washington without his reward."[22]

Small wonder that the defeated South chose Robert E. Lee as its symbol.

APPENDIX

LEE'S REFLECTIONS

J. William Jones (1836–1909) served as a chaplain in the Army of Northern Virginia and after the war as a Baptist minister in Lexington, Virginia, where he came to know and admire Lee. After Lee's death Jones was chosen by the trustees of Washington College to prepare a memorial volume. The book that resulted, *Personal Reminiscences of General Robert E. Lee*, was published in 1875.

The author's uncritical admiration for his subject makes the text of limited value today, but the book remains useful as a source of many of Lee's letters. Jones had unique access to some Lee material. In Jones's own words,

> It was my sad privilege, not long after General Lee's death, to look over some papers found in his army-satchel, together with his parole, and other things which had not been disturbed since his return from Appomattox Court House. On loose sheets he had written—evidently to amuse a leisure hour in camp—a great many maxims, proverbs,

quotations from the Psalms, selections from standard authors, and reflections of his own.[1]

Jones quoted three of Lee's reflections in his own book. Others are now in the Virginia Historical Society, but the fact that none of these are from the Scriptures, or from "standard authors," suggests that some of Lee's notes have been scattered. Those quoted here, all but one from the Virginia Historical Society, are highly eclectic, and in some instances obscure. It should be recalled that Lee meant these for his eyes only, and wrote accordingly.

Human Relations

My experience of men has neither disposed me to think worse of them, or indisposed me to serve them; nor in spite of failures which I lament, of errors which I now see & acknowledge; or of the present aspect of affairs; do I despair of the future. The truth is this, The march of Providence is so slow, and our desire so impatient, the work of progress is so immense & our means of aiding it so feeble; the life of humanity is so long & that of an individual so brief, that we often see only the ebb of the advancing wave, & are thus discouraged. It is history that teaches us to hope.[2]

Authority

The forbearing use of power does not only form a touchstone, but the manner in which an individual enjoys certain advantages over others, is a test of a *true gentleman.* The power which the strong have over the weak, the magistrate over the citizen, the employer over the employed, the educated over the unlettered, the experienced over the confiding, even the clever over the silly; the forbearing & inoffensive use of all this power or authority, or a total abstinence from it when the case admits it, will show the gentleman in a plain light. The gentleman does not needlessly and unnecessarily remind an offender of a wrong he may have committed against him. He can not only forgive, he can forget; & he strives for that nobleness of self and mildness of character which imparts sufficient strength to let the past be but the past. A true man of honor feels humbled himself when he cannot help humbling others.[3]

Virtue

Despise fickleness & fear. Let danger never turn you aside from the pursuit of honor or the service of your country. Know that death is inevitable & the fame of virtue immortal.

The man who possesses wealth without the capacity for active virtue, often learns to indulge in the vacancy of contemplative enjoyments, & slumbering on his post, abandons himself to pleasant dreams.

Politics and Politicians

Private & public life are subject to the same rules, & truth & manliness are two qualities that will carry you through this world, much better than . . . tact, or expediency, or any other word that was ever devised to conceal or mystify a deviation from a straight line.[4]

Whenever property, talent, & virtue are all on one side, & only ignorant members, with a mere sprinkling of property & talent to agitate them & make use of them, or misinformed or mistaken virtue to sanction them on the other side, no honest man can take long to deliberate which side he will choose.

Politicians are more or less so warped by party feeling, by selfishness, or prejudices, that their minds are not altogether truly balanced. They are the most difficult to cure of all insane people, politics having so much excitement in them.

Religion

Let religion wear the garb of gaiety & the daily thanksgiving to God be joyous & sincere. Nature always asserts her rights & abounds in means of gladness—

Time as it advances never reproduces an old piece, but unfolds new scenes in the grand drama of human existence. Scenes of mere glory, of mere wealth, of mere action, but not of tranquility & family.

The War

The war was occasioned by a doubtful question of construction of the Constitution which our wise & cautious forefathers differed about even while framing it, & which was transmitted unsettled to their descendants.

The purpose of the war has been perverted by the party in power. If the present policy had been announced at the time, I cannot believe that it would have been tolerated by the North, & it now seems to me so revolting to reason, & patriotism, that I cannot help wondering at its endorsement by men who must possess the common attributes of pride of race & country.

Philosophy

My Country, said the young William of Orange, trusts in me. I will not sacrifice it to any interests, but if need be die with it in the last ditch.

Grotius contended that right & wrong are not evanescent expressions of fluctuating opinion, but are endowed with an immortality of their own— Ideas once generated will live for ever.

Penn, Plato & Fénilon maintained that God is to be loved for his own sake, virtue to be practiced for its intrinsic loveliness.

Penn (1686) claimed for the Executive of the Country the prerogative of employing every person "according to his ability, & not according to his opinion."

Spiritual religion is an enfranchising power, expanding & elevating the Soul, & a service of forms is analogous to contracted understandings—

The selfishness of evil defeats itself, & God rules in the affairs of men.

The finite will of man, free in its individuality, is in the aggregate, subordinate to general laws. This is the reason why evil is self destructive; why truth when it is _____ is sure to live forever; why freedom & justice though resisted & restrained, renew the contest from age to age, confident that heaven fight[s] on their side, & that the stars in their courses war against their foes.

La Salle

La Salle, the daring adventurer, pursued the discovery of the Mississippi from the falls of St. Anthony to its mouth. Won the affections of the Gov. of Canada, the esteem of Colbert, the confidence of Seigrulay, the favor of Louis XIV; for force of will & vast conceptions; for various knowledge & quick adaptation of his genius to untried circumstances;

for a sublime magnanimity, that resigned itself, & yet triumphed over affliction by energy of purpose & unflattering hope, had no superior among his Countrymen. He was murdered in a branch of the Trinity River, Texas, by two mutineers, Derhand & L'Arshivegur, 17 March 1687.

A Soldier's Death[5]

The warmest instincts of every man's soul declare the glory of the soldier's death. It is more important to the Christian than to the Greek to sing:

> Glorious his fate, and envied is his lot,
> Who for his country fights and for it dies.

NOTES

Preface

1. Gary W. Gallagher, ed., *Lee the Soldier* (Lincoln: University of Nebraska Press, 1996), 279.

Chapter 1: The General and the Historians

1. Mary C. Lee to Edward C. Turner, Oct. ___ 1870, Christie's catalog #7700, June 9, 1993.
2. Douglas S. Freeman, *R. E. Lee* (New York: Charles Scribner's Sons, 1935), IV, 491.
3. *New York Times*, October 16, 1870.
4. Quoted in Richard Kenin and Justin Wintle, eds., *Dictionary of Biographical Quotations* (New York: Dorset Press, 1978), 483.
5. Garnet Wolseley, *The Story of a Soldier's Life* (London: Archibald Constable, 1903), I, 135.
6. Thomas L. Connelly, *The Marble Man* (New York: Alfred A. Knopf, 1977), 95.
7. John R. Young, *Around the World with General Grant* (New York: American News, 1879), II, 459.
8. Michael Fellman, *Citizen Sherman* (New York: Random House, 1995), 406.
9. Gallagher, *Lee the Soldier*, 425.

10. Alan T. Nolan, *Lee Considered* (Chapel Hill: University of North Carolina Press, 1991), 5.
11. David E. Johnson, "Character Confirmed: The Life of Douglas Southall Freeman," *Columbiad*, Fall 1997.
12. Freeman, *R. E. Lee*, IV, 494.
13. Connelly, *The Marble Man*, 84.
14. Ibid., xiv–xv.
15. Grady McWhiney and Perry D. Jamieson, *Attack and Die* (University of Alabama Press, 1982), 7, 71.
16. John Keegan, *The Mask of Command* (New York: Viking Books, 1987), 197.
17. Nolan, *Lee Considered*, 10.
18. Ibid., 42.
19. Ibid., 97.

Chapter 2: Son of the Old Dominion

1. Paul C. Nagel, *The Lees of Virginia* (New York: Oxford University Press, 1990), 166.
2. Charles Royster, *Light-Horse Harry Lee* (Baton Rouge: Louisiana State University Press, 1981), 62.
3. David Hackett Fischer, *Albion's Seed* (New York: Oxford University Press, 1989), 270.
4. Freeman, *R. E. Lee*, I, 31.
5. Fischer, *Albion's Seed*, 312.
6. Thomas J. Fleming, *West Point* (New York: William Morrow, 1969), 58.
7. Freeman, *R. E. Lee*, I, 74.
8. Clifford Dowdey, *Lee* (New York: Bonanza Books, 1965), 46.
9. Emory M. Thomas, *Robert E. Lee* (New York: W. W. Norton, 1995), 53.
10. Dowdey, *Lee*, 48.
11. Thomas, *Robert E. Lee*, 62.
12. Nagel, *The Lees of Virginia*, 237.
13. Nancy Scott Anderson and Dwight Anderson, *The Generals* (New York: Alfred A. Knopf, 1987), 44.
14. Anderson and Anderson, *The Generals*, 43.
15. Thomas, *Robert E. Lee*, 78.
16. Nagel, *The Lees of Virginia*, 240.

Chapter 3: The Young Soldier

1. Nagel, *The Lees of Virginia*, 206–7.
2. Ibid., 238.

3. Thomas, *Robert E. Lee*, 73.
4. Ibid., 83–84.
5. Robert E. Lee, Jr., *My Father, General Lee* (New York: Doubleday, 1960), 133.
6. Byron Farwell, *Stonewall: A Biography of General Thomas J. Jackson* (New York: W. W. Norton, 1992), 45.
7. Freeman, *R. E. Lee*, I, 239–40.
8. John S. D. Eisenhower, *So Far from God* (New York: Random House, 1989), xxiii.
9. Freeman, *R. E. Lee*, I, 272.
10. Dowdey, *Lee*, 93–94.
11. Ulysses S. Grant, *Memoirs* (New York: Charles L. Webster & Co., 1885) I, 49, 53.
12. Anderson and Anderson, *The Generals*, 95.
13. Freeman, *R. E. Lee*, I, 294.

Chapter 4: Duty, God, and Slavery

1. Anderson and Anderson, *The Generals*, 106.
2. Thomas, *Robert E. Lee*, 149.
3. Anderson and Anderson, *The Generals*, 107, 110.
4. Almira R. Hancock, *Reminiscences of Winfield Scott Hancock* (New York: Charles L. Webster, 1887), 46–47.
5. Anderson and Anderson, *The Generals*, 108.
6. Freeman, *R. E. Lee*, IV, 309.
7. REL to Rooney Lee, June 2, 1853. Christie's catalog #7700, June 9, 1993.
8. Nagel, *The Lees of Virginia*, 258.
9. Robert M. Utley, *Frontiersmen in Blue* (Lincoln: University of Nebraska Press, 1967), 29.
10. Thomas, *Robert E. Lee*, 68.
11. Connelly, *The Marble Man*, 118–19.
12. Anderson and Anderson, *The Generals*, 143.
13. Thomas, *Robert E. Lee*, 177.
14. Freeman, *R. E. Lee*, I, 372.
15. Clifford Dowdey and Louis H. Manarin, eds., *The Wartime Papers of Robert E. Lee* (New York: Da Capo Press, 1987), 378–79.
16. Nolan, *Lee Considered*, 10–11, 23.
17. Thomas, *Robert E. Lee*, 372.
18. Freeman, *R. E. Lee*, I, 370.
19. Thomas, *Robert E. Lee*, 173.
20. John M. Taylor, *William Henry Seward* (Washington, D.C.: Brassey's, 1996), 114.

Chapter 5: "I Shall Share the Miseries of My People"

1. Freeman, *R. E. Lee*, I, 411.
2. Dowdey, *Lee*, 122.
3. Freeman, *R. E. Lee*, I, 417.
4. Ibid., 420–21.
5. James M. McPherson, *Battle Cry of Freedom* (New York: Oxford University Press, 1988), 279.
6. Lee to Reverdy Johnson, Feb. 25, 1868, quoted in J. William Jones, *Personal Reminiscences of General Robert E. Lee* (Baton Rouge: Louisiana State University Press, 1989), 141.
7. Freeman, *R. E. Lee*, I, 437.
8. Charles B. Flood, *Lee: The Final Years* (Boston: Houghton Mifflin, 1981), 124.
9. Burke Davis, *Gray Fox* (New York: Holt, Rinehart and Winston, 1956), 15.
10. Freeman, *R. E. Lee*, I, 441.
11. Mary C. Lee to Winfield Scott, May 5, 1861, quoted in Anderson and Anderson, *The Generals*, 200.
12. Connelly, *The Marble Man*, 198.
13. Nolan, *Lee Considered*, 42.
14. Connelly, *The Marble Man*, 198.
15. Freeman, *R. E. Lee*, I, 466–67.

Chapter 6: War

1. Freeman, *R. E. Lee*, I, 450.
2. David J. Eicher, *Robert E. Lee: A Life Portrait* (Dallas, Tex.: Taylor Publishing Co., 1997), 64.
3. Ibid., 48.
4. A. L. Long, *Memoirs of Robert E. Lee* (Secaucus, N.J.: Blue and Grey Press, 1983), 112.
5. Freeman, *R. E. Lee*, I, 539.
6. Steven E. Woodworth, *Davis and Lee at War* (Lawrence: University Press of Kansas, 1995), 59.
7. Lee, *My Father, General Lee*, 46–47.
8. Freeman, *R. E. Lee*, I, 577–78.
9. Ibid., I, 602–3.
10. Lee, *My Father, General Lee*, 60–61.
11. Ibid., 83.
12. Stephen W. Sears, *To the Gates of Richmond* (New York: Ticknor & Fields, 1992), 24.
13. Dowdey, *Lee*, 183.
14. Walter H. Taylor, *General Lee: His Campaigns in Virginia* (Dayton, Ohio: Morningside Press, 1975), 25.

15. REL to Albert Sidney Johnston, March 26, 1862. Quoted in "The Rhodes Scholar" Catalog #3, September 1998.
16. Freeman, *R. E. Lee*, II, 21.
17. Dowdey, *Lee*, 189.
18. Woodworth, *Davis and Lee at War*, 115–16.
19. Stephen W. Sears, *Landscape Turned Red* (New York: Ticknor & Fields, 1983), 54.
20. McPherson, *Battle Cry of Freedom*, 457.
21. Freeman, *R. E. Lee*, II, 48.
22. Thomas, *Robert E. Lee*, 224.
23. Ernest B. Furgurson, *Ashes of Glory* (New York: Vintage Books, 1996), 139.

Chapter 7: Saving Richmond

1 Gary W. Gallagher, "When Lee Was Mortal," *MHQ (Military History Quarterly)*, Spring 1998, 51.
2. Stephen W. Sears, *George B. McClellan* (New York: Ticknor & Fields, 1988), 180.
3. Edward P. Alexander, *Fighting for the Confederacy* (Chapel Hill: University of North Carolina Press, 1989), 91.
4. Freeman, *R. E. Lee*, II, 347.
5. Davis, *Gray Fox*, 80.
6. Lee, *Wartime Papers*, 183–84.
7. Ibid.
8. William Allan, "Memoranda of Conversations with General Robert E. Lee," in Gallagher, *Lee the Soldier*, 15.
9. John M. Taylor, "Hawk in the Fowlyard," *MHQ*, Autumn 1994.
10. Sears, *To the Gates of Richmond*, 200.
11. Richard Wheeler, *Sword Over Richmond* (New York: Harper & Row, 1986), 303.
12. Freeman, *R. E. Lee*, II, 153.
13. Bruce Catton, *Terrible Swift Sword*, (New York: Doubleday, 1963), 331.
14. Benjamin P. Thomas and Harold M. Hyman, *Stanton* (New York: Alfred A. Knopf, 1962), 205–6.
15. Alexander, *Fighting for the Confederacy*, 117.
16. Freeman, *R. E. Lee*, II, 174.
17. Douglas S. Freeman, "Morale in the Army of Northern Virginia," in Stuart W. Smith, ed., *Douglas Southall Freeman on Leadership* (Newport, R.I.: Naval War College Press, 1990), 129.
18. Thomas, *Robert E. Lee*, 241.
19. Lee, *Wartime Papers*, 210.
20. McWhiney and Jamieson, *Attack and Die*, 18.

21. Sears, *To the Gates of Richmond*, 343–45.
22. Ibid., 442–43.
23. Gallagher, "When Lee Was Mortal" *MHQ*, Spring 1998, 53.

Chapter 8: Suppressing Pope

1. McPherson, *Battle Cry of Freedom*, 337.
2. Lee, *Wartime Papers*, 238.
3. Thomas, *Robert E. Lee*, 176.
4. Ibid., 249.
5. Farwell, *Stonewall*, 373.
6. Glenn Tucker, *High Tide at Gettysburg* (Dayton, Ohio: Morningside Book-shop, 1973), 5.
7. Lee, *Wartime Papers*, 235.
8. Ibid., 239.
9. Woodworth, *Davis and Lee at War*, 176.
10. Catton, *Terrible Swift Sword*, 419.
11. Jeffrey D. Wert, *General James Longstreet* (New York: Touchstone Books, 1993), 167.
12. Ibid., 169.
13. Farwell, *Stonewall*, 408.
14. Wert, *General James Longstreet*, 170.
15. Farwell, *Stonewall*, 414.
16. Lee, *Wartime Papers*, 268.
17. Wert, *General James Longstreet*, 178–79.
18. Freeman, *R. E. Lee*, II, 261.

Chapter 9: Determined Valor

1. McPherson, *Battle Cry of Freedom*, 532–33.
2. Lee, *Wartime Papers*, 295.
3. Keegan, *The Mask of Command*, 181.
4. Gallagher, *Lee the Soldier*, 13.
5. Taylor, *William Henry Seward*, 196.
6. Sears, *Landscape Turned Red*, 40.
7. Lee, *Wartime Papers*, 301.
8. Mary B. Mitchell, "A Woman's Recollections of Antietam," *Battles and Leaders*, II, 687–88.
9. Sears, *Landscape Turned Red*, 96.
10. Ibid., 68.
11. Freeman, *R. E. Lee*, II, 362.

12. McPherson, *Battle Cry of Freedom*, 537.
13. Thomas, *Robert E. Lee*, 261.
14. Freeman, *R. E. Lee*, II, 370.
15. Dowdey, *Lee*, 311–12.
16. Charles C. Coffin, "Antietam Scenes," *Battles and Leaders*, II, 684.
17. James I. Robertson Jr., *General A. P. Hill* (New York: Random House, 1987), 143.
18. Henry Kyd Douglas, *I Rode With Stonewall* (University of North Carolina Press, 1940), 174.
19. Lee, *Wartime Papers*, 322.
20. J. C. Levenson, ed., *The Letters of Henry Adams* (Cambridge, Mass.: 1982), I, 327.
21. Lee, *Wartime Papers*, 322.
22. Smith, *Douglas Southall Freeman on Leadership*, 130.

Chapter 10: High Tide at Fredericksburg

1. Lee papers, Virginia Historical Society.
2. Freeman, *On Leadership*, 111.
3. Letter signed "Personne," *Charleston Daily Courier*, Oct. 9, 1862.
4. Freeman, *R. E. Lee*, II, 355.
5. Walter H. Taylor, *Four Years with General Lee* (New York: 1877), 76.
6. Lee, *Wartime Papers*, 357.
7. Freeman, *R. E. Lee*, II, 428.
8. Bruce Catton, *Glory Road* (New York: Doubleday & Co., 1952), 65.
9. Thomas, *Robert E. Lee*, 271.
10. J. Cutler Andrews, *The North Reports the Civil War* (Pittsburgh, Pa.: University of Pittsburgh Press, 1985), 331.
11. Stephen W. Sears, *Chancellorsville* (Boston: Houghton Mifflin, 1996), 13.
12. Frederick D. Williams, ed., *The Wild Life of the Army: Civil War Letters of James A. Garfield* (Michigan State University Press, 1964), 173.
13. Samuel E. Morison and Henry S. Commager, *The Growth of the American Republic* (New York: Oxford University Press, 1962), I, 737.
14. Sears, *Chancellorsville*, 3–4.
15. Ibid., 26.
16. J. William Jones, *Personal Reminiscences of Gen. Robert E. Lee* (New York: D. Appleton and Co., 1874), 298.
17. James Longstreet, "The Battle of Fredericksburg," *Battles and Leaders*, III, 82–83.
18. Alexander, *Fighting for the Confederacy*, 167–68.
19. Lee, *Wartime Papers*, 364–65.

Chapter 11: "May God Have Mercy on General Lee"

1. John H. Munford to "My dear Sister," Jan. 28, 1863. Author's collection.
2. Catton, *Never Call Retreat*, 97.
3. Freeman, *R. E. Lee*, II, 496.
4. Thomas, *Robert E. Lee*, 279–80.
5. Dowdey, *Lee*, 335.
6. Long, *Memoirs of Robert E. Lee*, 241–42.
7. Samuel M. Bemiss to his children, April 10, 1863. Bemiss Family Papers, Virginia Historical Society.
8. Lee, *Wartime Papers*, 437–38.
9. Ibid., 430.
10. Catton, *Glory Road*, 140.
11. Archer Jones, *Civil War Command and Strategy* (New York: The Free Press, 1992), 112.
12. Ibid., 145.
13. McPherson, *Battle Cry of Freedom*, 585–86.
14. Alexander, *Fighting for the Confederacy*, 195.
15. Sears, *Chancellorsville*, 120.
16. Catton, *Never Call Retreat*, 144.
17. Lee, *Wartime Papers*, 449.
18. Freeman, *R. E. Lee*, II, 514.
19. Sears, *Chancellorsville*, 191–92.
20. Alexander, *Fighting for the Confederacy*, 196.
21. Thomas, *Robert E. Lee*, 282.
22. Alfred Pleasonton, "The Successes and Failures of Chancellorsville," *Battles and Leaders*, III, 177.
23. Alexander, *Fighting for the Confederacy*, 201.
24. John L. Collins, "When Stonewall Jackson Turned Our Right," *Battles and Leaders*, III, 183.
25. Catton, *Never Call Retreat*, 154.
26. Robert K. Krick, "Lee's Greatest Victory," *American Heritage*, March 1990.
27. *London Times*, June 16, 1863.
28. Sears, *Chancellorsville*, 444.
29. McPherson, *Battle Cry of Freedom*, 645.
30. Sears, *Chancellorsville*, 447–48.
31. George W. Doughty to his parents, May 9, 1863. Author's collection.
32. Lee, *Wartime Papers*, 462.
33. Paul D. Casdorph, *Lee and Jackson* (New York: Paragon House, 1992), 394.
34. Robert K. Krick, "Lee at Chancellorsville," in Gallagher, *Lee the Soldier*, 365.

Chapter 12: The Road to Gettysburg

1. Lee, *Wartime Papers*, 485.
2. Thomas, *Robert E. Lee*, 287.
3. William McWillie Notebooks, Mississippi D. A. H. McWillie was a member of Gen. Anderson's staff.
4. Anderson and Anderson, *The Generals*, 259.
5. Richard Taylor, *Destruction and Reconstruction* (New York: Da Capo Press, 1995), 37.
6. Freeman, *Lee's Dispatches*, 82.
7. Lee, *Wartime Papers*, 482.
8. Long, *Memoirs of Robert E. Lee*, 268–69.
9. Tucker, *High Tide at Gettysburg*, 20.
10. Ibid., 18.
11. McPherson, *Battle Cry of Freedom*, 590.
12. Ibid., 647.
13. Lee, *Wartime Papers*, 508.
14. Wert, *General James Longstreet*, 245.
15. Thomas, *Robert E. Lee*, 290–91.
16. Lee, *Wartime Papers*, 512.
17. Thomas, *Robert E. Lee*, 292.
18. Tucker, *High Tide at Gettysburg*, 24.
19. Taylor, "Hawk in the Fowlyard," *MHQ*, Autumn 1994.
20. Lee, *Wartime Papers*, 533–34.
21. Freeman, *R. E. Lee*, III, 59; Dowdey, *Lee*, 363.
22. Donald, *Lincoln*, 445; Tucker, *High Tide at Gettysburg*, 79.
23. Richard Wheeler, *Witness to Gettysburg* (New York: Harper and Row, 1987), 106.
24. Gary W. Gallagher, ed., *The First Day at Gettysburg* (Kent, Ohio: Kent State University Press, 1992), 115.
25. Lee, *Wartime Papers*, 490.
26. Gallagher, *The First Day at Gettysburg*, 67.
27. Thomas, *Robert E. Lee*, 292–93.
28. Ibid., 293.

Chapter 13: "This Is All My Fault"

1. Gallagher, *The First Day at Gettysburg*, 35.
2. Ibid., 40.
3. Freeman, *R. E. Lee*, III, 75.
4. Tucker, *High Tide at Gettysburg*, 221.
5. Ibid., 212.

6. Dowdey, *Lee*, 371.
7. Lee, *Wartime Papers*, 576.
8. Burke Davis, *Gray Fox: Robert E. Lee and the Civil War* (New York: Rinehart, 1956), 229.
9. Albert A. Nofi, *The Gettysburg Campaign* (Conshohocken, Pa.: Combined Books, 1986), 101.
10. Wert, *General James Longstreet*, 264.
11. Harry W. Pfanz, *Gettysburg: The Second Day* (Chapel Hill: University of North Carolina Press, 1987), 112.
12. Dowdey, *Lee*, 378.
13. Freeman, *R. E. Lee*, III, 150.
14. Tucker, *High Tide at Gettysburg*, 317.
15. Lee, *Wartime Papers*, 580.
16. James Longstreet, "Lee's Right Wing at Gettysburg," *Battles and Leaders*, III, 342–43.
17. Wert, *General James Longstreet*, 291.
18. Dowdey, *Lee*, 389; Thomas, *Robert E. Lee*, 300.
19. Gallagher, *Lee the Soldier*, 450.
20. Ibid., 13–14.
21. John J. Imboden, "The Confederate Retreat From Gettysburg," *Battles and Leaders*, III, 421.

Chapter 14: A Military Sacrament

1. Thomas, *Robert E. Lee*, 304–5.
2. Freeman, *R. E. Lee*, III, 131.
3. Gallagher, *Lee the Soldier*, 498.
4. Lee, *Wartime Papers*, 547–48.
5. Ibid., 565.
6. Taylor, "Hawk in the Fowlyard," *MHQ*, Autumn 1994.
7. Gallagher, *Lee the General*, 503.
8. McPherson, *Battle Cry of Freedom*, 664.
9. John B. Jones, *A Rebel War Clerk's Diary* (New York: Sagamore Press, 1958), 244.
10. Philip Van Doren Stern, *When the Guns Roared* (New York: Doubleday, 1965), 208.
11. Thomas, *Robert E. Lee*, 305, 319.
12. Lee, *Wartime Papers*, 413, 491.
13. Thomas, *Robert E. Lee*, 317.
14. Lee, *Wartime Papers*, 591.
15. Ibid., 589–90.
16. Dowdey, *Lee*, 403.
17. Woodworth, *Davis and Lee at War*, 254.

18. Lee, *Wartime Papers*, 596.
19. Freeman, *R. E. Lee*, III, 183.
20. Woodworth, *Davis and Lee at War*, 263.
21. Gary W. Gallagher, *The Confederate War* (Cambridge, Mass.: Harvard University Press, 1997), 47.
22. Lee, *Wartime Papers*, 659–60.
23. C. Vann Woodward, ed., *Mary Chesnut's Civil War* (New Haven: Yale University Press, 1981), 509.
24. Alexander, *Fighting for the Confederacy*, 345–46.
25. Freeman, *R. E. Lee*, III, 267.
26. Wert, *General James Longstreet*, 377.

Chapter 15: "We Have Got to Whip Them"

1. McPherson, *Battle Cry of Freedom*, 722.
2. Noah A. Trudeau, *Bloody Roads South* (Boston: Little, Brown, 1989), 13.
3. Thomas, *Robert E. Lee*, 320.
4. J. Tracy Power, *Lee's Miserables* (University of North Carolina Press, 1998), 2.
5. Lee, *Wartime Papers*, 700.
6. Freeman, *R. E. Lee*, III, 264.
7. Dowdey, *Lee*, 421.
8. Gordon C. Rhea, *The Battle of the Wilderness* (Baton Rouge: Louisiana State University Press, 1994), 300.
9. Power, *Lee's Miserables*, 44.
10. Noah Andre Trudeau, "The Walls of 1864," *MHQ*, Winter 1994.
11. McPherson, *Battle Cry of Freedom*, 728.
12. John B. Gordon, *Reminiscences of the Civil War* (New York: Charles Scribner's, 1903), 278.
13. Cicero D. Gilbert, undated manuscript, SHC-068, Northwest Georgia Document Preservation Project, Shorter College, Rome, Georgia.
14. Gordon, *Reminiscences of the Civil War*, 278–79.
15. Richard Wheeler, *On Fields of Fury* (New York: HarperCollins, 1991), 209.
16. Power, *Lee's Miserables*, 35.
17. Trudeau, *Bloody Roads South*, 192.
18. McPherson, *Battle Cry of Freedom*, 732.
19. Taylor, "Hawk in the Fowlyard," *MHQ*, Autumn 1994.

Chapter 16: Never Call Retreat

1. George C. Eggleston, "Notes on Cold Harbor," *Battles and Leaders*, IV, 230.
2. Lee, *Wartime Papers*, 733.
3. Eggleston, "Notes on Cold Harbor," 231.

4. Trudeau, *Bloody Roads South*, 235.
5. Freeman, *R. E. Lee*, III, 359.
6. Freeman and McWhiney, *Lee's Dispatches*, 195.
7. Lee, *Wartime Papers*, 758–59.
8. Ibid., 759–60.
9. McPherson, *Battle Cry of Freedom*, 735.
10. Trudeau, *Bloody Roads South*, 278–79.
11. Lee, *Wartime Papers*, 752.
12. Power, *Lee's Miserables*, 65.
13. Freeman, *R. E. Lee*, III, 389.
14. McPherson, *Battle Cry of Freedom*, 735.
15. J. Cutler Andrews, *The North Reports the Civil War* (University of Pittsburgh Press, 1983), 541.
16. Grant, *Memoirs*, II, 280–81.
17. Catton, *Never Call Retreat*, 366.

Chapter 17: Siege

1. Douglas S. Freeman, *Lee's Dispatches*, 254.
2. Furgurson, *Ashes of Glory*, 275.
3. Lee, *Wartime Papers*, 821–22.
4. Noah Andre Trudeau, *The Last Citadel* (Boston: Little, Brown, 1991), 240.
5. Dowdey, *Lee*, 494.
6. Power, *Lee's Miserables*, 126.
7. Lee, *Wartime Papers*, 811.
8. John M. Taylor, "The Crater," *MHQ*, Winter 1998.
9. Power, *Lee's Miserables*, 139.
10. Ibid.
11. Lee, *Wartime Papers*, 828.
12. Ibid., 843–44.
13. Charles C. Osborne, *Jubal* (Chapel Hill, N.C.: Algonquin Books, 1992), 353.
14. Ibid., 347.
15. Ibid., 353.
16. Power, *Lee's Miserables*, 167.
17. Jones, *A Rebel War Clerk's Diary*, 412.
18. Trudeau, *The Last Citadel*, 220.
19. Donald, *Lincoln*, 529.
20. Thomas, *Robert E. Lee*, 318.
21. Ibid.
22. Sotheby's Catalog #7058, Nov. 25, 1997.
23. Taylor, *Four Years with General Lee*, 146.
24. Freeman, *R. E. Lee*, III, 507.

25. McPherson, *Battle Cry of Freedom*, 836.
26. Catton, *Never Call Retreat*, 427.
27. McPherson, *Battle Cry of Freedom*, 837.

Chapter 18: A Surrender of Quality

1. James G. Randall and David Donald, *The Civil War and Reconstruction* (New York: Heath, 1969), 516–17.
2. Jones, *A Rebel War Clerk's Diary*, 469.
3. Lee, *Wartime Papers*, 892.
4. Freeman, *R. E. Lee*, IV, 3–4.
5. Wert, *General James Longstreet*, 397.
6. Dowdey, *Lee*, 509.
7. Power, *Lee's Miserables*, 203.
8. Ibid.
9. John M. Taylor, *Confederate Raider* (Washington, D.C.: Brassey's, 1994), 225.
10. Gordon, *Reminiscences*, 387.
11. Ibid., 390.
12. Woodworth, *Davis and Lee at War*, 315.
13. Freeman, *R. E. Lee*, III, 538.
14. Lee, *Wartime Papers*, 917.
15. Dowdey, *Lee*, 560.
16. Charles B. Flood, *Lee: The Last Years* (Boston: Houghton Mifflin, 1981), 20.
17. Thomas, *Robert E. Lee*, 360.
18. Horace Porter, "The Surrender at Appomattox Court House," *Battles and Leaders*, IV, 732–33.
19. Freeman, *R. E. Lee*, IV, 122–23.
20. Thomas, *Robert E. Lee*, 362.
21. Eicher, *Robert E. Lee: A Life Portrait*, 145.
22. Nolan, *Lee Considered*, 129–30.
23. Freeman, *R. E. Lee*, IV, 144.

Chapter 19: A Dry and Thirsty Land

1. Dowdey, *Lee*, 583.
2. Flood, *Lee: The Last Years*, 43.
3. L. Guild to REL, [April 1865], National Archives RG 109, Chap. VI, vol. 642.
4. Dowdey, *Lee*, 595.
5. Freeman, *R. E. Lee*, IV, 204.
6. Flood, *Lee: The Last Years*, 79–80.
7. Ibid., 84.

8. R. Lockwood Tower, ed., *Lee's Adjutant* (Columbia: University of South Carolina Press, 1995), 203.

9. Flood, *Lee: The Last Years*, 110.

10. Freeman, *R. E. Lee*, IV, 278.

11. Dowdey, *Lee*, 605.

12. Rose M. E. MacDonald, *Mrs. Robert E. Lee* (Pikesville, Md.: Robert B. Poisal, 1973), 245.

13. Freeman, *R. E. Lee*, IV, 375–77.

14. Dowdey, *Lee*, 687.

15. Freeman, *Lee*, IV, 276–77.

16. Gallagher, *Lee the Soldier*, 27.

17. Ibid., 13–15.

18. Dowdey, *Lee*, 729.

19. Freeman, *R. E. Lee*, IV, 475.

20. J. William Jones, *Life and Letters of Robert Edward Lee* (Washington, D.C.: 1906), 390.

21. Thomas, *Robert E. Lee*, 407.

22. Dowdey, *Lee*, 725.

23. Freeman, *R. E. Lee*, IV, 487.

Chapter 20: Meet General Lee

1. Freeman, *R. E. Lee*, III, 242.

2. Ibid., 492.

3. Connelly, *The Marble Man*, 3.

4. Kenin and Wintle, *The Dictionary of Biographical Quotations*, 652.

5. McWhiney and Jamieson, *Attack and Die*, xiii.

6. Gallagher, *The Confederate War*, 134.

7. McWhiney and Jamieson, *Attack and Die*, 7.

8. Ibid., 19–20.

9. Freeman, *R. E. Lee*, IV, 178.

10. Ibid., 168.

11. Gallagher, *Lee the Soldier*, 280.

12. Burke Davis, *Gray Fox* (New York: The Fairfax Press, 1961), 385.

13. Gallagher, *Lee the Soldier*, 184.

14. Lee, *Wartime Papers*, 482.

15. Gallagher, *Lee the Soldier*, 219.

16. Woodward, ed., *Mary Chesnut's Civil War*, 116.

17. Taylor, *Four Years with General Lee*, 77.

18. Lee papers, Virginia Historical Society.

19. R. Lockwood Tower, ed., *Lee's Adjutant*, 273.

20. Freeman, *R. E. Lee*, IV, 505.

21. Thomas, *Robert E. Lee*, 392.
22. Robert Heinl, *Dictionary of Military and Naval Quotations* (Annapolis, Md.: U.S. Naval Institute Press, 1966), 173.

Appendix: Lee's Reflections

1. J. William Jones, *Personal Reminiscences of General Robert E. Lee* (Baton Rouge: Louisiana State University Press, 1989), 145.
2. Lee used this identical language in a letter to his aide, Charles Marshall, after the war.
3. A slightly variant version appears in Jones, p. 163.
4. Quoted in Jones, p. 145.
5. Quoted in Jones but not in the Virginia Historical Society.

INDEX

Abolitionists, 29, 43, 45, 102

Adams, Charles Francis, 5

Adams, Henry, 99

Alexander, Edward P., 8, 68, 74, 111, 117, 120, 123, 151, 165, 211–12

Alexandria, 13

Alexandria Academy, 16

Allan, William, 90–91, 155, 225

Amelia Courthouse, 209

American Colonization Society, 38

American Revolution, 89

Anderson, Richard H., 129–30, 210; at Chancellorsville, 119–21; at Cold Harbor, 183; Lee and, 199, 210; at Petersburg, 187; at Spotsylvania, 174

Anderson, Robert, 47

Antietam, battle of, 7–8, 90–99; and Lee's popularity, 105

Appomattox, 213–14

Arlington (Lee home), 20, 39–40, 52f, 222

Army of Northern Virginia, 67; after Gettysburg, 156, 160; at Antietam, 97–98; brigades of, 103–4; disintegration of, 209–10; at Gettysburg, 142–49; Grant and, 168; Lee's appointment as commander of, 52–53; Lee's farewell to, 215–16; morale in, 202–3; numbers of, 102, 168–69, 184, 192, 195, 206; problems of, 179–80; reorganization of, 81, 102–3, 129–30; in retreat, 156; siege of, 189–201; state of, 138; structure of, 70–71, 93, 169; in winters, 112, 164–66, 200

Army of the Potomac, 80, 90, 93, 116, 139, 180; Grant and, 167; numbers of, 168, 184, 206; offensive by, 171–74; state of, 192

Army of Virginia, 80

Atlanta, 190, 198

authority, Lee on, 241

balloons, observation, 74

Banks, Nathaniel P., 64, 84

Beauregard, P. G. T., 55, 115, 161, 170, 179, 181–83, 187; at Fort Sumter, 47; Lee and, 226; in Mexican War, 27–28

Bell, John, 45

Bermuda Hundred, 171, 177, 180, 187

Bigelow, John, 92

Blackford, Charles M., 129
black soldiers, 194; Confederacy and,
  195–96, 200; Lee and, 200
Blair, Francis P., Sr., 48, 50
Bradford, Gamaliel, 4
Brady, Mathew, 218
Bragg, Braxton, 131–32, 162–63, 190
Brandy Station, battle of, 135
Bratton, John, 205
Breckinridge, John C., 45, 192, 205
Bristoe Station, 162–63
Britain, and Confederacy, 91–92, 152, 159
Brockenbough, John, 219
Browning, Orville, 109
Brown, John, 43
Buchanan, James, 42
Buford, John, 142
Burnside, Ambrose E., 106–7, 112; at
  Antietam, 97–99; character of, 110; at
  siege of Richmond, 194; at Spotsylva-
  nia, 176
Butler, Benjamin, 168, 171, 177, 179–80,
  182–83

Cameron, Simon, 49
Carter, Charles, 10, 12
Castel, Albert, 9
casualties: at Antietam, 98–99; at Chan-
  cellorsville, 125; at Cold Harbor, 185;
  at Fisher's Hill and Winchester, 196;
  at Fredericksburg, 108; at Gettysburg,
  156; Lee and, 77, 231–32; at Malvern
  Hill, 76; in Pickett's Charge, 152; at
  Second Manassas, 88, 90; at Spotsyl-
  vania, 173, 177
Catton, Bruce, 188, 200
cavalry, 116, 135, 144, 146, 150, 178, 191
Cemetery Ridge, 146, 148, 150–51
Cerro Gordo, battle of, 27–28
Chamberlain, Joshua, 148, 212
Chancellor house, 119–20, 123–24
Chancellorsville, battle of, 5, 7, 116–27
Charleston, 58–59, 161
Chase, Salmon P., 109
Chattanooga, 163
Cheat Mountain, 56–57
Chesnut, Mary, 160, 165, 236
Chickamauga, 163, 165
Chilton, Robert, 131, 217
The Chimneys, 69
Christ Church, Alexandria, 51

Civil War: beginning of, 47–48; early
  days of, 54–66; end of, 202–14
Clay, Henry, 29
Cleburne, Patrick, 195
Cobb, Howell, 200
Cockspur Island, 20
Coffin, Charles, 97
Cold Harbor, battle of, 181–88
Commager, Henry Steele, 5
Compromise of 1850, 42
Confederacy: after Gettysburg, 156–57;
  on arming slaves, 195–96, 200; assets
  of, 89; European nations and, 91–92;
  Fort Sumter and, 47–48; prospects of,
  59–60, 134; strategy of, 65, 69–70,
  79–80, 94, 131, 182, 185, 190, 199–200,
  230, 232; surrender of, 202–14; tactics
  of, 7
Confederate Army: casualties of, 76–77,
  88, 98, 103, 108, 125, 156, 173, 177;
  numbers of, 61; organization of, 55–
  56; problems of, 179–80; state of, 56,
  89–90, 138–39, 167–68. *See also* Army
  of Northern Virginia
Connelly, Thomas L., 6–7, 15, 50–51,
  228
conscription, 61, 133, 158, 167, 195, 200
Cooke, John Esten, 205
Cooper, Samuel, 55
Cortinas, Juan, 45
Crater, battle of, 194
Culpeper, 136
Curtin, Andrew, 94
Custis, George Washington Parke, 15,
  20–22, 38–39
Custis, Mary Fitzhugh, 16, 20, 38

Dabb's House, 71
Dabney, Robert, 126
Dahlgren, Ulrich, 164
Davis, Burke, 6
Davis, Jefferson, 47; and army, 55, 58,
  62–63; correspondence with Lee, 90,
  92–93, 102, 157–58, 169–70, 180, 182–
  83, 187, 189, 192–93, 195; criticism
  of, 203; education of, 17; and Fredericksburg, 110; and generals, 163; and
  Gettysburg, 134, 157; and Lee, 59, 61,
  65, 68, 82, 136, 160–61; and race, 195–
  96; strategy of, 70, 79–80, 94, 190,
  199–200, 235; and surrender, 203–4,

206, 213; and Western campaign, 131, 162, 164
Davis, William C., 9
death, Lee on, 244
desertion, 93, 160, 210
desertions, 108, 202–3
Devil's Den, 146, 148
Donnally, Jim, 31
Douglas, Henry Kyd, 98
Douglas, Stephen A., 45
Dowdey, Clifford, 6
draft riots, in New York, 133, 158
duty, Lee and, 6, 35, 222, 238–39

Early, Jubal A., 4, 131, 133, 177, 183, 186; at Chancellorsville, 124; at Gettysburg, 143–45; at Malvern Hill, 75; in Shenandoah Valley, 192–93, 196–97
Eggleston, George C., 179
elections: of 1860, 45; of 1862, 99–100; of 1864, 186, 197–99, 213
emancipation, Lee on, 164, 200
Emancipation Proclamation, 93, 99, 109, 116, 133; Lee on, 101–2
entrenchments, 174, 191
Ewell, Richard S., 64, 130, 136, 139–40, 169, 183, 209; at Briscoe Station, 162; character of, 145; at Gettysburg, 143–47, 149, 151, 153; Lee and, 6, 226; at Spotsylvania, 171, 173–75

Fair Oaks, battle of, 66
Farragut, David G., 198
Federal Army: after Gettysburg, 158; casualties of, 76–77, 88, 90, 98, 108, 125, 156, 173, 177, 185; dissension in, 109–10; failures in East, 133; Lee's refusal of command of, 3, 48–49; state of, 167–68; strategy of, 80. *See also* Army of the Potomac
Fisher's Hill, battle of, 196
Fitzhugh, Anna, 20
Fitzhugh, William Henry, 13, 16
Five Forks, battle of, 209
Floyd, John B., 42, 56
food for Lee's army, 102, 114, 116, 133, 137, 160, 197; shortages of, 164, 181, 190, 204, 206, 209–10
Fort Donelson, 79
Fort Hamilton, 27
Fort Harrison, 200

Fort Henry, 79
Fort Mason, 46
Fort McHenry, 20
Fort Pickens, 47
Fort Pulaski, 20, 58
Fortress Monroe, 22, 25, 38, 60, 113, 159
Fort Stedman, 208–9
Fort Sumter, 46–47
France, and Confederacy, 91–92, 159
Franklin, William B., 66, 107, 116
Fredericksburg, 109*f*, 112; battle of, 101–11
Freeman, Douglas Southall, 5–6, 149
Freemantle, Arthur, 157, 164
Fuller, John F. C., 234
Furlough system, 113, 116, 160

Gaines's Mill, battle of, 72–74, 73*f*
Gallagher, Gary W., 9, 230
Garfield, James A., 108
Gettysburg (movie), 8–9
Gettysburg, battle of, 6–8, 76, 142–55; analysis of, 152–55; controversy over, 3–4, 86, 147; Lee on, 154–55, 157–58; preparations for, 128–41; terrain of, 146
Giddings, Joshua, 43
Gordon, Edward, 225
Gordon, John B., 2, 169, 173, 176, 206–8, 211
Grant, Ulysses S., 8, 209, 225; character of, 167–68, 199; at Chatanooga, 163; at Cold Harbor, 182–85; and Lee, 3, 192, 217–19, 238; in Mexican War, 29, 31; offensive towards Richmond, 167–78; at Petersburg, 186–87; and Shenandoah Valley, 180; at siege of Richmond, 191–94, 196; and surrender, 210–11, 213; at Vicksburg, 115, 131, 157
Great Revival, 113
Greene, Nathanael, 15
Gregg, David, 172

Halleck, Henry W., 80, 83, 88, 167, 186
Halstead, Murat, 108
Hampton Roads conference, 203–4
Hancock, Almira, 34
Hancock, Winfield S., 34, 143, 175–76
Hanover Junction, 180–81
Hanson, Alexander, 13

Hardee, William J., 190
Harpers Ferry, 94–95, 98–100; Brown's raid at, 42–43
Harrisburg, 139
Harrison, Henry, 140
Heintzelman, Samuel, 66
Heth, Henry, 130, 133; at Briscoe Station, 163; at Gettysburg, 142, 150; Lee and, 158
Hill, Ambrose Powell, 88, 105, 130, 140–41, 169, 177, 181; at Antietam, 98; at Briscoe Station, 162–63; at Gettysburg, 142, 147, 149, 151; at Petersburg, 187; at Second Manassas, 83; at Seven Days' campaign, 71–72; at Sharpsburg, 95; at siege of Richmond, 191–93; at Spotsylvania, 171–72
Hill, Benjamin H., 239
Hill, D. H., 71, 95; at Antietam, 96–97; at Harpers Ferry, 95; at Malvern Hill, 74–76; at Second Manassas, 83
Hoke, Robert, 183, 187
Hood, John B., 96, 104, 190–91; and casualties, 231; at Gettysburg, 146, 148; in North Carolina, 113; at Seven Days' campaign, 73
Hooker, Joseph, 110, 117f, 136–38; at Antietam, 96; at Chancellorsville, 116–20, 123, 125; character of, 115–16; at Fredericksburg, 107; Lee and, 118–19; in Mexican War, 31
Hotchkiss, Jed, 121
Howard, O. O., 122, 143
Huger, Benjamin, 81
Human relations, Lee on, 241
Humphreys, Milton, 225
Hunter, David, 186, 192
Hunter, Robert M. T., 204
Huntersville, 56
Hunt, Henry J., 215

Imboden, John D., 155
intelligence: of Federal Army, 85, 95, 118, 136; of Lee's army, 70, 74, 76, 82, 140, 146–47, 150, 170, 187
Ives, Joseph, 68

Jackson, Andrew, 25, 48
Jackson, Thomas J. "Stonewall," 6, 8, 70, 124f; at Antietam, 97; at Blue Ridge, 106; at Chancellorsville, 119–23; char-

acter of, 83–84, 103, 108, 113, 129; command of, 81–82; criticism of, 126–27; death of, 123, 125–26, 128; at Fredericksburg, 107–8; at Harpers Ferry, 95; and Lee, 5, 88, 104; Lee and, 82, 128–29, 226; at Malvern Hill, 74; in Mexican War, 27; promotion of, 102–3; at Second Manassas, 83–87; at Seven Days' campaign, 71–73, 76; at Sharpsburg, 95; in Shenandoah Valley, 64
Jamieson, Perry D., 7, 77, 230–31
Janney, John, 52–53
Johns, John, 35
Johnson, Andrew, 217
Johnson, Bushrod, 210
Johnson, Edward "Allegheny," 151, 175
Johnston, Albert Sidney, 55, 61
Johnston, Joseph E., 3, 55, 61, 115, 190, 203; and Army of Northern Virginia, 67; and casualties, 231; Davis and, 163–64; and defense of Richmond, 63; education of, 17; and Lee, 65; and Richmond, 66, 77; at Vicksburg, 131; and Western campaign, 168
Johnston, Samuel R., 146–47
Johnston, William P., 1–2
Jones, David, 97
Jones, John B., 158, 198, 203
Jones, J. William, 240–41
Jones, William E., 141, 186

Keegan, John, 8
Kennesaw Mountain, 190
Keyes, Erasmus D., 17–18, 30, 66
Krick, Robert, 127

Lacy, Beverly Tucker, 121, 126
La Salle, 243–44
Lee, Agnes (daughter), 26, 159, 198, 207, 226–27
Lee, Ann Carter (mother), 10, 12–13, 15–16, 18–20
Lee, Annie (daughter), 26, 35, 236
Lee, Ann McCarty, 24
Lee, Carter (brother), 16, 20, 22
Lee, Charlotte, 105, 135
Lee, Fitzhugh (brother), 37, 122, 211
Lee, George Washington Custis (son), 25, 37, 39, 45, 207–8, 216; correspondence with Lee, 113–14, 171, 192

Lee, Henry "Black-Horse Harry," 13, 24–25

Lee, Henry "Light-Horse Harry" (father), 10–15, 11f, 18–19, 24, 58

Lee, Mary (daughter), 25–26, 35, 159, 207

Lee, Mary Custis (wife), 20, 21, 25, 32–34, 39, 51, 159–60, 198, 219, 222–23, 236; character of, 21–23; correspondence with Lee, 29–30, 39–40, 55–56, 58–59, 111, 114–15, 135, 157, 159–60, 194; and death of Lee, 1–2; health of, 26, 44, 223; and Lee's resignation, 49; and McClellan, 81; and Yankees, 216, 223

Lee, Matilda, 12–13, 24

Lee, Mildred (daughter), 26, 198, 207, 217

Lee, Robert E., 19f, 36f, 218f, 221f; after war, 215–27; appointment as commander, 52–53; birth of, 12; boyhood of, 14–15; character of, 5–7, 17–18, 32, 35, 54–55, 105, 108, 113–14, 129, 198–99, 236–39; children of, 25–26, 32, 38–40, 105, 159, 207–8, 215, 237; correspondence, 33, 38–39, 46, 59, 105, 113–14, 135, 171, 192, 219; correspondence with Davis, 90, 92–93, 102, 157–58, 169–70, 180, 182–83, 187, 189, 192–93, 195; correspondence with Mary Custis Lee, 29–30, 39–40, 55–56, 58–59, 111, 114–15, 135, 157, 159–60, 194; councils of war, 69, 71, 144–45, 163–64, 211; criticism of, 3–4, 49–51, 77, 110, 126–27, 212–13; death of, 1–2, 244; on defense of Richmond, 62–64; depression and, 33–35; early military career, 24–31, 33–34, 68; education of, 15–18, 30–31; as engineer, 20; eulogies for, 2–3; evaluation of, 228–39; faith and philosophy of, 2–3, 6, 14, 34–35, 41–42, 45–46, 113, 204, 222, 229, 236–38, 241–44; farewell tour by, 226–27; faults of, 5–7, 233; on field duty, 37–38; and government, 205–7, 238; headquarters staff of, 130–31; health of, 114, 161, 181, 183, 226; historians and, 1–9; indictment for treason, 217, 222; legend of, 165, 228–29; marriage of, 7, 20–23, 25–26, 32–33, 222–23; and

McClellan, 63–65; military career of, 44; military skills of, 67–68, 234; offer to resign after Gettysburg, 160–61; and officers, 145; pardon of, 217–19; on politics, 223–25, 242; refusal of Federal command, 3, 48–49; relations with generals, 96, 196; relations with officers, 31, 103, 169, 210, 234; relations with troops, 57, 104–5, 139, 165–66, 205, 212–13, 216–17, 228, 234, 236; resignation from U.S. Army, 8, 49–51; as soldier, 29–30, 238; as strategist, 3–5, 8, 30, 69–70, 76–77, 89–91, 100, 131, 152, 229–35; surrender of, 202–14; as tactician, 97, 111, 120–21, 135, 232; and Virginia, 23, 48–49, 51, 226, 235–36

Lee, Robert E., Jr., 26, 39–40, 216

Lee, Smith (brother), 16, 20, 22, 32, 37, 236

Lee, William Henry Fitzhugh "Rooney" (son), 26, 37, 39–40, 81, 105, 236; in battle, 135, 159, 187, 216; correspondence with Lee, 38–39, 46, 219

Letcher, John, 51–52, 57

Lincoln, Abraham, 186; and army, 80, 88, 93, 105, 116; character of, 236; and Congress, 109; and conscription, 133; and election of 1860, 45; and election of 1864, 198; and Emancipation Proclamation, 93, 99; and Grant, 167–68; at Hampton Roads conference, 203–4; historians and, 229; inauguration of, 47; Lee and, 102; and Maryland, 91; McClellan and, 68; on race, 41

Little Round Top, 146, 148, 149f

Long, Armistead, 55, 58, 97, 131–32, 146

Longstreet, James, 134–36, 141, 169; after war, 224; at Antietam, 97; character of, 82, 103; command of, 81–82, 130; and defense of Richmond, 62; at Fair Oaks, 66; at Fredericksburg, 107, 110–11; at Gettysburg, 4, 6, 86, 142–43, 145, 147–51, 154; at Harpers Ferry, 94–95; historians and, 6–7, 229; and Lee, 69, 88, 104–5, 165–66; Lee and, 158, 225–26; at Malvern Hill, 75; in North Carolina, 113; promotion of, 102–3; resignation from U.S. Army, 50; at Second Manassas, 84–87; at Seven Days' campaign, 71–72; at

Longstreet, James, *continued*
  Sharpsburg, 96; at Spotsylvania,
  171–73; and surrender, 204–5, 210–11;
  as tactician, 135; and Western campaign, 132, 162, 165; wounding of,
  173, 177
Loring, William W., 56
Lost Order, 94–95

Mackay family, 20
Mackay, Jack, 17, 25, 33
Magruder, John, 62, 69, 74–76, 81
Mahan, Dennis Hart, 90
Mahone, William, 169, 194, 211
Malone, Dumas, 5
Malvern Hill, battle of, 7, 74–78
Manassas, first battle of, 55
Manassas, second battle of, 5, 7, 82–88,
  86f, 90
Marcy, William, 27
Marshall, Charles, 61, 131, 212–13, 215,
  222
Marshall, George C., 223
Maryland, 91, 93
Mason, Charles, 18
McCarty, Elizabeth, 24–25
McClellan, George B., 7, 56, 60f, 113,
  198; at Antietam, 96–97, 99; and
  Army of the Potomac, 93; career of,
  44; and casualties, 231; at Harpers
  Ferry, 95; Lee and, 63–65, 71, 74, 76–
  77, 105–6, 226; and Lincoln, 80; and
  Mary Lee, 81; in Mexican War, 31;
  and Pope, 90; and Richmond, 59–60,
  62, 66, 68; at Second Manassas, 83,
  88; at Seven Days' campaign, 72
McCormick, Cyrus, 220
McDowell, Irvin, 62, 64, 66, 90; at Sec-
  ond Manassas, 85
McLaws, Lafayette: at Chancellorsville,
  121, 125; at Gettysburg, 147–48; at
  Harpers Ferry, 94
McLean house, 213–14, 214f
McLellan, Mrs., 137–38
McPherson, James, 174, 177, 201
McWhiney, Grady, 7, 77, 230–31
Meade, George G., 4, 138–40, 156, 165,
  167–68, 185, 193; at Bristoe Station,
  162–63; and Lee, 215; in Mexican
  War, 31

Medill, Joseph, 108, 133
Mexican War, 26–31
Mexico City, 27–29
Miley, Michael, 221
Mines, 193–94
Monroe, James, 14
Morgan, John T., 80
Mule Shoe at Spotsylvania, 174–78

Napoleon III, emperor of France, 92,
  159
Newport News, 113
Nolan, Alan T., 8, 41, 50, 200, 212
Noncombatants, 81, 137
North: after Gettysburg, 158; disillu-
  sionment in, 186; economy of, 159;
  strategy of, 168
Northrop, Lucius, 165

Ord, E. O. C., 205

Palmerston, Lord, 92
Patton, George, 223
peace movement in North, 133–34
Peach Orchard, 148
Pemberton, John C., 235
Pender, Dorsey, 88, 125, 150
Pendleton, William, 2
Petersburg, 180; battle of, 186–88; siege
  of, 189, 191, 199, 209
Pettigrew, James, 141–42
Pickens, Francis, 58
Pickett, George E., 180, 191; at Gettys-
  burg, 147, 150–51; Lee and, 158, 210;
  in North Carolina, 113; at Seven
  Days' campaign, 73
Pickett's Charge, 4, 151–52, 154; Lee
  and, 155
Pillow, Gideon, 28, 31
politics, Lee on, 223–25, 242
Polk, James K., 27, 29
Pollard, Edward, 58
Pope, John, 79–88, 90
Porter, Fitz John, 66, 71–73, 85

race, Lee on, 41–42, 222, 224
Randolph, Elizabeth Carter, 14
Randolph, George W., 62, 64
Ravensworth, 16, 22
Reagan, John H., 64, 134, 185

Reid, Whitelaw, 138
religion, Lee on, 242
repeating rifle, 31
Richmond, 54; defense of, 66–78, 136,
    170, 189, 191; evacuation of, 209;
    Grant's offensive and, 167–78; threat
    to, 59–60, 62–65, 182–83
Robertson, Beverly, 141
Rodes, Robert E., 144, 169
Roebuck, John, 159
Roosevelt, Theodore, 4
Rosecrans, William S., 115, 131–32,
    161–63, 223
rotation system, 191
Russell, John, 92

St. Paul's Episcopal Church, Richmond,
    41–42, 54
Sandburg, Carl, 229
Santa Anna, Antonio López de, 28–29
Savage Station, 74
Savannah, 58–59, 202
Saylor's Creek, 210
Scott, Winfield, 3, 27, 31; and Lee, 30,
    47, 49; in Mexican War, 28–29; and
    Virginia, 51
Sears, Stephen W., 95
secession, 45; Lee and, 51, 223–24
Seddon, James A., 115, 132, 134, 156,
    165, 195, 200
Sedgwick, John, 118–19, 124–25, 171
Seminole War, 24
Semmes, Raphael, 206
Seven Days' campaign, 5, 71–74, 76
Seward, William Henry, 43, 92–93, 159,
    203–4
sharpshooters, 192
Shaw, Mrs. James, 15
Shenandoah Valley, 63, 80, 168, 180, 186,
    196
Sheridan, Philip H., 168, 177–78, 186,
    193, 209; in Shenandoah Valley, 196–
    97
Sherman, William T., 3, 116, 167–68,
    177, 190, 198, 202
shortages in Lee's army, 139, 164, 181,
    204, 206, 209–10
Sickles, Daniel, 121, 125, 148, 154
Sigel, Franz, 168, 177
slavery, Lee and, 8, 38–42, 223–24, 238

Smith, Channing, 217
Smith, Gerrit, 43
Smith, Gustavus W., 62, 66
Smith, William, 196
Sorrel, Moxley, 55
South: after war, 215–27; characteristics
    of, 4, 79; Lee on, 45
Spotsylvania: battle of, 171–74; salient at,
    174–78
Stanton, Edwin, 74, 80, 93
Stoneman, George, 118
Stratford Hall, 10, 12–13, 24
Strong, George Templeton, 90, 158
Stuart, "Jeb," 42–43; at Chancellorsville,
    121, 123; character of, 108; death of,
    177–78; at Gettysburg, 150; and intel-
    ligence, 70, 74, 106, 130, 136, 141, 144,
    146, 153, 155; Lee and, 135, 158, 163–
    64; at Second Manassas, 84–85
Stuart, Richard, 25
Sumner, Edwin V., 66, 107–8, 116
surrender, 202–14; criticism of, 212–13;
    Lee and, 171

Talcott, Andrew, 23, 25
Talcott, T. M. R., 131
Taylor, Walter H., 55, 61, 105, 119, 131,
    143, 170, 172, 174, 199–200, 216, 220,
    236
Taylor, Zachary, 26–27
Terry, Alfred H., 3
Texas, 44–45; secession of, 45–47
Thomas, Emory, 198
Thomas, George H., 51
"Traveller," 2, 59, 98, 151, 172, 174, 176,
    184, 221, 221f, 225
Tredegar Iron Works, 54, 65
Trimble, Isaac, 140
Turner, Nat, 38
Twiggs, David, 27–28, 46

United States Army, 24, 33–34, 37; Lee's
    resignation from, 8, 49–51
United States Military Academy, 16–18,
    35–38, 138
Utley, Robert, 37–38

Venable, Charles, 131, 146, 166, 174, 181
Veracruz, 27

Vicksburg, 115, 134, 157, 159
Virginia, Lee and, 23, 48–49, 51, 226,
   235–36
Virginia Military Institute, 2, 177
virtue, Lee on, 242

Walker, John G., 94–95
war, Lee and, 65–66, 81, 225–26, 242–43
War of 1812, 13, 20
Warren, Gouverneur K., 148, 171
Washington College, 1, 35, 219–22,
   226–27
Washington, George, 89; Henry Lee
   and, 10–12; Lee and, 14–15, 26
Washington, Martha, 20
Watters, James D., 144
Waud, Alfred, 175
Weldon Railroad, 195

Western campaign, 115, 131–32, 138,
   152, 161–65, 167, 202, 235–36
West Point. *See* U.S. Military Academy
Whiting, William H. C., 69
Whitman, George, 177
Wigfall, Louis, 134
Wilcox, Cadmus, 125
Wilderness campaign, 6, 117–18, 120, 171
Williams, Martha "Markie," 33, 59
Wilson, Edmund, 229
Wilson, James H., 178
Wilson, Woodrow, 4
Winchester, 196
Wise, Henry A., 56, 234
Wolseley, Garnet, 2–3, 100
Worth, William, 29

Zoan Church, 119–20

ABOUT THE AUTHOR

John M. Taylor graduated from Williams College in 1952 with honors in history, and subsequently earned a master's degree in history from George Washington University. From 1952 until 1987 he was employed by the U.S. government in agencies concerned with intelligence and foreign affairs.

Mr. Taylor is the author of eight books of history and biography. His most recent biography, *Confederate Raider: Raphael Semmes of the Alabama*, was a 1995 selection of the History Book Club. His immediately previous book was another Civil War biography, *William Henry Seward: Lincoln's Right Hand*.

Mr. Taylor's other works include a biography of his father, *General Maxwell Taylor*, and a collection of articles about the Civil War, *While Cannons Roared*. He is a frequent contributor to historical publications and has served as an interviewee and historical consultant for television documentaries on Raphael Semmes and William Henry Seward. He is also coauthor, with William N. Still Jr. and Norman C. Delaney, of *Raiders and Blockaders: The American Civil War Afloat*.

The author and his wife, Priscilla, live in McLean, Virginia.